D0997770

> # If mankind does not end war, war will end mankind.
>
> This has not been true in the past. But it is true in the present. For the present has produced something new. It has produced science. And if science is the principal hope of mankind, it is also the principal menace. For it can destroy as easily as it can create; and all that it creates is useless, if it creates only to destroy. But *destruction is what war means; and all its other meanings are made meaningless by this.*
>
> —G. Lowes Dickinson
> from *Three Notes on War*

This is a book about war. Past and present. As seen through the prose and poetry of the gifted and the great. Past and present.

It is their investment against war in our future. And your only obligation is to read it.

WAR:
AN ANTHOLOGY

edited by
**Edward and Elizabeth
Huberman**

WSP
Ⱶ WASHINGTON SQUARE PRESS · NEW YORK

WAR: AN ANTHOLOGY

A *Washington Square Press* edition
1st printing .... September, 1969

Published by
Washington Square Press, a division of Simon & Schuster, Inc.,
630 Fifth Avenue, New York, N.Y.

L

WASHINGTON SQUARE PRESS editions are distributed in the
U.S. by Simon & Schuster, Inc., 630 Fifth Avenue, New
York, N.Y. 10020 and in Canada by Simon & Schuster
of Canada, Ltd., Richmond Hill, Ontario, Canada.

ACKNOWLEDGMENTS

For arrangements made with various publishing houses whereby certain
copyrighted material was permitted to be reprinted, and for the courtesy
extended by them and by several authors and others, the following
acknowledgments are gratefully made:

GEORGE ALLEN & UNWIN LTD. (London). The short story by Alun
Lewis entitled *The Raid* from *In the Green Tree* by Alun Lewis.

GEORGE ALLEN & UNWIN LTD. The essay by G. Lowes Dickinson
entitled *Three Notes on War* from *War: Its Nature Cause and Cure* by
G. Lowes Dickinson.

ASHLEY FAMOUS AGENCY, INC. The short story by Walter Van Tilburg
Clark entitled *The Portable Phonograph* from *The Watchful Gods and
Other Stories* by Walter Van Tilburg Clark (New York: Random House,
1950), copyright, 1941, by Walter Van Tilburg Clark.

THE ATLANTIC MONTHLY and THE HARVARD COLLEGE LIBRARY. The
letter by Leo Tolstoy entitled "Advice to a Draftee" as it appeared in
The Atlantic Monthly, translated by Rodney Dennis, copyright, ©,
February, 1968, by *The Atlantic Monthly*.

BRANDT & BRANDT. The poem by Stephen Vincent Benét entitled
"Nightmare for Future Reference" from *The Selected Works of Stephen*

Vincent Benét (New York: Holt, Rinehart and Winston, 1959), copyright, 1938, by Stephen Vincent Benét; copyright renewed, ©, 1965, by Thomas C. Benét, Stephanie B. Mahin, and Rachel Benét Lewis.

CURTIS BROWN LTD. (London). The poem by Roy Fuller entitled "Epitaph on a Bombing Victim" from *Collected Poems 1936-1961* by Roy Fuller.

JONATHAN CAPE LIMITED (London). The poems by Sagittarius entitled "Now We Are Six" and "Prologue to a Murder in the Cathedral" from *Strasbourg Geese* by Sagittarius.

JONATHAN CAPE LIMITED, HENRY REED, and HARCOURT, BRACE & WORLD, INC. The poem by Henry Reed entitled "Naming of Parts" from *A Map of Verona* by Henry Reed, copyright, 1947, by Henry Reed.

CHATTO & WINDUS LTD. (London) and MR. HAROLD OWEN. The poems by Wilfred Owen entitled "Anthem for Doomed Youth," "Dulce et Decorum Est," and "Strange Meeting" from *The Collected Poems of Wilfred Owen*.

COLUMBIA UNIVERSITY FORUM and LEO HAMALIAN. The poem by Leo Hamalian entitled "Nursery Rhyme" from *Columbia University FORUM* (Fall 1966, Vol. IX, No. 4), copyright, ©, 1966, by the Trustees of Columbia University in the City of New York.

ALFRED DUGAN and YALE UNIVERSITY PRESS. The poem by Alfred Dugan entitled "How We Heard the Name" from *Poems* by Alfred Dugan.

FABER & FABER LTD. (London). The poem by Robert Lowell entitled "Christmas Eve Under Hooker's Statue" from *Poems 1938-1949* by Robert Lowell; the poem by Stephen Spender entitled "The War God" from *Collected Poems 1928-1953* by Stephen Spender.

SENATOR J. W. FULBRIGHT. The essay entitled *The Price of Empire* from *Congressional Record* (Senate), Vol. 113, No. 125 (August 9, 1967).

E. Y. HARBURG. The poems entitled "Fission Fashion," "*Go to the Lexicon, Thou Sluggard," and "Pox or Pax."

HARCOURT, BRACE & WORLD, INC. The poem by E. E. Cummings entitled "i sing of Olaf" from *Poems, 1923-1954* by E. E. Cummings, copyright, 1931, copyright renewed, ©, 1959, by E. E. Cummings; the poem by Robert Lowell entitled "Christmas Eve Under Hooker's Statue" from *Lord Weary's Castle* by Robert Lowell, copyright, 1944, 1946, by Robert Lowell.

HARPER & ROW, PUBLISHERS, INC. The poem by Robert Bly entitled "Driving through Minnesota during the Hanoi Bombings" from *The Light around the Body* by Robert Bly, copyright, ©, 1967, by Robert Bly; the essay by Randolph S. Bourne entitled *Below the Battle* from *War and the Intellectuals* by Randolph S. Bourne.

HARPER & ROW, PUBLISHERS, INC., MRS. LAURA HUXLEY, and CHATTO & WINDUS LTD. The essay by Aldous Huxley entitled *Ethics and War* from *An Encyclopedia of Pacifism* by Aldous Huxley.

HARPER'S MAGAZINE and LOUIS SIMPSON. The essay by Louis Simpson entitled *The Making of a Soldier USA*.

HARVARD UNIVERSITY PRESS. The poem by Theodore Spencer entitled "The Inflatable Globe" from *Poems 1940-1947* by Theodore Spencer, copyright, 1944, 1948, by the President and Fellows of Harvard College.

DAVID HIGHAM ASSOCIATES, LTD. (London). The poem by Charles Causley entitled "I Saw a Shot-Down Angel" from *Union Street* by Charles Causley, published by Hart-Davis; the poems by D. J. Enright entitled "Parliament of Cats" and "Apocalypse" from *Addictions* by D. J. Enright, published by Chatto & Windus Ltd.; the poem by Dame Edith Sitwell entitled "Lullaby" from *Collected Poems* by Dame Edith Sitwell, published by The Macmillan Company.

HOLT, RINEHART AND WINSTON, INC. The poem by Carl Sandburg entitled "Buttons" from *Chicago Poems* by Carl Sandburg, copyright, 1916, by Holt, Rinehart and Winston, Inc., copyright, 1944, by Carl Sandburg.

HOUGHTON MIFFLIN COMPANY. The poem by Archibald MacLeish entitled "The End of the World."

MRS. RANDALL JARRELL. The poems by Randall Jarrell entitled "The Death of the Ball Turret Gunner" and "Eighth Air Force."

ALFRED A. KNOPF, INC. The poem by Witter Bynner entitled "To a President" from *A Canticle of Pan* by Witter Bynner; the poem by Wallace Stevens entitled "The Death of a Soldier" from *The Collected Poems of Wallace Stevens,* copyright, 1923, copyright renewed, 1951, by Wallace Stevens.

LITTLE, BROWN AND COMPANY and ELAINE GREENE LTD. The short story by William Sansom entitled *How Claeys Died* from *The Stories of William Sansom,* copyright, ©, 1960, by William Sansom.

MACGIBBON & KEE (London). The poem by E. E. Cummings entitled "i sing of Olaf" from *Complete Poems* by E. E. Cummings.

McGRAW-HILL BOOK COMPANY. The poem by Richard Armour entitled "Hiding Place" from *Light Armour* by Richard Armour, copyright, 1954, by Richard Armour.

MACMILLAN & CO., LTD. (London) and THE MACMILLAN COMPANY OF CANADA LIMITED. The short story by Frank O'Connor entitled *Guests of the Nation* from *Collection One* by Frank O'Connor.

THE MACMILLAN COMPANY. The essay by G. Lowes Dickinson entitled *Three Notes on War* from *War: Its Nature Cause and Cure* by G. Lowes Dickinson; the poems by Hugh MacDiarmid entitled "Reflections in an Ironworks" and "If I Was Not a Soldier" from *Collected Poems* by Hugh MacDiarmid, copyright, ©, 1962, by Christopher Murray Grieve.

NEW DIRECTIONS PUBLISHING CORPORATION. The poem by Denise Levertov entitled "What Were They Like?" from *The Sorrow Dance* by Denise Levertov, copyright, ©, 1966, by Denise Levertov Goodman; the poem by Thomas Merton entitled "Chant to Be Used in Processions around a Site with Furnaces" from *Emblems of a Season of Fury* by Thomas Merton, copyright, ©, 1961, by The Abbey of Gethsemani, Inc.; the poems by Wilfred Owen entitled "Anthem for Doomed Youth," "Dulce et Decorum Est," and "Strange Meeting" from *Collected Poems* by Wilfred Owen, copyright, 1946, ©, 1963, by Chatto & Windus Ltd.; the poem by Kenneth Patchen entitled "In Order To" from *The Collected Poems* by Kenneth Patchen, copyright, 1954, by New Directions Publishing Corporation.

NEW DIRECTIONS PUBLISHING CORPORATION, J. M. DENT & SONS LTD.: PUBLISHERS (London), and THE TRUSTEES FOR THE COPYRIGHTS OF THE LATE DYLAN THOMAS. The poem by Dylan Thomas entitled "A Refusal to Mourn the Death, by Fire, of a Child in London" from *Collected Poems* by Dylan Thomas, copyright, 1952, by Dylan Thomas.

THE NEW YORK TIMES MAGAZINE and CHARLES C. MOSKOS, JR. The essay by Charles C. Moskos, Jr., entitled *A Sociologist Appraises the G.I.* from *The New York Times Magazine,* September 24, 1967, copyright, ©, 1967, by The New York Times Company.

NORTH AMERICAN NEWSPAPER ALLIANCE. The dispatch from Spain by Ernest Hemingway entitled "Jay Raven from Pittsburgh," datelined April 24, 1937, copyright, 1937, by North American Newspaper Alliance, copyright renewed, ©, 1965, by Mary Hemingway.

W. W. NORTON & COMPANY, INC. The essay by Edith Hamilton entitled *A Pacifist in Periclean Athens* from *Three Greek Plays,* translated and with Introductions by Edith Hamilton, copyright, 1937, by W. W. Norton & Company, Inc., copyright renewed, ©, 1965, by Doris Fielding Reid.

W. W. NORTON & COMPANY, INC., and RUSSELL & VOLKENING, INC. The poem by May Sarton entitled "The Tortured" from *Cloud, Stone, Sun, Vine* by May Sarton, copyright, ©, 1961, by May Sarton.

HAROLD OBER ASSOCIATES INCORPORATED. The short story by William March entitled *The Unknown Soldier* from *Company K* by William March, copyright, 1933, by William March Campbell, copyright renewed.

HARRIET O'DONOVAN. The short story by Frank O'Connor entitled *Guests of the Nation* from *More Stories* by Frank O'Connor, copyright, 1954, by Frank O'Connor.

OXFORD UNIVERSITY PRESS, INC., and FABER & FABER LTD. The poem by Louis MacNeice entitled "The Conscript" from *The Collected Poems of*

Louis MacNeice, edited by E. R. Dodds, copyright, ©, 1966, by The Estate of Louis MacNeice; the poems by Edwin Muir entitled "The Interrogation," "The Combat," and "The Horses" from *Collected Poems* by Edwin Muir, copyright, ©, 1960, by Willa Muir.

LAURENCE POLLINGER LIMITED (London). The poem by Laurie Lee entitled "The Long War" from *The Sun My Monument* by Laurie Lee, published by The Hogarth Press, Ltd.; the poem by Denise Levertov entitled "What Were They Like?" from *The Sorrow Dance* by Denise Levertov, published by Jonathan Cape Limited; the poem by Carl Sandburg entitled "Buttons" from *Chicago Poems* by Carl Sandburg, published by Jonathan Cape Limited.

RANDOM HOUSE, INC. The poem by Stephen Spender entitled "The War God" from *Selected Poems* by Stephen Spender, copyright, 1942, by Stephen Spender.

RANDOM HOUSE, INC., and THE ESTATE OF GERTRUDE STEIN. The essay by Gertrude Stein entitled *I Was Talking* from *Wars I Have Seen* by Gertrude Stein.

WILLIAM SANSOM and ELAINE GREENE LTD. The short story by William Sansom entitled *How Claeys Died* from *The Stories of William Sansom*, published by The Hogarth Press, London, copyright, ©, 1963, by William Sansom.

GEORGE SASSOON. The poems by Siegfried Sassoon entitled "The Rear-Guard," "The Effect," "Base Details," "The General," and "Everyone Sang" from *Collected Poems 1908-56* by Siegfried Sassoon, published by Faber & Faber Ltd.

SCHOCKEN BOOKS, INC. THE AUTHOR'S LITERARY ESTATE, and CHATTO & WINDUS LTD. The poem by Isaac Rosenberg entitled "Break of Day in the Trenches" from *Collected Poems* by Isaac Rosenberg, copyright, 1949, by Schocken Books, Inc.

CHARLES SCRIBNER'S SONS. The poem by Louis Simpson entitled "The Ash and the Oak" from *Good News of Death and Other Poems* by Louis Simpson (*Poets of Today II*), copyright, 1951, by Louis Simpson.

SWALLOW PRESS INCORPORATED and DON GORDON. The poem by Don Gordon entitled "The Kimono" from *Displaced Persons* by Don Gordon (Chicago: Swallow Press Incorporated, 1958).

MRS. JAMES THURBER and HAMISH HAMILTON, LTD. (London). The story and drawings by James Thurber entitled *The Last Flower* from *Alarms and Diversions* by James Thurber (New York: Harper & Row, 1957), copyright, 1939, by James Thurber, copyright, ©, 1967, by Helen W. Thurber and Rosemary Thurber Sauers; from *Vintage Thurber* by James Thurber, copyright, ©, 1963, by Hamish Hamilton, Ltd.

THE TRUSTEES OF THE HARDY ESTATE, MACMILLAN & CO., LTD., THE MACMILLAN COMPANY OF CANADA LIMITED, and THE MACMILLAN COMPANY. The poems by Thomas Hardy entitled "Channel Firing" and "The Man He Killed" from *Collected Poems* by Thomas Hardy, copyright, 1925, by The Macmillan Company.

THE VIKING PRESS, INC. The short story by Dorothy Parker entitled *Soldiers of the Republic* from *The Portable Dorothy Parker*, copyright, 1938, copyright renewed, ©, 1966, by Dorothy Parker (originally appeared in *The New Yorker*); the poems by Siegfried Sassoon entitled "The Rear-Guard," "The Effect," "Base Details," "The General," and "Everyone Sang" from *Collected Poems* by Siegfried Sassoon, copyright, 1918, by E. P. Dutton & Co., copyright renewed, 1946, by Siegfried Sassoon.

CHARLES E. WYZANSKI, JR. The essay entitled *On Civil Disobedience*, as it originally appeared in *The Atlantic Monthly*.

MR. M. B. YEATS, MACMILLAN & CO., LTD., THE MACMILLAN COMPANY OF CANADA LIMITED, and THE MACMILLAN COMPANY. The poems by William Butler Yeats entitled "An Irish Airman Foresees His Death," "On Being Asked for a War Poem," and "The Stare's Nest by My Window" from *Collected Poems of William Butler Yeats*, copyright, 1919, by The Macmillan Company, copyright renewed, 1946, by Bertha Georgie Yeats.

Contents

x • Contents

Introduction

We read of the disasters of war every morning in our newspapers, hear of them on the radio, see them on television. They are as familiar to us as vitamins, toothpaste, and zippers, and we take them as much for granted. When an individual act of violence unexpectedly strikes one of our public heroes—John or Robert Kennedy or Martin Luther King— for a few days we are aroused to the meaning of the general condition of violence in which we live. We even enjoy an orgy of self-condemnation and remorse. But immediately thereafter we relapse into our customary indifference. Murder on a New York street, terrorist bombings in Jerusalem, destruction by napalm of a Vietnamese village—we are accustomed to them all, and we turn the page or the dial to something that more immediately concerns us: the latest baseball scores or ads for refrigerator sales.

Indifference like ours, of course, is not exactly a new phenomenon. Undoubtedly there were cavemen who preferred gnawing the bones of their delicious roast mammoth to interfering in the next cave, where the more than usually unpleasant noises indicated that the male was doing away with the female who had burned his supper. At the same time, however, since as long ago as the days of Isaiah or of Homer, there have always been some few human beings not blinded by this indifference. Some few who have been constantly aware of the suffering and degradation caused by man's aggressiveness toward man, particularly by the large-scale, organized aggressiveness known as war. It is a sampling of what these few have written across the centuries that this anthology has gathered together.

There is very little in these pages of the excitement, the splendor, that many writers and many generals have found in war. Instead, above all, there is the "pity of War," as Wilfred Owen wrote in the Preface to his volume of war poems; the "Poetry," he said, was "in the pity." There is the futility of war, symbolized, for instance, in the magnanimous but futile gallantry of Yeats's "An Irish Airman Foresees His Death." There is the brutality of war, brutally stated in e. e. cummings' poem of a stubborn, heroic pacifist, "i sing of Olaf glad and big." There is the sheer perversity—brilliantly mocked in satires like Byron's or Johnson's, or in Thurber's child's-eye view—which engenders war in the first place. And there is the enormous waste which is war's result: waste of lives, frustration of love, destruction of values, ravaging of the very earth that breeds and feeds us. Only the young soldier who speaks in Robert Burns's "The Silver Tassie" seems to take war lightly, and he is clearly a lad who has not yet been under fire. Only Whitman in "Beat! Beat! Drums" summons men to arms in a supposedly righteous cause; and although this cause was the preservation of the Union and the abolition of slavery in the United States—certainly as righteous a cause as one could wish for—nevertheless, in the end, after four years of the war and all the horrors he himself had seen on the battlefield and in hospital, it is not a justification of the war or a celebration of victory that Whitman writes, but rather a poem of forgiveness and brotherhood, "Reconciliation." What we tried to buy by war could only be built by peace, and that has not yet, as we all know, been truly built.

It goes without saying that a writer's reluctance to glorify war is not in itself enough to guarantee that he is one of those few not blinded by indifference to violence. Since the mass slaughter of the first World War, and even more since Hiroshima, glorification of war has become unfashionable. Voices such as Mussolini's and Hitler's which tried to revive the old glamor have been recognized as echoes of our barbaric past or of the primitive instincts most of us fortunately succeed in controlling. Because not many of our writers and statesmen care to advocate any doctrines reminiscent of Hitler's, they must as a matter of course make the ritual observations that they hate war, that war is hell, that it is better to reason together, and that peace is wonderful. If, however, these sentiments in no way prevent them from either acquiescing in or initiating policies calculated to lead to war; if they accept war and the threat of war as a way of life, a foundation for our politics and our economics, then obviously they do not belong with that small number who through the years have been appalled by the effects of violence on man. Perhaps it is an indication of some slight enlightenment on all our parts that antiwar platitudes are now expected in political platforms, popular magazine articles, Broadway plays, and children's literature; but between these platitudes, which cloak an underlying compliance, and a true insight into the horror of violence, there is a vast difference, as there always is between platitude and insight on any subject. Insight alone is not art, but art cannot exist without it.

Which brings us again to the contents of this anthology. For the pieces we have included here, whether stories, essays, or poems, have all had to meet a certain requirement: they had to show the insight that must accompany a work of art. Not all of them stand among the world's masterpieces. But in all of them there is at least some degree of that imaginative power that dispels indifference, that opens the inward eye to the fears and sufferings, the hopes and delights of our fellow man, whether he lives next door today or lived a thousand years ago on another continent. Nor is that all. Just as platitude without insight is insufficient, so insight is insufficient without form. The cry of sympathy that any of us, even the most apathetic, gives at the sight of a hurt child is not art. Neither are most of the letters that so many of us hopefully write to newspapers and legislators, in behalf of nuclear disarmament, or in opposition to tyranny in one part of the globe and violence in another. This sympathy, this understanding that so laudably moves us, achieves the condition of art only when it has been given objective shape; only when it has been crystallized into some form that at once contains and expresses the imaginative vision which is the content.

Thus no trace of emotional "outcry" remains in Erasmus' "Letter to Anthony a Bergis," nor in Thoreau's "Battles of Ants." No sentimentality mars Walter van Tilburg Clark's picture of the desolate, dehumanized world that will face the survivors of any future wars. No sermonizing distracts us from the mysterious terror of the image of endless conflict in Edwin Muir's "The Combat," or from the photographic realism of Crane's image of death on the battlefield in "The Upturned Face." The cutting wit of Richard Armour's or E. Y. Harburg's verses is unblunted by what Ezra Pound once called "emotional slither." In each case the raw personal feeling that undoubtedly accompanied the initial experience of insight, whether imaginary or actual, has been transmuted, embodied in some timeless and universal pattern, whether of logical reasoning or of dramatic or poetic structure. And, so embodied, so transmuted, that insight into the meaning of violence in human lives becomes not only the most powerful kind of argument against such violence, but also, and equally important, an enduring work of art.

Whatever the date of composition of each of the pieces presented here, whatever its national or sectional origin, it is our feeling that it speaks as sharply to our own time and place as it did to the era and location in which it was written. Whatever his approach—in the vast range from the factual and objective to the imaginative and transforming—each writer represented in this volume has displayed in his own way his reaction and his response to the horror and futility of war and violence. The reader must decide for himself whether the prognosis is peace for mankind or an escalation of violence to the point of self-annihilation. Let these writers show us the way.

ELIZABETH HUBERMAN
EDWARD HUBERMAN

Richard Armour

HIDING PLACE

A speaker at a meeting of the New York Frozen Food Locker Association declared that the best hiding place in event of an atomic explosion is a frozen food locker, where "radiation will not penetrate."

—NEWS ITEM

Move over, ham
    And quartered cow,
My Geiger says
    The time is now.

Yes, now I lay me
    Down to sleep,
And if I die,
    At least I'll keep.

Stephen Vincent Benét

NIGHTMARE FOR FUTURE REFERENCE

That was the second year of the Third World War,
The one between Us and Them.
                        Well, we've gotten used.
We don't talk much about it, queerly enough.
There was all sorts of talk the first years after the Peace,
A million theories, a million wild suppositions,
A million hopeful explanations and plans,
But we don't talk about it, now. We don't even ask.
We might do the wrong thing. I don't guess you'd under-
    stand that.
But you're eighteen, now. You can take it. You'd better know.

You see, you were born just before the war broke out.
Who started it? Oh, they said it was Us or Them
And it looked like it at the time. You don't know what that's
    like.
But anyhow, it started and there it was,
Just a little worse, of course, than the one before,
But mankind was used to that. We didn't take notice.
They bombed our capital and we bombed theirs.
You've been to the Broken Towns? Yes, they take you there.
They show you the look of the tormented earth.
But they can't show the smell or the gas or the death
Or how it felt to be there, and a part of it.
But we didn't know. I swear that we didn't know.

I remember the first faint hint there was something wrong,
Something beyond all wars and bigger and strange,
Something you couldn't explain.
                        I was back on leave—
Strange, as you felt on leave, as you always felt—
But I went to see the Chief at the hospital

And there he was, in the same old laboratory,
A little older, with some white in his hair
But the same eyes that went through you and the same tongue.
They hadn't been able to touch him—not the bombs
Nor the ruin of his life's work nor anything.
He blinked at me from behind his spectacles
And said, "Huh. It's you. They won't let me have guinea pigs
Except for the war work, but I steal a few.
And they've made me a colonel—expect me to salute.
Damn fools. A damn-fool business. I don't know how.
Have you heard what Erickson's done with the ductless glands?
The journals are four months late. Sit down and smoke."
And I did and it was like home.

                    He was a great man.
You might remember that—and I'd worked with him.
Well, finally he said to me, "How's your boy?"
"Oh—healthy," I said. "We're lucky."

                         "Yes," he said,
And a frown went over his face. "He might even grow up,
Though the intervals between wars are getting shorter.
I wonder if it wouldn't simplify things
To declare mankind in a permanent state of siege.
It might knock some sense in their heads."

                         "You're cheerful," I said.
"Oh, I'm always cheerful," he said. "Seen these, by the way?"
He tapped some charts on a table.

                       "Seen what?" I said.
"Oh," he said, with that devilish, sidelong grin of his,
"Just the normal city statistics—death and birth.
You're a soldier now. You wouldn't be interested.
But the birth rate's dropping—"

                       "Well, really, sir," I said,
"We know that it's always dropped, in every war."

"Not like this," he said. "I can show you the curve.
It looks like the side of a mountain, going down.
And faster, the last three months—yes, a good deal faster.
I showed it to Lobenheim and he was puzzled.
It makes a neat problem—yes?" He looked at me.

"They'd better make peace," he said. "They'd better make
    peace."

"Well, sir," I said, "if we break through, in the spring—"

"Break through?" he said. "What's that? They'd better make
     peace.
The stars may be tired of us. No, I'm not a mystic.
I leave that to the big scientists in bad novels.
But I never saw such a queer maternity curve.
I wish I could get to Ehrens, on their side.
He'd tell me the truth. But the fools won't let me do it."

His eyes looked tired as he stared at the careful charts.
"Suppose there are no more babies?" he said. "What then?
It's one way of solving the problem."
                                        "But, sir—" I said.
"But, sir!" he said. "Will you tell me, please, what is life?
Why it's given, why it's taken away?
Oh, I know—we make a jelly inside a test tube,
We keep a cock's heart living inside a jar.
We know a great many things and what do we know?
We think we know what finished the dinosaurs,
But do we? Maybe they were given a chance
And then it was taken back. There are other beasts
That only kill for their food. No, I'm not a mystic,
But there's a certain pattern in nature, you know,
And we're upsetting it daily. Eat and mate
And go back to the earth after that, and that's all right.
But now we're blasting and sickening earth itself.
She's been very patient with us. I wonder how long."

Well, I thought the Chief had gone crazy, just at first,
And then I remembered the look of no man's land,
That bitter landscape, pockmarked like the moon,
Lifeless as the moon's face and horrible,
The thing we'd made with the guns.
                                        If it were earth,
It looked as though it hated.
                                        "Well?" I said,
And my voice was a little thin. He looked hard at me.
"Oh—ask the women," he grunted. "Don't ask me.
Ask them what they think about it."
                                        I didn't ask them,
Not even your mother—she was strange, those days—

But, two weeks later, I was back in the lines
And somebody sent me a paper—
Encouragement for the troops and all of that—
All about the fall of Their birth rate on Their side.

I guess you know, now. There was still a day when we fought
And the next day, the women knew. I don't know how they
    knew,
But they smashed every government in the world
Like a heap of broken china, within two days,
And we'd stopped firing by then. And we looked at each
    other.

We didn't talk much, those first weeks. You couldn't talk.
We started in rebuilding and that was all,
And at first, nobody would even touch the guns,
Not even to melt them up. They just stood there, silent,
Pointing the way they had and nobody there.
And there was a kind of madness in the air,
A quiet, bewildered madness, strange and shy.
You'd pass a man who was muttering to himself
And you'd know what he was muttering, and why.
I remember coming home and your mother there.
She looked at me, at first didn't speak at all,
And then she said, "Burn those clothes. Take them off and
    burn them
Or I'll never touch you or speak to you again."
And then I knew I was still in my uniform.

Well, I've told you, now. They tell you now at eighteen.
There's no use telling before.
                 Do you understand?
That's why we have the Ritual of the Earth,
The Day of Sorrow, the other ceremonies.
Oh yes, at first people hated the animals
Because they still bred, but we've gotten over that.
Perhaps they can work it better, when it's their turn,
If it's their turn—I don't know. I don't know at all.
You can call it a virus, of course, if you like the word,
But we haven't been able to find it. Not yet. No.
It isn't as if it had happened all at once.
There were a few children born in the last six months

Before the end of the war, so there's still some hope.
But they're almost grown. That's the trouble. They're almost
    grown.
Well, we had a long run. That's something. At first they
    thought
There might be a nation somewhere—a savage tribe.
But we were all in it, even the Eskimos,
And we keep the toys in the stores, and the colored books,
And people marry and plan and the rest of it,
But, you see, there aren't any children. They aren't born.

Ambrose Bierce

THE COUP DE GRÂCE

The fighting had been hard and continuous; that was attested by all the senses. The very taste of battle was in the air. All was now over; it remained only to succor the wounded and bury the dead—to "tidy up a bit," as the humorist of a burial squad put it. A good deal of "tidying up" was required. As far as one could see through the forests, among the splintered trees, lay wrecks of men and horses. Among them moved the stretcher-bearer, gathering and carrying away the few who showed signs of life. Most of the wounded had died of neglect while the right to minister to their wants was in dispute. It is an army regulation that the wounded must wait; the best way to care for them is to win the battle. It must be confessed that victory is a distinct advantage to a man requiring attention, but many do not live to avail themselves of it.

The dead were collected in groups of a dozen or a score and laid side by side in rows while the trenches were dug to receive them. Some, found at too great a distance from these rallying points, were buried where they lay. There was little attempt at identification, though in most cases, the burial parties being detailed to glean the same ground which they had assisted to reap, the names of the victorious dead were known and listed. The enemy's fallen had to be content with counting. But of that they got enough—many of them were counted several times, and the total, as given afterward in the official report of the victorious commander, denoted rather a hope than a result.

At some little distance from the spot where one of the burial parties had established its "bivouac of the dead," a man in the uniform of a federal officer stood leaning against a tree. From his feet upward to his neck his attitude was that of weariness reposing; but he turned his head uneasily from side to side; his mind was apparently not at rest. He was perhaps uncertain in which direction to go: he was not likely to remain long where he was, for already the level rays of the setting sun straggled redly through the open spaces of the wood, and the weary soldiers were quitting their task for the day. He would hardly make a night of it alone there among the dead. Nine men in ten whom you meet after a battle inquire the way to some fraction of the army—as if any one could know. Doubtless this officer was lost. After resting himself a moment he would presumably follow one of the retiring burial squads.

When all were gone he walked straight away into the forest toward the red west, its light staining his face like blood. The air of confidence with which he now strode along showed that he was on familiar ground; he had recovered his bearings. The dead on his right and on his left were unregarded as he passed. An occasional low moan from some sorely-stricken wretch whom the relief-parties had not reached, and who would have to pass a comfortless night beneath the stars with his thirst to keep him company, was equally unheeded. What, indeed, could the officer have done, being no surgeon and having no water?

At the head of a shallow ravine, a mere depression of the ground, lay a small group of bodies. He saw, and swerving suddenly from his course walked rapidly toward them. Scanning each one sharply as he passed, he stopped at last above one which lay at a slight remove from the others, near a clump of small trees. He looked at it narrowly. It seemed to stir. He stopped and laid his hand upon its face. It screamed.

The officer was Captain Downing Madwell, of a Massachusetts regiment of infantry, a daring and intelligent soldier, an honorable man.

In the regiment were two brothers named Halcrow— Caffal and Creede Halcrow. Caffal Halcrow was a sergeant in Captain Madwell's company, and these two men, the sergeant and the captain, were devoted friends. In so far as disparity of rank, difference in duties, and considerations of military discipline would permit, they were commonly together. They had, indeed, grown up together from childhood. A habit of the heart is not easily broken off. Caffal Halcrow had nothing military in his taste nor disposition, but the thought of separation from his friend was disagreeable; he enlisted in the company in which Madwell was second lieutenant. Each had taken two steps upward in rank, but between the highest noncommissioned and the lowest commissioned officer the gulf is deep and wide, and the old relation was maintained with difficulty and a difference.

Creede Halcrow, the brother of Caffal, was the major of the regiment—a cynical, saturnine man between whom and Captain Madwell there was a natural antipathy which circumstances had nourished and strengthened to an active animosity. But for the restraining influence of their mutual relation to Caffal these two patriots would doubtless have endeavored to deprive their country of each other's services.

At the opening of the battle that morning the regiment was performing outpost duty a mile away from the main army. It was attacked and nearly surrounded in the forest, but stubbornly held its ground. During a lull in the fighting Major Halcrow came to Captain Madwell. The two exchanged formal salutes, and the major said: "Captain, the colonel directs that you push your company to the head of this ravine and hold your place there until recalled. I need hardly apprise you of the dangerous character of the movement, but if you wish, you can, I suppose, turn over the command to your first lieutenant. I was not, however, directed to authorize the substitution; it is merely a suggestion of my own, unofficially made."

To this deadly insult Captain Madwell coolly replied: "Sir, I invite you to accompany the movement. A mounted officer would be a conspicuous mark, and I have long held the opinion that it would be better if you were dead."

The art of repartee was cultivated in military circles as early as 1862.

A half-hour later Captain Madwell's company was driven from its position at the head of the ravine, with a loss of one-third its number. Among the fallen was Sergeant Halcrow. The regiment was soon afterward forced back to the main line, and at the close of the battle was miles away. The captain was now standing at the side of his subordinate and friend.

Sergeant Halcrow was mortally hurt. His clothing was deranged; it seemed to have been violently torn apart, exposing the abdomen. Some of the buttons of his jacket had been pulled off and lay on the ground beside him, and fragments of his other garments were strewn about. His leather belt was parted and had apparently been dragged from beneath him as he lay. The only visible wound was a wide, ragged opening in the abdomen. It was defiled with earth and dead leaves. Protruding from it was a loop of small intestine. In all his experience Captain Madwell had not seen a wound like this. He could neither conjecture how it was made nor explain the attendant circumstances— the strangely torn clothing, the parted belt, the besmirching of the white skin. He knelt and made a closer examination. When he rose to his feet, he turned his eyes in different directions as if looking for an enemy. Fifty yards away, on the crest of a low, thinly-wooded hill, he saw several dark objects moving about among the fallen men—a herd of swine. One stood with its back to him, its shoulders sharply elevated. Its forefeet were upon a human body, its head was depressed and invisible. The bristly ridge of its chin showed black against the red west. Captain Madwell drew away his eyes and fixed them again upon the thing which had been his friend.

The man who had suffered these monstrous mutilations was alive. At intervals he moved his limbs; he moaned at every breath. He stared blankly into the face of his friend and if touched screamed. In his giant agony he had torn up the ground on which he lay; his clenched hands were full of leaves and twigs and earth. Articulate speech was beyond his power; it was impossible to know if he were sensible to anything but pain. The expression of his face was an appeal: his eyes were full of prayer. For what?

There was no misreading that look; the captain had too frequently seen it in eyes of those whose lips had still the power to formulate it by an entreaty for death. Consciously or unconsciously, this writhing fragment of humanity, this type and example of acute sensation, this handiwork of man and beast, this humble, unheroic Prometheus, was imploring everything, all, the whole non-ego, for the boon of oblivion. To the earth and the sky alike, to the trees, to the man, to whatever took form in sense or consciousness, this incarnate suffering addressed that silent plea.

For what, indeed? For that which we accord to even the meanest creature without sense to demand it, denying it only to the wretched of our own race: For the blessed release, the rite of uttermost compassion, the coup de grâce.

Captain Madwell spoke the name of his friend. He repeated it over and over without effect, until emotion choked his utterance. His tears plashed upon the livid face beneath his own and blinded himself. He saw nothing but a blurred and moving object, but the moans were more distinct than ever, interrupted at briefer intervals by sharper shrieks. He turned away, struck his hand upon his forehead, and strode from the spot. The swine, catching sight of him, threw up their crimson muzzles, regarding him suspiciously a second, and then with a gruff, concerted grunt, raced away out of sight. A horse, its foreleg splintered by a cannon shot, lifted its head sidewise from the ground and neighed piteously. Madwell stepped forward, drew his revolver and shot the poor beast between the eyes, narrowly observing its death struggle, which, contrary to his expectation, was violent and long; but at last it lay still. The tense muscles of its lips, which had uncovered the teeth in a horrible grin, relaxed; the sharp, clean-cut profile took on a look of profound peace and rest.

Along the distant, thinly-wooded crest to westward the fringe of sunset fire had now nearly burned itself out. The light upon the trunks of the trees had faded to a tender gray; shadows were in their tops, like great dark birds aperch. Night was coming and there were miles of haunted forest between Captain Madwell and camp. Yet he stood there at the side of the dead animal, apparently lost to all sense of his surroundings. His eyes were bent upon the earth at his feet; his left hand hung loosely at his side, his right still held the pistol. Presently he lifted his face, turned it toward his dying friend and walked rapidly back to his side. He knelt upon one knee, cocked the weapon, placed the muzzle against the man's forehead, and turning away his eyes pulled the trigger. There was no report. He had used his last cartridge for the horse.

The sufferer moaned and his lips moved convulsively. The froth that ran from them had a tinge of blood.

Captain Madwell rose to his feet and drew his sword from the scabbard. He passed the fingers of his left hand along the edge from hilt to point. He held it out straight before him, as if to test his nerves. There was no visible tremor of the blade: the ray of bleak skylight that it reflected was steady and true. He stooped and with his left hand tore away the dying man's shirt, rose and placed the point of the sword just over the heart. This time he did not withdraw his eyes. Grasping the hilt with both hands, he thrust downward with all his strength and weight. The blade sank into the man's body—through his body into the earth; Captain Madwell came near falling forward upon his work. The dying man drew up his knees and at the same time threw his right arm across his breast and grasped the steel so tightly that the knuckles of the hand visibly whitened. By a violent but vain effort to withdraw the blade the wound was enlarged; a rill of blood escaped, running sinuously down into the deranged clothing. At that moment three men stepped silently forward from behind the clump of young trees which had concealed their approach. Two were hospital attendants and carried a stretcher.

The third was Major Creede Halcrow.

A SON OF THE GODS

A Study in the Present Tense

A breezy day and a sunny landscape. An open country to right and left and forward; behind, a wood. In the edge of this wood, facing the open but not venturing into it, long lines of troops, halted. The wood is alive with them, and full of confused noises—the occasional rattle of wheels as a battery of artillery goes into position to cover the advance; the hum and murmur of the soldiers talking; a sound of innumerable feet in the dry leaves that strew the interspaces among the trees; hoarse commands of officers. Detached groups of horsemen are well in front—not altogether exposed—many of them intently regarding the crest of a hill a mile away in the direction of the interrupted advance. For this powerful army, moving in battle order through a forest, has met with a formidable obstacle—the open country. The crest of that gentle hill a mile away has a sinister look; it says, Beware! Along it runs a stone wall extending to left and right a great distance. Behind the wall is a hedge;

behind the hedge are seen the tops of trees in rather straggling order. Among the trees—what? It is necessary to
know.

Yesterday, and for many days and nights previously, we
were fighting somewhere; always there was cannonading,
with occasional keen rattlings of musketry, mingled with
cheers, our own or the enemy's, we seldom knew, attesting
some temporary advantage. This morning at daybreak the
enemy was gone. We have moved forward across his earth-
works, across which we have so often vainly attempted to
move before, through the débris of his abandoned camps,
among the graves of his fallen, into the woods beyond.

How curiously we had regarded everything! how odd it
all had seemed! Nothing had appeared quite familiar; the
most commonplace objects—an old saddle, a splintered
wheel, a forgotten canteen—everything had related something of the mysterious personality of those strange men
who had been killing us. The soldier never becomes wholly
familiar with the conception of his foes as men like himself;
he cannot divest himself of the feeling that they are another
order of beings, differently conditioned, in an environment
not altogether of the earth. The smallest vestiges of them
rivet his attention and engage his interest. He thinks of them
as inaccessible; and, catching an unexpected glimpse of
them, they appear farther away, and therefore larger, than
they really are—like objects in a fog. He is somewhat in awe
of them.

From the edge of the wood leading up the acclivity are
the tracks of horses and wheels—the wheels of cannon. The
yellow grass is beaten down by the feet of infantry. Clearly
they have passed this way in thousands; they have not
withdrawn by the country roads. This is significant—it is
the difference between retiring and retreating.

That group of horsemen is our commander, his staff and
escort. He is facing the distant crest, holding his field-glass
against his eyes with both hands, his elbows needlessly
elevated. It is a fashion; it seems to dignify the act; we
are all addicted to it. Suddenly he lowers the glass and says
a few words to those about him. Two or three aides detach
themselves from the group and canter away into the woods,
along the lines in each direction. We did not hear his words,
but we know them: "Tell General X. to send forward the

skirmish line." Those of us who have been out of place resume our positions; the men resting at ease straighten themselves and the ranks are re-formed without a command. Some of us staff officers dismount and look at our saddle girths; those already on the ground remount.

Galloping rapidly along in the edge of the open ground comes a young officer on a snow-white horse. His saddle blanket is scarlet. What a fool! No one who has ever been in action but remembers how naturally every rifle turns toward the man on a white horse; no one but has observed how a bit of red enrages the bull of battle. That such colors are fashionable in military life must be accepted as the most astonishing of all the phenomena of human vanity. They would seem to have been devised to increase the death-rate.

This young officer is in full uniform, as if on parade. He is all agleam with bullion—a blue-and-gold edition of the Poetry of War. A wave of derisive laughter runs abreast of him all along the line. But how handsome he is!—with what careless grace he sits his horse!

He reins up within a respectful distance of the corps commander and salutes. The old soldier nods familiarly; he evidently knows him. A brief colloquy between them is going on; the young man seems to be preferring some request which the elder one is indisposed to grant. Let us ride a little nearer. Ah! too late—it is ended. The young officer salutes again, wheels his horse, and rides straight toward the crest of the hill!

A thin line of skirmishers, the men deployed at six paces or so apart, now pushes from the wood into the open. The commander speaks to his bugler, who claps his instrument to his lips. *Tra-la-la! Tra-la-la!* The skirmishers halt in their tracks.

Meantime the young horseman has advanced a hundred yards. He is riding at a walk, straight up the long slope, with never a turn of the head. How glorious! Gods! what would we not give to be in his place—with his soul! He does not draw his sabre; his right hand hangs easily at his side. The breeze catches the plume in his hat and flutters it smartly. The sunshine rests upon his shoulder-straps, lovingly, like a visible benediction. Straight on he rides. Ten thousand pairs of eyes are fixed upon him with an intensity that he can hardly fail to feel; ten thousand hearts keep quick time to the inaudible hoof-beats of his snowy steed. He is not alone—he draws all souls after him. But we remember that we laughed! On and on, straight for the hedge-lined wall, he rides. Not a look backward. O, if he would but turn—if he could but see the love, the adoration, the atonement!

Not a word is spoken; the populous depths of the forest still murmur with their unseen and unseeing swarm, but all along the fringe is silence. The burly commander is an equestrian statue of himself. The mounted staff officers, their field-glasses up, are motionless all. The line of battle in the edge of the wood stands at a new kind of "attention," each man in the attitude in which he was caught by the consciousness of what is going on. All these hardened and impenitent man-killers, to whom death in its awfulest forms is a fact familiar to their every-day observation; who sleep on hills trembling with the thunder of great guns, dine in the midst of streaming missiles, and play at cards among the dead faces of their dearest friends—all are watching with suspended breath and beating hearts the outcome of an act involving the life of one man. Such is the magnetism of courage and devotion.

If now you should turn your head you would see a simultaneous movement among the spectators—a start, as if they had received an electric shock—and looking forward again to the now distant horseman you would see that he has in that instant altered his direction and is riding at an angle to his former course. The spectators suppose the sudden deflection to be caused by a shot, perhaps a wound; but take this field-glass and you will observe that he is riding toward a break in the wall and hedge. He means, if not killed, to ride through and overlook the country beyond.

You are not to forget the nature of this man's act; it is not permitted to you to think of it as an instance of bravado, nor, on the other hand, a needless sacrifice of self. If the enemy has not retreated he is in force on that ridge. The investigator will encounter nothing less than a line-of-battle; there is no need of pickets, videttes, skirmishers, to give warning of our approach; our attacking lines will be visible, conspicuous, exposed to an artillery fire that will shave the ground the moment they break from cover, and for half the distance to a sheet of rifle bullets in which nothing

can live. In short, if the enemy is there, it would be madness to attack him in front; he must be manœuvred out by
the immemorial plan of threatening his line of communication, as necessary to his existence as to the diver at the bottom
of the sea his air tube. But how ascertain if the enemy is
there? There is but one way,—somebody must go and see.
The natural and customary thing to do is to send forward
a line of skirmishers. But in this case they will answer in
the affirmative with all their lives; the enemy, crouching
in double ranks behind the stone wall and in cover of the
hedge, will wait until it is possible to count each assailant's
teeth. At the first volley a half of the questioning line will
fall, the other half before it can accomplish the predestined
retreat. What a price to pay for gratified curiosity! At what
a dear rate an army must sometimes purchase knowledge!
"Let me pay all," says this gallant man—this military Christ!

There is no hope except the hope against hope that the
crest is clear. True, he might prefer capture to death. So
long as he advances, the line will not fire—why should it?
He can safely ride into the hostile ranks and become a prisoner of war. But this would defeat his object. It would not
answer our question; it is necessary either that he return
unharmed or be shot to death before our eyes. Only so shall
we know how to act. If captured—why, that might have been
done by a half-dozen stragglers.

Now begins an extraordinary contest of intellect between
a man and an army. Our horseman, now within a quarter of
a mile of the crest, suddenly wheels to the left and gallops
in a direction parallel to it. He has caught sight of his an-
tagonist; he knows all. Some slight advantage of ground has
enabled him to overlook a part of the line. If he were here
he could tell us in words. But that is now hopeless; he must
make the best use of the few minutes of life remaining to
him, by compelling the enemy himself to tell us as much and
as plainly as possible—which, naturally, that discreet power
is reluctant to do. Not a rifleman in those crouching ranks,
not a cannoneer at those masked and shotted guns, but knows
the needs of the situation, the imperative duty of forbear-
ance. Besides, there has been time enough to forbid them all
to fire. True, a single rifle-shot might drop him and be no
great disclosure. But firing is infectious—and see how rapidly
he moves, with never a pause except as he whirls his horse

about to take a new direction, never directly backward toward us, never directly forward toward his executioners. All
this is visible through the glass; it seems occurring within
pistol-shot; we see all but the enemy, whose presence, whose
thoughts, whose motives we infer. To the unaided eye there is
nothing but a black figure on a white horse, tracing slow zig-
zags against the slope of a distant hill—so slowly they seem
almost to creep.

Now—the glass again—he has tired of his failure, or sees
his error, or has gone mad; he is dashing directly forward
at the wall, as if to take it at a leap, hedge and all! One
moment only and he wheels right about and is speeding like
the wind straight down the slope—toward his friends, toward
his death! Instantly the wall is topped with a fierce roll of
smoke for a distance of hundreds of yards to right and left.
This is as instantly dissipated by the wind, and before the
rattle of the rifle reaches us he is down. No, he recovers his
seat; he has but pulled his horse upon its haunches. They are
up and away! A tremendous cheer bursts from our ranks,
relieving the insupportable tension of our feelings. And the
horse and its rider? Yes, they are up and away. Away, indeed—they are making directly to our left, parallel to the
now steadily blazing and smoking wall. The rattle of the
musketry is continuous, and every bullet's target is that
courageous heart.

Suddenly a great bank of white smoke pushes upward from
behind the wall. Another and another—a dozen roll up before the thunder of the explosions and the humming of the
missiles reach our ears and the missiles themselves come
bounding through clouds of dust into our covert, knocking
over here and there a man and causing a temporary distrac-
tion, a passing thought of self.

The dust drifts away. Incredible!—that enchanted horse
and rider have passed a ravine and are climbing another
slope to unveil another conspiracy of silence, to thwart the
will of another armed host. Another moment and that crest
too is in eruption. The horse rears and strikes the air with
its forefeet. They are down at last. But look again—the man
has detached himself from the dead animal. He stands erect,
motionless, holding his sabre in his right hand straight above
his head. His face is toward us. Now he lowers his hand to
a level with his face and moves it outward, the blade of the

sabre describing a downward curve. It is a sign to us, to the world, to posterity. It is a hero's salute to death and history.

Again the spell is broken; our men attempt to cheer; they are choking with emotion; they utter hoarse, discordant cries; they clutch their weapons and press tumultuously forward into the open. The skirmishers, without orders, against orders, are going forward at a keen run, like hounds unleashed. Our cannon speak and the enemy's now open in full chorus; to right and left as far as we can see, the distant crest, seeming now so near, erects its towers of cloud and the great shot pitch roaring down among our moving masses. Flag after flag of ours emerges from the wood, line after line sweeps forth, catching the sunlight on its burnished arms. The rear battalions alone are in obedience; they preserve their proper distance from the insurgent front.

The commander has not moved. He now removes his field-glass from his eyes and glances to the right and left. He sees the human current flowing on either side of him and his huddled escort, like tide waves parted by a rock. Not a sign of feeling in his face; he is thinking. Again he directs his eyes forward; they slowly traverse that malign and awful crest. He addresses a calm word to his bugler. *Tra-la-la! Tra-la-la!* The injunction has an imperiousness which enforces it. It is repeated by all the bugles of all the subordinate commanders; the sharp metallic notes assert themselves above the hum of the advance and penetrate the sound of the cannon. To halt is to withdraw. The colors move slowly back; the lines face about and sullenly follow, bearing their wounded; the skirmishers return, gathering up the dead.

Ah, those many, many needless dead! That great soul whose beautiful body is lying over yonder, so conspicuous against the sere hillside—could it not have been spared the bitter consciousness of a vain devotion? Would one exception have marred too much the pitiless perfection of the divine, eternal plan?

Robert Bly

DRIVING THROUGH MINNESOTA
DURING THE HANOI BOMBINGS

We drive between lakes just turning green;
Late June. The white turkeys have been moved
To new grass.
How long the seconds are in great pain!
Terror just before death,
Shoulders torn, shot
From helicopters, the boy
Tortured with the telephone generator,
"I felt sorry for him,
And blew his head off with a shotgun."
These instants become crystals,
Particles
The grass cannot dissolve. Our own gaiety
Will end up
In Asia, and in your cup you will look down
And see
Black Starfighters.
We were the ones we intended to bomb!
Therefore we will have
To go far away
To atone
For the sufferings of the stringy-chested
And the small rice-fed ones, quivering
In the helicopter like wild animals,
Shot in the chest, taken back to be questioned.

Randolph S. Bourne

BELOW THE BATTLE

He is one of those young men who, because his parents happened to mate during a certain ten years of the world's history, has had now to put his name on a wheel of fate, thereby submitting himself to be drawn into a brief sharp course of military training before being shipped across the sea to kill Germans or be killed by them. He does not like this fate that menaces him, and he dislikes it because he seems to find nothing in the programme marked out for him which touches remotely his aspirations, his impulses, or even his desires. My friend is not a happy young man, but even the unsatisfactory life he is living seems supplemented at no single point by the life of the drill-ground or the camp or the stinking trench. He visualizes the obscenity of the battlefield and turns away in nausea. He thinks of the weary regimentation of young men, and is filled with disgust. His mind has turned sour on war and all that it involves. He is poor material for the military proclamation and the drill-sergeant.

I want to understand this friend of mine, for he seems rather typical of a scattered race of young Americans of today. He does not fall easily into the categories of patriot and coward which the papers are making popular. He feels neither patriotism nor fear, only an apathy toward the war, faintly warmed into a smouldering resentment at the men who have clamped down the war-pattern upon him and that vague mass of people and ideas and workaday living around him that he thinks of as his country. Now that resentment has knotted itself into a tortured tangle of what he should do, how he can best be true to his creative self? I should say that his apathy cannot be imputed to cowardly ease. My friend earns about fifteen hundred dollars a year as an architect's assistant, and he lives alone in a little room over a fruitshop. He worked his way through college, and he has ever known even a leisurely month. There is nothing rhæacian about his life. It is scarcely to save his skin for riotous living that he is reluctant about war. Since he left college he has been trying to find his world. He is often seriously depressed and irritated with himself for not having hewed out a more glorious career for himself. His work is just interesting enough to save it from drudgery, and yet not nearly independent and exacting enough to give him a confident professional sense. Outside his work, life is deprived and limited rather than luxurious. He is fond of music and goes to cheap concerts. He likes radical meetings, but never could get in touch with the agitators. His friends are seeking souls just like himself. He likes midnight talks in cafés and studios, but he is not especially amenable to drink. His heart of course is hungry and turbid, but his two or three love-affairs have not clarified anything for him. He eats three rather poor restaurant meals a day. When he reads, it is philosophy—Nietzsche, James, Bergson—or the novels about youth—Rolland, Nexö, Cannan, Frenssen, Beresford. He has a rather constant mood of futility, though he is in unimpeachable health. There are moments when life seems quite without sense or purpose. He has enough friends, however, to be not quite lonely, and yet they are so various as to leave him always with an ache for some more cohesive, purposeful circle. His contacts with people irritate him without rendering him quite unhopeful. He is always expecting he doesn't know quite what, and always being frustrated of he doesn't quite know what would have pleased him. Perhaps he never had a moment of real external or internal ease in his life.

Obviously a creature of low vitality, with neither the broad vision to be stirred by the President's war message, nor the red blood to itch for the dummy bayonet-charge. Yet somehow he does not seem exactly weak, and there is a consistency about his attitude which intrigues me. Since he left college eight years ago, he has been through most of the intellectual and emotional fads of the day. He has always cursed himself for being so superficial and unrooted, and he has tried to write a little of the thoughts that stirred him. What he got down on paper was, of course, the usual large vague feeling of a new time that all of us feel. With the outbreak of the Great War, most of his socialist and pacifist theories were knocked flat. The world turned out to be an entirely different place from what he had thought. Progress and uplift seemed to be indefinitely suspended, though it was a long time before he realized how much he had been corroded by the impact of news and the endless discussions he heard. I think he gradually worked himself into a truly neutral indifference. The reputable people and the comfortable classes who were having all the conventional emotions rather disgusted him. The neurotic fury about self-defence seemed to come from types and classes that he instinctively detested. He was not scared, and somehow he could not get enthusiastic about defending himself with "preparedness" unless he were badly scared. Things got worse. All that he valued seemed frozen until the horrible mess came to a close. He had gone to an unusually intelligent American college, and he had gotten a feeling for a humane civilization that had not left him. The war, it is true, bit away piece by piece every ideal that made this feeling seem plausible. Most of the big men—intellectuals—whom he thought he respected had had so much of their idealism hacked away and got their nerves so frayed that they became at last, in their panic, willing and even eager to adopt the war-technique in aid of their government's notions of the way to impose democracy on the world.

My poor young friend can best be understood as too naive and too young to effect this metamorphosis. Older men might mix a marvellous intellectual brew of personal anger, fear, a sense of "dishonor," fervor for a League of Peace, and set going a machinery that crushed everything intelligent, humane and civilized. My friend was less flexible. War simply did not mix with anything that he had learned to feel was desirable. Something in his mind spewed it out whenever it was suggested as a cure for our grievous American neutrality. As I got all this from our talks, he did not seem weak. He merely had no notion of the patriotism that meant the springing of a nation to arms. He read conscientiously *The New Republic's* feast of eloquent idealism, with its appealing harbingers of a cosmically efficacious and well-bred war. He would often say, This is all perfectly convincing; why, then, are we not all convinced? He seemed to understand the argument for American participation. We both stood in awe at the superb intellectual structure that was built up. But my friend is one of those unfortunate youths whose heart has to pprehend as well as his intellect, and it was his heart that inexorably balked. So he was in no mood to feel the worth of American participation, in spite of the infinite tact and Fabian strategy of the Executive and his intellectualist backers. He felt apart from it all. He had not the imagination to see a healed world-order built out of the rotten materials of armaments, diplomacy and "liberal" statesmanship. And he wasn't affected by the psychic complex of panic, hatred, rage, class-arrogance and patriotic swagger that was creating in newspaper editors and in the *"jeunesse dorée"* around us the authentic *élan* for war.

My friend is thus somehow in the nation but not of the nation. The war has as yet got no conceivable clutch on his soul. He knows that theoretically he is united with a hundred million in purpose, sentiment and deed for an idealistic war to defend democracy and civilization against predatory autocracy. Yet somehow, in spite of all the excitement, nobody has yet been able to make this real to him. He is healthy, intelligent, idealistic. The irony is that the demand which his country now makes on him is one to which not one single cell or nerve of idealism or desire responds. The cheap and silly blare of martial life leaves him cold. The easy inflation of their will-to-power which is coming to so many people from their participation in volunteer or government service, or, better still, from their urging others to farm, enlist, invest, retrench, organize,—none of this allures him. His life is uninteresting and unadventurous, but it is not quite dull enough to make this activity or anything he knows about war seem a release into lustier expression. He has ideals but he cannot see their realization through a desperate struggle to the uttermost. He doubts the "saving" of an America which can only be achieved through world-suicide. He wants democracy, but he does not want the kind of democracy we will get by this war enough to pay the suicidal cost of getting it in the way we set about it.

Dulce et decorum est pro patria mori, sweet and becoming is it to die for one's country. This is the young man who is suddenly asked to die for his country. My friend was much concerned about registration. He felt coercive forces closing in upon him. He did not want to register for the purposes of being liable to conscription. It would be doing something positive when he felt only apathy. Furthermore, if he was to resist, was it not better to take a stand now than to wait to be drafted? On the other hand, was it not too much of a concession to rebel at a formality? He did not really wish to be a martyr. Going to prison for a year for merely refusing to register was rather a grotesque and futile gesture. He did not see himself as a hero, shedding inspiration by his example to his fellows. He did not care what others did. His objection to prison was not so much fear perhaps as contempt for a silly sacrifice. He could not keep up his pose of complete aliency from the war-enterprise, now that registration was upon him. Better submit stoically, he thought, to the physical pressure, mentally reserving his sense of spiritual aliency from the enterprise into which he was being remorselessly moulded. Yet my friend is no arrant prig. He does not pretend to be a "world-patriot," or a servant of some higher law than his country's. Nor does he feel blatantly patriotic. With his groping philosophy of life, patriotism has merely died as a concept of significance for him. It is to him merely the emotion that fills the herd when it imagines itself engaged in massed defence or massed attack. Having no such images, he has no feeling of patriotism. He still feels himself inextricably a part of this blundering, wistful, crass civilization we call America. All he asks is not to be identified with it for warlike ends. He does not feel pro-German. He tells me there is not a drop of any but British blood in his veins. He does not love the Kaiser. He is quite willing to believe that it is the German government and not the German people whom he is asked to fight, although it may be the latter whom he is obliged to kill. But he cannot forget that it is the American government rather than the American people who got up the animus to fight the German government. He does not forget that the American government, having through tragic failure slipped into the war-technique, is now trying to manipulate him into that war-technique. And my friend's idea of *patria* does not include the duty of warlike animus, even when the government decides such animus is necessary to carry out its theories of democracy and the future organization of the world. There are ways in which my friend would probably be willing to die for his country. If his death now meant the restoration of those ravaged lands and the bringing back of the dead, that would be a cause to die for. But he knows that dead cannot be brought back or the brotherly currents restored. The work of madness will not be undone. Only a desperate war will be prolonged. Everything seems to him so mad that there is nothing left worth dying for. *Pro patria mori*, to my friend, means something different from lying gaunt as a conscript on a foreign battlefield, fallen in the last desperate fling of an interminable world-war.

Does this mean that if he is drafted he will refuse to serve? I do not know. It will not be any plea of "conscientious objection" that keeps him back. That phrase to him has already an archaic flavor which implies a ruling norm, a stiff familiar war-machine. If he were merely afraid of death, he would be delighted to work up one's blood-lust for the business, except that this unaccountable conscience, like a godly grandmother, absolutely forbids. In the case of my friend, it will not be any objective "conscience." It will be something that is woven into his whole modern philosophic feel for life. This is what paralyzes him against taking one step toward the war-machine. If he were merely afraid of death, he would seek some alternative service. But he does not. He remains passive and apathetic, waiting for the knife to fall. There is a growing cynicism in him about the brisk and inept bustle of war-organization. His attitude suggests that if he is worked into war-service, he will have to be coerced every step of the way.

Yet he may not even rebel. He may go silently into the ranks in a mood of cold contempt. His horror of useless sacrifice may make even the bludgeoning of himself seem futile. He may go in the mood of so many young men in the other countries, without enthusiasm, without idealism, without hope and without belief, victims of a tragically blind force behind them. No other government, however, has had to face from the very start quite this appalling skepticism of youth. My friend is significant because all the shafts of panic, patriotism and national honor have been discharged at him without avail. All the seductions of "liberal" idealism leave him cold. He is to be susceptible to nothing but the use of crude, rough, indefeasible violence. Nothing could be more awkward for a "democratic" President than to be faced with this cold, staring skepticism of youth, in the prosecution of his war. The attitude of my friend suggests that there is a personal and social idealism in America which is out of reach of the most skilful and ardent appeals of the older order, an idealism that cannot be hurt by the taunts of cowardice and slacking or kindled by the slogans of capitalistic democracy. This is the cardinal fact of our war—the non-mobilization of the younger intelligentsia.

What will they do to my friend? If the war goes on they will need him. Pressure will change skepticism into bitterness. That bitterness will well and grow. If the country submissively pours month after month its wealth of life and resources into the work of annihilation, that bitterness will spread out like a stain over the younger American generation. If the enterprise goes on endlessly, the work, so blithely undertaken for the defence of democracy, will have crushed out the only genuinely precious thing in a nation, the hope and ardent idealism of its youth.

Robert Burns

THE SILVER TASSIE

Go, fetch to me a pint o' wine,
    An' fill it in a silver tassie;
That I may drink, before I go,
    A service to my bonnie lassie.
The boat rocks at the pier o' Leith,
    Fu' loud the wind blaws frae the ferry,
The ship rides by the Berwick-law
    And I maun leave my bonnie Mary.

The trumpets sound, the banners fly,
    The glittering spears are rankèd ready;
The shouts o' war are heard afar,
    The battle closes thick and bloody;
But it's no the roar o' sea or shore
    Wad mak me langer wish to tarry,
Nor shout o' war that's heard afar,
    It's leaving thee, my bonnie Mary.

Witter Bynner

TO A PRESIDENT

If this was our battle, if these were our friends,
Which were our enemies, which were our friends?

George Noel Gordon, Lord Byron

DON JUAN

From Canto the Seventh

LXXIX

Oh, thou eternal Homer! who couldst charm
   All ears, though long; all ages, though so short,
By merely wielding with poetic arm
   Arms to which men will never more resort,
Unless gunpowder should be found to harm
   Much less than is the hope of every court,
Which now is leagued young Freedom to annoy;
But they will not find Liberty a Troy:—

LXXX

Oh, thou eternal Homer! I have now
   To paint a siege, wherein more men were slain,
With deadlier engines and a speedier blow,
   Than in thy Greek gazette of that campaign;
And yet, like all men else, I must allow,
   To vie with thee would be about as vain
As for a brook to cope with ocean's flood;
But still we moderns equal you in blood;

LXXXI

If not in poetry, at least in fact;
   And fact is truth, the grand desideratum!
Of which, howe'er the Muse describes each act,
   There should be ne'ertheless a slight substratum.
But now the town is going to be attack'd;
   Great deeds are doing—how shall I relate 'em?
Souls of immortal generals! Phœbus watches
To colour up his rays from your despatches.

LXXXII

Oh, ye great bulletins of Bonaparte!
  Oh, ye less grand long lists of kill'd and wounded!
Shade of Leonidas, who fought so hearty,
  When my poor Greece was once, as now, surrounded!
Oh, Cæsar's Commentaries! now impart, ye
  Shadows of glory! (lest I be confounded)
A portion of your fading twilight hues,
So beautiful, so fleeting, to the Muse.

LXXXIII

When I call 'fading' martial immortality,
  I mean, that every age and every year,
And almost every day, in sad reality,
  Some sucking hero is compell'd to rear,
Who, when we come to sum up the totality
  Of deeds to human happiness most dear,
Turns out to be a butcher in great business,
Afflicting young folks with a sort of dizziness.

LXXXIV

Medals, rank, ribands, lace, embroidery, scarlet,
  Are things immortal to immortal man,
As purple to the Babylonian harlot:
  An uniform to boys is like a fan
To women; there is scarce a crimson varlet
  But deems himself the first in Glory's van.
But Glory's glory; and if you would find
What that is—ask the pig who sees the wind!

LXXXV

At least *he feels it,* and some say he *sees,*
  Because he runs before it like a pig;
Or, if that simple sentence should displease,
  Say, that he scuds before it like a brig,
A schooner, or—but it is time to ease
  This Canto, ere my Muse perceives fatigue.
The next shall ring a peal to shake all people,
Like a bob-major from a village steeple.

LXXXVI

Hark! through the silence of the cold, dull night,
   The hum of armies gathering rank on rank!
Lo! dusky masses steal in dubious sight
   Along the leaguer'd wall and bristling bank
Of the arm'd river, while with straggling light
   The stars peep through the vapours dim and dank,
Which curl in curious wreaths:—how soon the smoke
Of Hell shall pall them in a deeper cloak!

LXXXVII

Here pause we for the present—as even then
   That awful pause, dividing life from death,
Struck for an instant on the hearts of men,
   Thousands of whom were drawing their last breath!
A moment—and all will be life again!
   The march! the charge! the shouts of either faith!
Hurra! and Allah! and—one moment more,
The death-cry drowning in the battle's roar.

From Canto the Eighth

I

Oh blood and thunder! and oh blood and wounds!
   These are but vulgar oaths, as you may deem,
Too gentle reader! and most shocking sounds:
   And so they are; yet thus is Glory's dream
Unriddled, and as my true Muse expounds
   At present such things, since they are her theme,
So be they her inspirers! Call them Mars,
Bellona, what you will—they mean but wars.

II

All was prepared—the fire, the sword, the men
   To wield them in their terrible array.
The army, like a lion from his den,
   March'd forth with nerve and sinews bent to slay,—

A human Hydra, issuing from its fen
   To breathe destruction on its winding way,
Whose heads were heroes, which cut off in vain
Immediately in others grew again.

III

History can only take things in the gross;
   But could we know them in detail, perchance
In balancing the profit and the loss,
   War's merit it by no means might enhance,
To waste so much gold for a little dross,
   As hath been done, mere conquest to advance.
The drying up a single tear has more
Of honest fame, than shedding seas of gore.

IV

And why?—because it brings self-approbation;
   Whereas the other, after all its glare,
Shouts, bridges, arches, pensions from a nation,
   Which (it may be) has not much left to spare,
A higher title, or a loftier station,
   Though they may make Corruption gape or stare,
Yet, in the end, except in Freedom's battles,
Are nothing but a child of Murder's rattles.

V

And such they are—and such they will be found:
   Not so Leonidas and Washington,
Whose every battle-field is holy ground,
   Which breathes of nations saved, not worlds undone.
How sweetly on the ear such echoes sound!
   While the mere victor's may appal or stun
The servile and the vain, such names will be
A watchword till the future shall be free.

VI

The night was dark, and the thick mist allow'd
   Nought to be seen save the artillery's flame,
Which arch'd the horizon like a fiery cloud,
   And in the Danube's waters shone the same—

A mirror'd hell! the volleying roar, and loud
    Long booming of each peal on peal, o'ercame
The ear far more than thunder; for Heaven's flashes
Spare, or smite rarely—man's make millions ashes!

VII

The column order'd on the assault scarce pass'd
    Beyond the Russian batteries a few toises,
When up the bristling Moslem rose at last,
    Answering the Christian thunders with like voices:
Then one vast fire, air, earth, and stream embraced,
    Which rock'd as 'twere beneath the mighty noises;
While the whole rampart blazed like Etna, when
The restless Titan hiccups in his den.

VIII

And one enormous shout of 'Allah!' rose
    In the same moment, loud as even the roar
Of war's most mortal engines, to their foes
    Hurling defiance: city, stream, and shore
Resounded 'Allah!' and the clouds which close
    With thick'ning canopy the conflict o'er,
Vibrate to the Eternal name. Hark! through
All sounds it pierceth 'Allah! Allah! Hu!'

IX

The columns were in movement one and all,
    But of the portion which attack'd by water,
Thicker than leaves the lives began to fall,
    Though led by Arseniew, that great son of slaughter,
As brave as ever faced both bomb and ball.
    'Carnage' (so Wordsworth tells you) 'is God's daugh-
        ter:'
If *he* speaks truth, she is Christ's sister, and
Just now behaved as in the Holy Land.

X

The Prince de Ligne was wounded in the knee;
    Count Chapeau-Bras, too, had a ball between

His cap and head, which proves the head to be
   Aristocratic as was ever seen,
Because it then received no injury
   More than the cap; in fact, the ball could mean
No harm unto a right legitimate head:
'Ashes to ashes'—why not lead to lead?

XI

Also the General Markow, Brigadier,
   Insisting on removal of *the prince*
Amidst some groaning thousands dying near,—
   All common fellows, who might writhe and wince,
And shriek for water into a deaf ear,—
   The General Markow, who could thus evince
His sympathy for rank, by the same token,
To teach him greater, had his own leg broken.

XII

Three hundred cannon threw up their emetic,
   And thirty thousand muskets flung their pills
Like hail, to make a bloody diuretic.
   Mortality! thou hast thy monthly bills;
Thy plagues, thy famines, thy physicians, yet tick,
   Like the death-watch, within our ears the ills
Past, present, and to come;—but all may yield
To the true portrait of one battle-field.

XIII

There the still varying pangs, which multiply
   Until their very number makes men hard
By the infinities of agony,
   Which meet the gaze whate'er it may regard—
The groan, the roll in dust, the all-white eye
   Turn'd back within its socket,—these reward
Your rank and file by thousands, while the rest
May win perhaps a riband at the breast!

XIV

Yet I love glory;—glory's a great thing:—
   Think what it is to be in your old age

Maintain'd at the expense of your good king:
  A moderate pension shakes full many a sage,
And heroes are but made for bards to sing,
  Which is still better; thus in verse to wage
Your wars eternally, besides enjoying
Half-pay for life, make mankind worth destroying.

XV

The troops, already disembark'd, push'd on
  To take a battery on the right; the others,
Who landed lower down, their landing done,
  Had set to work as briskly as their brothers:
Being grenadiers, they mounted one by one,
  Cheerful as children climb the breasts of mothers,
O'er the entrenchment and the palisade,
Quite orderly, as if upon parade.

XVI

And this was admirable; for so hot
  The fire was, that were red Vesuvius loaded,
Besides its lava, with all sorts of shot
  And shell or hells, it could not more have goaded.
Of officers a third fell on the spot,
  A thing which victory by no means boded
To gentlemen engaged in the assault:
Hounds, when the huntsman tumbles, are at fault.

XVII

But here I leave the general concern,
  To track our hero on his path of fame:
He must his laurels separately earn;
  For fifty thousand heroes, name by name,
Though all deserving equally to turn
  A couplet, or an elegy to claim,
Would form a lengthy lexicon of glory,
And what is worse still, a much longer story. . . .

WHEN A MAN HATH NO FREEDOM

When a man hath no freedom to fight for at home,
    Let him combat for that of his neighbors;
Let him think of the glories of Greece and of Rome,
    And get knocked on the head for his labors.

To do good to mankind is the chivalrous plan,
    And is always as nobly requited;
Then battle for freedom wherever you can,
    And, if not shot or hanged, you'll get knighted.

Thomas Campbell

THE SOLDIER'S DREAM

Our bugles sang truce, for the night-cloud had lower'd,
   And the sentinel stars set their watch in the sky;
And thousands had sunk on the ground overpower'd,
   The weary to sleep, and the wounded to die.

When reposing that night on my pallet of straw
   By the wolf-scaring faggot that guarded the slain,
At the dead of the night a sweet vision I saw;
   And thrice ere the morning I dreamt it again.

Methought from the battle-field's dreadful array
   Far, far I had roam'd on a desolate track:
'Twas autumn,—and sunshine arose on the way
   To the home of my fathers, that welcomed me back.

I flew to the pleasant fields traversed so oft
   In life's morning march, when my bosom was young;
I heard my own mountain-goats bleating aloft,
   And knew the sweet strain that the corn-reapers sung.

Then pledged we the wine-cup, and fondly I swore
   From my home and my weeping friends never to part;
My little ones kissed me a thousand times o'er,
   And my wife sobb'd aloud in her fullness of heart.

'Stay—stay with us!—rest!—thou art weary and worn!—
   And fain was their war-broken soldier to stay;—
But sorrow return'd with the dawning of morn,
   And the voice in my dreaming ear melted away.

Charles Causley

I SAW A SHOT-DOWN ANGEL

I saw a shot-down angel in the park
His marble blood sluicing the dyke of death,
A sailing tree firing its brown sea-mark
Where he now wintered for his wounded breath.

I heard the bird-noise of his splintered wings
Sawing the steep sierra of the sky,
On his fixed brow the jewel of the Kings
Reeked the red morning with a starving eye.

I stretched my hand to hold him from the heat,
I fetched a cloth to bind him where he bled,
I brought a bowl to wash his golden feet,
I shone my shield to save him from the dead.

My angel spat my solace in my face
And fired my fingers with his burning shawl,
Crawling in blood and silver to a place
Where he could turn his torture to the wall.

Alone I wandered in the sneaking snow
The signature of murder on my day,
And from the gallows-tree, a careful crow
Hitched its appalling wings and flew away.

Walter Van Tilburg Clark

THE PORTABLE PHONOGRAPH

The red sunset, with narrow black cloud strips like threats across it, lay on the curved horizon of the prairie. The air was still and cold, and in it settled the mute darkness and greater cold of night. High in the air there was wind, for through the veil of the dusk the clouds could be seen gliding rapidly south and changing shapes. A queer sensation of torment, of two-sided, unpredictable nature, arose from the stillness of the earth air beneath the violence of the upper air. Out of the sunset, through the dead, matted grass and isolated weed stalks of the prairie, crept the narrow and deeply rutted remains of a road. In the road, in places, there were crusts of shallow, brittle ice. There were little islands of an old oiled pavement in the road too, but most of it was mud, now frozen rigid. The frozen mud still bore the toothed impress of great tanks, and a wanderer on the neighboring undulations might have stumbled, in this light, into large, partially filled-in and weed-grown cavities, their banks channeled and beginning to spread into badlands. These pits were such as might have been made by falling meteors, but they were not. They were the scars of gigantic bombs, their rawness already made a little natural by rain, seed, and time. Along the road there were rakish remnants of fence. There was also, just visible, one portion of tangled and multiple barbed wire still erect, behind which was a shelving ditch with small caves, now very quiet and empty, at intervals in its back wall. Otherwise there was no structure or remnant of a structure visible over the dome of the darkling earth, but only, in sheltered hollows, the darker shadows of young trees again.

Under the wuthering arch of a high wind a V of wild geese fled south. The rush of their pinions sounded briefly, and the faint, plaintive notes of their expeditionary talk. Then they left a still greater vacancy. There was the smell and expectation of snow, as there is likely to be when the wild geese fly south. From the remote distance, towards the red sky, came faintly the protracted howl and quick yap-yap of a prairie wolf.

North of the road, perhaps a hundred yards, lay the parallel and deeply intrenched course of a small creek, lined with leafless alders and willows. The creek was already silent under ice. Into the bank above it was dug a sort of cell, with a single opening, like the mouth of a mine tunnel. Within the cell there was a little red of fire, which showed dully through the opening, like a reflection or a deception of the imagination. The light came from the chary burning of four blocks of poorly aged peat, which gave off a petty warmth and much acrid smoke. But the precious remnants of wood, old fenceposts and timbers from the long-deserted dugouts, had to be saved for the real cold, for the time when a man's breath blew white, the moisture in his nostrils stiffened at once when he stepped out, and the expansive blizzards paraded for days over the vast open, swirling and settling and thickening, till the dawn of the cleared day when the sky was thin blue-green and the terrible cold, in which a man could not live for three hours unwarmed, lay over the uniformly drifted swell of the plain.

Around the smoldering peat four men were seated crosslegged. Behind them, traversed by their shadows, was the earth bench, with two old and dirty army blankets, where the owner of the cell slept. In a niche in the opposite wall were a few utensils which caught the glint of the coals. The host was rewrapping in a piece of daubed burlap four fine, leather-bound books. He worked slowly and very carefully and at last tied the bundle securely with a piece of grass-woven cord. The other three looked intently upon the process, as if a great significance lay in it. As the host tied the cord he spoke. He was an old man, his long, matted beard and hair gray to nearly white. The shadows made his brows and cheekbones appear gnarled, his eyes and cheeks deeply sunken. His big hands, rough with frost and swollen by rheumatism, were awkward but gentle at their task. He was like a prehistoric priest performing a fateful ceremonial rite. Also his voice had in it a suitable quality of deep, reverent despair, yet perhaps at the moment a sharpness of selfish satisfaction.

"When I perceived what was happening," he said, "I told myself, 'It is the end. I cannot take much; I will take these.'"

"Perhaps I was impractical," he continued. "But for myself, I do not regret, and what do we know of those who will come after us? We are the doddering remnant of a race of mechanical fools. I have saved what I love; the soul of what was good in us is here; perhaps the new ones will make a strong enough beginning not to fall behind when they become clever."

He rose with slow pain and placed the wrapped volumes in the niche with his utensils. The others watched him with the same ritualistic gaze.

"Shakespeare, the Bible, *Moby Dick, The Divine Comedy*," one of them said softly. "You might have done worse, much worse."

"You will have a little soul left until you die," said another harshly. "That is more than is true of us. My brain becomes thick, like my hands." He held the big, battered hands, with their black nails, in the glow to be seen.

"I want paper to write on," he said. "And there is none."

The fourth man said nothing. He sat in the shadow farthest from the fire, and sometimes his body jerked in its rags from the cold. Although he was still young, he was sick and coughed often. Writing implied a greater future than he now felt able to consider.

The old man seated himself laboriously and reached out, groaning at the movement, to put another block of peat on the fire. With bowed heads and averted eyes his three guests acknowledged his magnanimity.

"We thank you, Dr. Jenkins, for the reading," said the man who had named the books.

They seemed then to be waiting for something. Dr. Jenkins understood but was loath to comply. In an ordinary moment he would have said nothing. But the words of *The Tempest*, which he had been reading, and the religious attention of the three made this an unusual occasion.

"You wish to hear the phonograph," he said grudgingly.

The two middle-aged men stared into the fire, unable to formulate and expose the enormity of their desire.

The young man, however, said anxiously, between suppressed coughs, "Oh, please," like an excited child.

The old man rose again in his difficult way and went to the back of the cell. He returned and placed tenderly upon the packed floor, where the firelight might fall upon it, an old portable phonograph in a black case. He smoothed the top with his hand and then opened it. The lovely green-felt-covered disk became visible.

"I have been using thorns as needles," he said. "But tonight, because we have a musician among us"—he bent his head to the young man, almost invisible in the shadow—"I will use a steel needle. There are only three left."

The two middle-aged men stared at him in speechless adoration. The one with the big hands, who wanted to write, moved his lips, but the whisper was not audible.

"Oh, don't!" cried the young man, as if he were hurt. "The thorns will do beautifully."

"No," the old man said. "I have become accustomed to the thorns, but they are not really good. For you, my young friend, we will have good music tonight.

"After all," he added generously, and beginning to wind the phonograph, which creaked, "they can't last forever."

"No, nor we," the man who needed to write said harshly. "The needle, by all means."

"Oh, thanks," said the young man. "Thanks," he said again in a low, excited voice, and then stifled his coughing with a bowed head.

"The records, though," said the old man when he had finished winding, "are a different matter. Already they are very worn. I do not play them more than once a week. One, once a week, that is what I allow myself.

"More than a week I cannot stand it; not to hear them," he apologized.

"No, how could you?" cried the young man. "And with them here like this."

"A man can stand anything," said the man who wanted to write, in his harsh, antagonistic voice.

"Please, the music," said the young man.

"Only the one," said the old man. "In the long run, we will remember more that way."

He had a dozen records with luxuriant gold and red seals. Even in that light the others could see that the threads of the records were becoming worn. Slowly he read out the titles and the tremendous, dead names of the composers and the artists and the orchestras. The three worked upon the names in their minds, carefully. It was difficult to select from such a wealth what they would at once most like to remember. Finally the man who wanted to write named Gershwin's "New York."

"Oh, no!" cried the sick young man, and then could say nothing more because he had to cough. The others understood him, and the harsh man withdrew his selection and waited for the musician to choose.

The musician begged Dr. Jenkins to read the titles again, very slowly, so that he could remember the sounds. While they were read he lay back against the wall, his eyes closed, his thin, horny hand pulling at his light beard, and listened to the voices and the orchestras and the single instruments in his mind.

When the reading was done he spoke despairingly. "I have forgotten," he complained. "I cannot hear them clearly.

"There are things missing," he explained.

"I know," said Dr. Jenkins. "I thought that I knew all of Shelley by heart. I should have brought Shelley."

"That's more soul than we can use," said the harsh man. *"Moby Dick* is better.

"By God, we can understand that," he emphasized.

The Doctor nodded.

"Still," said the man who had admired the books, "we need the absolute if we are to keep a grasp on anything.

"Anything but these sticks and peat clods and rabbit snares," he said bitterly.

"Shelley desired an ultimate absolute," said the harsh man. "It's too much," he said. "It's no good; no earthly good."

The musician selected a Debussy nocturne. The others considered and approved. They rose to their knees to watch the Doctor prepare for the playing, so that they appeared to be actually in an attitude of worship. The peat glow showed the thinness of their bearded faces, and the deep lines in them, and revealed the condition of their garments. The other two continued to kneel as the old man carefully lowered the needle onto the spinning disk, but the musician suddenly drew back against the wall again, with his knees up, and buried his face in his hands.

At the first notes of the piano the listeners were startled. They stared at each other. Even the musician lifted his head in amazement but then quickly bowed it again, strainingly, as if he were suffering from a pain he might not be able to endure. They were all listening deeply, without movement. The wet, blue-green notes tinkled forth from the old machine and were individual, delectable presences in the cell. The individual, delectable presences swept into a sudden tide of unbearably beautiful dissonance and then continued fully the swelling and ebbing of that tide, the dissonant inpourings, and the resolutions, and the diminishments, and the little, quiet wavelets of interlude lapping between. Every sound was piercing and singularly sweet. In all the men except the musician there occurred rapid sequences of tragically heightened recollection. He heard nothing but what was there. At the final, whispering disappearance, but moving quietly so that the others would not hear him and look at him, he let his head fall back in agony, as if it were drawn there by the hair, and clenched the fingers of one hand over his teeth. He sat that way while the others were silent and until they began to breathe again normally. His drawn-up legs were trembling violently.

Quickly Dr. Jenkins lifted the needle off, to save it and not to spoil the recollection with scraping. When he had stopped the whirling of the sacred disk he courteously left the phonograph open and by the fire, in sight.

The others, however, understood. The musician rose last, but then abruptly, and went quickly out at the door without saying anything. The others stopped at the door and gave their thanks in low voices. The Doctor nodded magnificently.

"Come again," he invited, "in a week. We will have the 'New York.' "

When the two had gone together, out towards the rimed road, he stood in the entrance, peering and listening. At first there was only the resonant boom of the wind overhead, and then far over the dome of the dead, dark plain the wolf cry lamenting. In the rifts of clouds the Doctor saw four stars flying. It impressed the Doctor that one of them had just been obscured by the beginning of a flying cloud at the very moment he heard what he had been listening for, a sound of suppressed coughing. It was not near by, however. He believed that down against the pale alders he could see the moving shadow.

With nervous hands he lowered the piece of canvas which served as his door and pegged it at the bottom. Then quickly and quietly, looking at the piece of canvas frequently, he slipped the records into the case, snapped the lid shut, and carried the phonograph to his couch. There, pausing often to stare at the canvas and listen, he dug earth from the wall and disclosed a piece of board. Behind this there was a deep hole in the wall, into which he put the phonograph. After a moment's consideration he went over and reached down his bundle of books and inserted it also. Then, guardedly, he once more sealed up the hole with the board and the earth. He also changed his blankets and the grass-stuffed sack which served as a pillow, so that he could lie facing the entrance. After carefully placing two more blocks of peat upon the fire he stood for a long time watching the stretched canvas, but it seemed to billow naturally with the first gust of a lowering wind. At last he prayed, and got in under his blankets, and closed his smoke-smarting eyes. On the inside of the bed, next the wall, he could feel with his hand the comfortable piece of lead pipe.

Stephen Crane

WAR IS KIND

Do not weep, maiden, for war is kind.
Because your lover threw wild hands toward the sky
And the affrighted steed ran on alone,
Do not weep.
War is kind.

> Hoarse, booming drums of the regiment,
> Little souls who thirst for fight,
> These men were born to drill and die.
> The unexplained glory flies above them,
> Great is the battle god, great, and his kingdom
> A field where a thousand corpses lie.

Do not weep, babe, for war is kind.
Because your father tumbled in the yellow trenches,
Raged at his breast, gulped and died,
Do not weep.
War is kind.

> Swift blazing flag of the regiment,
> Eagle with crest of red and gold,
> These men were born to drill and die.
> Point for them the virtue of slaughter,
> Make plain to them the excellence of killing
> And a field where a thousand corpses lie.

Mother whose heart hung humble as a button
On the bright splendid shroud of your son,
Do not weep.
War is kind.

AN EPISODE OF WAR

The lieutenant's rubber blanket lay on the ground, and upon it he had poured the company's supply of coffee. Corporals and other representatives of the grimy and hot-throated men who lined the breast-work had come for each squad's portion.

The lieutenant was frowning and serious at this task of division. His lips pursed as he drew with his sword various crevices in the heap, until brown squares of coffee, astoundingly equal in size, appeared on the blanket. He was on the verge of a great triumph in mathematics, and the corporals were thronging forward, each to reap a little square, when suddenly the lieutenant cried out and looked quickly at a man near him as if he suspected it was a case of personal assault. The others cried out also when they saw blood upon the lieutenant's sleeve.

He had winced like a man stung, swayed dangerously, and then straightened. The sound of his hoarse breathing was plainly audible. He looked sadly, mystically, over the breast-work at the green face of a wood, where now were many little puffs of white smoke. During this moment the men about him gazed statuelike and silent, astonished and awed by this catastrophe which happened when catastrophes were not expected—when they had leisure to observe it.

As the lieutenant stared at the wood, they too swung their heads, so that for another instant all hands, still silent, contemplated the distant forest as if their minds were fixed upon the mystery of a bullet's journey.

The officer had, of course, been compelled to take his sword into his left hand. He did not hold it by the hilt. He gripped it at the middle of the blade, awkwardly. Turning his eyes from the hostile wood, he looked at the sword as he held it there, and seemed puzzled as to what to do with it, where to put it. In short, this weapon had of a sudden become a strange thing to him. He looked at it in a kind of stupefaction, as if he had been endowed with a trident, a sceptre, or a spade.

Finally he tried to sheathe it. To sheathe a sword held by the left hand, at the middle of the blade, in a scabbard hung at the left hip, is a feat worthy of a sawdust ring. This wounded officer engaged in a desperate struggle with the sword and the wobbling scabbard, and during the time of it he breathed like a wrestler.

But at this instant the men, the spectators, awoke from their stonelike poses and crowded forward sympathetically. The orderly-sergeant took the sword and tenderly placed it in the scabbard. At the time, he leaned nervously backward, and did not allow even his finger to brush the body of the lieutenant. A wound gives strange dignity to him who bears it. Well men shy from this new and terrible majesty. It is as if the wounded man's hand is upon the curtain which hangs before the revelations of all existence—the meaning of ants, potentates, wars, cities, sunshine, snow, a feather dropped from a bird's wing; and the power of it sheds radiance upon a bloody form, and makes the other men understand sometimes that they are little. His comrades look at him with large eyes thoughtfully. Moreover, they fear vaguely that the weight of a finger upon him might send him headlong, precipitate the tragedy, hurl him at once into the dim, grey unknown. And so the orderly-sergeant, while sheathing the sword, leaned nervously backward.

There were others who proffered assistance. One timidly presented his shoulder and asked the lieutenant if he cared to lean upon it, but the latter waved him away mournfully. He wore the look of one who knows he is the victim of a terrible disease and understands his helplessness. He again stared over the breast-work at the forest, and then, turning, went slowly rearward. He held his right wrist tenderly in his left hand as if the wounded arm was made of very brittle glass.

And the men in silence stared at the wood, then at the departing lieutenant; then at the wood, then at the lieutenant.

As the wounded officer passed from the line of battle, he was enabled to see many things which as a participant in the fight were unknown to him. He saw a general on a black horse gazing over the lines of blue infantry at the green woods which veiled his problems. An aide galloped furiously, dragged his horse suddenly to a halt, saluted, and presented a paper. It was, for a wonder, precisely like a historical painting.

To the rear of the general and his staff a group, composed of a bugler, two or three orderlies, and the bearer of the corps standard, all upon maniacal horses, were working like slaves to hold their ground, preserve their respectful interval, while the shells boomed in the air about them, and caused their chargers to make furious quivering leaps.

A battery, a tumultuous and shining mass, was swirling toward the right. The wild thud of hoofs, the cries of the riders shouting blame and praise, menace and encouragement, and, last, the roar of the wheels, the slant of the glistening guns, brought the lieutenant to an intent pause. The battery swept in curves that stirred the heart; it made halts as dramatic as the crash of a wave on the rocks, and when it fled onward this aggregation of wheels, levers, motors had a beautiful unity, as if it were a missile. The sound of it was a war-chorus that reached into the depths of man's emotion.

The lieutenant, still holding his arm as if it were of glass, stood watching this battery until all detail of it was lost, save the figures of the riders, which rose and fell and waved lashes over the black mass.

Later, he turned his eyes toward the battle, where the shooting sometimes crackled like bush-fires, sometimes sputtered with exasperating irregularity, and sometimes reverberated like the thunder. He saw the smoke rolling upward and saw crowds of men who ran and cheered, or stood and blazed away at the inscrutable distance.

He came upon some stragglers, and they told him how to find the field hospital. They described its exact location. In fact, these men, no longer having part in the battle, knew more of it than others. They told the performance of every corps, every division, the opinion of every general. The lieutenant, carrying his wounded arm rearward, looked upon them with wonder.

At the roadside a brigade was making coffee and buzzing with talk like a girls' boarding school. Several officers came out to him and inquired concerning things of which he knew nothing. One, seeing his arm, began to scold. "Why, man, that's no way to do. You want to fix that thing." He appropriated the lieutenant and the lieutenant's wound. He cut the sleeve and laid bare the arm, every nerve of which softly fluttered under his touch. He bound his handkerchief over the wound, scolding away in the meantime. His tone allowed one to think that he was in the habit of being wounded every day. The lieutenant hung his head, feeling, in this presence, that he did not know how to be correctly wounded.

The low white tents of the hospital were grouped around an old schoolhouse. There was here a singular commotion. In the foreground two ambulances interlocked wheels in the deep mud. The drivers were tossing the blame of it back and forth, gesticulating and berating, while from the ambulances, both crammed with wounded, there came an occasional groan. An interminable crowd of bandaged men were coming and going. Great numbers sat under the trees nursing heads or arms or legs. There was a dispute of some kind raging on the steps of the schoolhouse. Sitting with his back against a tree a man with a face as grey as a new army blanket was serenely smoking a corncob pipe. The lieutenant wished to rush forward and inform him that he was dying.

A busy surgeon was passing near the lieutenant. "Good-morning," he said, with a friendly smile. Then he caught sight of the lieutenant's arm, and his face at once changed. "Well, let's have a look at it." He seemed possessed suddenly of a great contempt for the lieutenant. This wound evidently placed the latter on a very low social plane. The doctor cried out impatiently: "What mutton-head had tied it up that way anyhow?" The lieutenant answered, "Oh, a man."

When the wound was disclosed the doctor fingered it disdainfully. "Humph," he said. "You come along with me and I'll tend to you." His voice contained the same scorn as if he were saying: "You will have to go to jail."

The lieutenant had been very meek, but now his face flushed, and he looked into the doctor's eyes. "I guess I won't have it amputated," he said.

"Nonsense, man! Nonsense! Nonsense!" cried the doctor. "Come along, now. I won't amputate it. Come along. Don't be a baby."

"Let go of me," said the lieutenant, holding back wrathfully, his glance fixed upon the door of the old schoolhouse, as sinister to him as the portals of death.

And this is the story of how the lieutenant lost his arm. When he reached home, his sisters, his mother, his wife, sobbed for a long time at the sight of the flat sleeve. "Oh, well," he said, standing shamefaced amid these tears, "I don't suppose it matters so much as all that."

THE UPTURNED FACE

"What will we do now?" said the adjutant, troubled and excited.

"Bury him," said Timothy Lean.

The two officers looked down close to their toes where lay the body of their comrade. The face was chalk-blue; gleaming eyes stared at the sky. Over the two upright figures was a windy sound of bullets, and on the top of the hill Lean's prostrate company of Spitzbergen infantry was firing measured volleys.

"Don't you think it would be better—" began the adjutant. "We might leave him until to-morrow."

"No," said Lean. "I can't hold that post an hour longer. I've got to fall back, and we've got to bury old Bill."

"Of course," said the adjutant, at once. "Your men got entrenching tools?"

Lean shouted back to his little line, and two men came slowly, one with a pick, one with a shovel. They started in the direction of the Rostina sharpshooters. Bullets cracked near their ears. "Dig here," said Lean gruffly. The men, thus caused to lower their glances to the turf, became hurried and frightened, merely because they could not look to see whence the bullets came. The dull beat of the pick striking the earth sounded amid the swift snap of close bullets. Presently the other private began to shovel.

"I suppose," said the adjutant, slowly, "we'd better search his clothes for—things."

Lean nodded. Together in curious abstraction they looked at the body. Then Lean stirred his shoulders suddenly, arousing himself.

"Yes," he said, "we'd better see what he's got." He

dropped to his knees, and his hands approached the body of the dead officer. But his hands wavered over the buttons of the tunic. The first button was brick-red with drying blood, and he did not seem to dare touch it.

"Go on," said the adjutant, hoarsely.

Lean stretched his wooden hand, and his fingers fumbled the bloodstained buttons. At last he rose with ghastly face. He had gathered a watch, a whistle, a pipe, a tobacco-pouch, a handkerchief, a little case of cards and papers. He looked at the adjutant. There was a silence. The adjutant was feeling that he had been a coward to make Lean do all the grisly business.

"Well," said Lean, "that's all, I think. You have his sword and revolver?"

"Yes," said the adjutant, his face working, and then he burst out in a sudden strange fury at the two privates. "Why don't you hurry up with that grave? What are you doing, anyhow? Hurry, do you hear? I never saw such stupid—"

Even as he cried out in his passion the two men were labouring for their lives. Ever overhead the bullets were spitting.

The grave was finished. It was not a masterpiece—a poor little shallow thing. Lean and the adjutant again looked at each other in a curious silent communication.

Suddenly the adjutant croaked out in a weird laugh. It was a terrible laugh, which had its origin in that part of the mind which is first moved by the singing of the nerves. "Well," he said humorously to Lean, "I suppose we had best tumble him in."

"Yes," said Lean. The two privates stood waiting, bent over their implements. "I suppose," said Lean, "it would be better if we laid him in ourselves."

"Yes," said the adjutant. Then, apparently remembering that he had made Lean search the body, he stooped with great fortitude and took hold of the dead officer's clothing. Lean joined him. Both were particular that their fingers should not feel the corpse. They tugged away; the corpse lifted, heaved, toppled, flopped into the grave, and the two officers, straightening, looked again at each other—they were always looking at each other. They sighed with relief.

The adjutant said, "I suppose we should—we should say something. Do you know the service, Tim?"

"They don't read the service until the grave is filled in," said Lean, pressing his lips to an academic expression.

"Don't they?" said the adjutant, shocked that he had made the mistake. "Oh, well," he cried, suddenly, "let us— let us say something—while he can hear us."

"All right," said Lean. "Do you know the service?"

"I can't remember a line of it," said the adjutant.

Lean was extremely dubious. "I can repeat two lines, but—"

"Well, do it," said the adjutant. "Go as far as you can. That's better than nothing. And the beasts have got our range exactly."

Lean looked at his two men, "Attention," he barked. The privates came to attention with a click, looking much aggrieved. The adjutant lowered his helmet to his knee. Lean, bareheaded, stood over the grave. The Rostina sharp-shooters fired briskly.

"O Father, our friend has sunk in the deep waters of death, but his spirit has leaped toward Thee as the bubble arises from the lips of the drowning. Perceive, we beseech, O Father, the little flying bubble, and—"

Lean, although husky and ashamed, had suffered no hesitation up to this point, but he stopped with a hopeless feeling and looked at the corpse.

The adjutant moved uneasily. "And from Thy superb heights—" he began, and then he too came to an end.

"And from Thy superb heights," said Lean.

The adjutant suddenly remembered a phrase in the back of the Spitzbergen burial service, and he exploited it with the triumphant manner of a man who has recalled everything, and can go on.

"O God, have mercy—"

"O God, have mercy—" said Lean.

"Mercy," repeated the adjutant, in quick failure.

"Mercy," said Lean. And then he was moved by some violence of feeling, for he turned upon his two men and tigerishly said, "Throw the dirt in."

The fire of the Rostina sharpshooters was accurate and continuous.

One of the aggrieved privates came forward with his
shovel. He lifted his first shovel-load of earth, and for a
moment of inexplicable hesitation it was held poised above
his corpse, which from its chalk-blue face looked keenly
out from the grave. Then the soldier emptied his shovel on
—on the feet.

Timothy Lean felt as if tons had been swiftly lifted from
off his forehead. He had felt that perhaps the private might
empty the shovel on—on the face. It had been emptied on
the feet. There was a great point gained there—ha, ha!—
the first shovelful had been emptied on the feet. How
satisfactory!

The adjutant began to babble. "Well, of course—a man
we've messed with all these years—impossible—you can't,
you know, leave your intimate friends rotting on the field.
Go on, for God's sake, and shovel, you."

The man with the shovel suddenly ducked, grabbed his
left arm with his right arm, and looked at his officer for
orders. Lean picked the shovel from the ground. "Go to the
rear," he said to the wounded man. He also addressed the
other private, "You get under cover, too; I'll finish this
business."

The wounded man scrambled hard still for the top of the
ridge without devoting any glances to the direction from
where the bullets came, and the other man followed at an
equal pace; but he was different, in that he looked back
anxiously three times.

This is merely the way—often—of the hit and unhit.

Timothy Lean filled the shovel, hesitated, and then, in a
movement which was like a gesture of abhorrence, he
flung the dirt into the grave, and as it landed it made a
sound—plop. Lean suddenly stopped and mopped his brow—
a tired labourer.

"Perhaps we have been wrong," said the adjutant. His
glance wavered stupidly. "It might have been better if we
hadn't buried him just at this time. Of course, if we advance
to-morrow the body would have been—"

"Damn you," said Lean, "shut your mouth." He was not
the senior officer.

He again filled the shovel and flung the earth. Always the
earth made that sound—plop. For a space Lean worked fran-
tically, like a man digging himself out of danger.

Soon there was nothing to be seen but the chalk-blue fac[e]
Lean filled the shovel. "Good God," he cried to the adjutar[t]
"Why didn't you turn him somehow when you put him i[n]
This—" Then Lean began to stutter.

The adjutant understood. He was pale to the lips. "Go o[n]
man," he cried, beseechingly, almost in a shout.

Lean swung back the shovel. It went forward in a pendulu[m]
curve. When the earth landed it made a sound—plop.

e. e. cummings

I SING OF OLAF

i sing of Olaf glad and big
whose warmest heart recoiled at war:
a conscientious object-or

his wellbbelovéd colonel (trig
westpointer most succinctly bred)
took erring Olaf soon in hand;
but—though an host of overjoyed
noncoms (first knocking on the head
him) do through icy waters roll
that helplessness which others stroke
with brushes recently employed
anent this muddy toiletbowl,
while kindred intellects evoke
allegiance per blunt instruments—
Olaf (being to all intents
a corpse and wanting any rag
upon what God unto him gave)
responds, without getting annoyed
"I will not kiss your f.ing flag"

straightway the silver bird looked grave
(departing hurriedly to shave)

but—though all kinds of officers
(a yearning nation's blueeyed pride)
their passive prey did kick and curse
until for wear their clarion
voices and boots were much the worse,
and egged the firstclassprivates on
his rectum wickedly to tease
by means of skilfully applied

bayonets roasted hot with heat—
Olaf (upon what were once knees)
does almost ceaselessly repeat
"there is some s. I will not eat"

our president, being of which
assertions duly notified
threw the yellowsonofabitch
into a dungeon, where he died

Christ (of His mercy infinite)
i pray to see; and Olaf, too

preponderatingly because
unless statistics lie he was
more brave than me: more blond than you

Alphonse Daudet

THE LAST LESSON

I started for school very late that morning and was in great dread of a scolding, especially because M. Hamel had said that he would question us on participles, and I did not know the first word about them. For a moment I thought of running away and spending the day out of doors. It was so warm, so bright! The birds were chirping at the edge of the woods; and in the open field back of the saw-mill the Prussian soldiers were drilling. It was all much more tempting than the rule for participles, but I had the strength to resist, and hurried off to school.

When I passed the town hall there was a crowd in front of the bulletin-board. For the last two years all our bad news had come from there—the lost battles, the draft, the orders of the commanding officer—and I thought to myself, without stopping:

"What can be the matter now?"

Then, as I hurried by as fast as I could go, the blacksmith, Wachter, who was there, with his apprentice, reading the bulletin, called after me:

"Don't go so fast, bub; you'll get to your school in plenty of time!"

I thought he was making fun of me, and reached M. Hamel's little garden all out of breath.

Usually, when school began, there was a great bustle, which could be heard out in the street, the opening and closing of desks, lessons repeated in unison, very loud, with our hands over our ears to understand better, and the teacher's great ruler rapping on the table. But now it was all so still! I had counted on the commotion to get to my desk without being seen; but, of course, that day everything had to be as quiet as Sunday morning. Through the window I saw my classmates, already in their places, and M. Hamel walking up and down with his terrible iron ruler under his arm. I had to open the door and go in before everybody. You can imagine how I blushed and how frightened I was.

But nothing happened. M. Hamel saw me and said very kindly:

"Go to your place quickly, little Franz. We were beginning without you."

I jumped over the bench and sat down at my desk. Not till then, when I had got a little over my fright, did I see that our teacher had on his beautiful green coat, his frilled shirt, and the little black silk cap, all embroidered, that he never wore except on inspection and prize days. Besides, the whole school seemed so strange and solemn. But the thing that surprised me most was to see, on the back benches that were always empty, the village people sitting quietly like ourselves; old Hauser, with his three-cornered hat, the former mayor, the former postmaster, and several others besides. Everybody looked sad; and Hauser had brought an old primer, thumbed at the edges, and he held it open on his knees with his great spectacles lying across the pages.

While I was wondering about it all, M. Hamel mounted his chair, and, in the same grave and gentle tone which he had used to me, said:

"My children, this is the last lesson I shall give you. The order has come from Berlin to teach only German in the schools of Alsace and Lorraine. The new master comes tomorrow. This is your last French lesson. I want you to be very attentive."

What a thunderclap these words were to me!

Oh, the wretches; that was what they had put up at the town hall!

My last French lesson! Why, I hardly knew how to write! I should never learn any more! I must stop there, then! Oh, how sorry I was for not learning my lessons, for seeking birds' eggs, or going sliding on the Saar! My books, that had seemed such a nuisance a while ago, so heavy to carry, my grammar, and my history of the saints, were old friends now that I couldn't give up. And M. Hamel, too; the idea that he was going away, that I should never see him again, made me forget all about his ruler and how cranky he was.

Poor man! It was in honor of this last lesson that he had put on his fine Sunday clothes, and now I understood why the old men of the village were sitting there in the back of the room. It was because they were sorry, too, that they had not gone to school more. It was their way of thanking our master for his forty years of faithful service and of showing their respect for the country that was theirs no more.

While I was thinking of all this, I heard my name called. It was my turn to recite. What would I not have given to be able to say that dreadful rule for the participle all through, very loud and clear, and without one mistake? But I got mixed up on the first words and stood there, holding on to my desk, my heart beating, and not daring to look up. I heard M. Hamel say to me:

"I won't scold you, little Franz; you must feel bad enough. See how it is! Every day we have said to ourselves: 'Bah! I've plenty of time. I'll learn it to-morrow.' And now you see where we've come out. Ah, that's the great trouble with Alsace; she puts off learning till to-morrow. Now those fellows out there will have the right to say to you: 'How is it; you pretend to be Frenchmen, and yet you can neither speak nor write your own language?' But you are not the worst, poor little Franz. We've all a great deal to reproach ourselves with.

"Your parents were not anxious to have you learn. They preferred to put you to work on a farm or at the mills, so as to have a little more money. And I? I've been to blame also. Have I not often sent you to water my flowers instead of learning your lessons? And when I wanted to go fishing, did I not just give you a holiday?"

Then, from one thing to another, M. Hamel went on to talk of the French language, saying that it was the most beautiful language in the world—the clearest, the most logical; that we must guard it among us and never forget it, because when a people are enslaved, as long as they hold fast to their language it is as if they had the key to their prison. Then he opened a grammar and read us our lesson. I was amazed to see how well I understood it. All he said seemed so easy, so easy! I think, too, that I had never listened so carefully, and that he had never explained everything with so much patience. It seemed almost as if the poor man wanted to give us all he knew before going away, and to put it all into our heads at one stroke.

After the grammar, we had a lesson in writing. That day M. Hamel had new copies for us, written in a beautiful round hand: France, Alsace, France, Alsace. They looked like little flags, floating everywhere in the school-room, hung from the rod at the top of our desks. You ought to have seen how every one set to work, and how quiet it was! The only sound was the scratching of the pens over the paper. Once some beetles flew in; but nobody paid any attention to them, not even the littlest ones, who worked right on tracing their fish-hooks, as if that was French, too. On the roof the pigeons cooed very low, and I thought to myself:

"Will they make them sing in German, even the pigeons?"

Whenever I looked up from my writing I saw M. Hamel sitting motionless in his chair and gazing first at one thing, then at another, as if he wanted to fix in his mind just how everything looked in that little school-room. Fancy! For forty years he had been there in the same place, with his garden outside the window and his class in front of him, just like that. Only the desks and benches had been worn smooth; the walnut-trees in the garden were taller, and the hop-vine that he had planted himself twined about the windows to the roof. How it must have broken his heart to leave it all, poor man; to hear his sister moving about in the room above, packing their trunks! For they must leave the country next day.

But he had the courage to hear every lesson to the very last. After the writing, we had a lesson in history, and then the babies chanted their ba, be, bi, bo, bu. Down there at the back of the room old Hauser had put on his spectacles and, holding his primer in both hands, spelled the letters with them. You could see that he, too, was crying; his voice trembled with emotion, and it was so funny to hear him that we all wanted to laugh and cry. Ah, how well I remember it, that last lesson!

All at once the church-clock struck twelve. Then the Angelus. At the same moment the trumpets of the Prussians, returning from drill, sounded under our windows. M. Hamel stood up, very pale, in his chair. I never saw him look so tall.

"My friends," said he, "I—I—" But something choked him. He could not go on.

Then he turned to the blackboard, took a piece of chalk, and, bearing on with all his might, he wrote as large as he could:

"Vive La France!"

Then he stopped and leaned his head against the wall, and, without a word, he made a gesture to us with his hand:

"School is dismissed—you may go."

G. Lowes Dickinson

THREE NOTES ON WAR

I. WAR MEANS THE DESTRUCTION OF MANKIND

My theme may be put in a sentence:—If mankind does not end war, war will end mankind. This has not been true in the past. But it is true in the present. For the present has produced something new. It has produced science. And if science is the principal hope of mankind, it is also the principal menace. For it can destroy as easily as it can create; and all that it creates is useless, if it creates only to destroy. But destruction is what war means; and all its other meanings are made meaningless by this.

Let me illustrate. On this day, March 22, 1922, I read in my newspaper a discussion in the House of Commons on the Aircraft Force. A member (says the account) "drew attention to the probable horrors of the next war. Vast fleets of aeroplanes would come over our towns with bombs of 4,000 or 5,000 pounds containing high explosives, poison gas, and probably cholera germs, and the women and children in those towns would suffer as much as the men engaged in actual warfare." Or take another statement, by Major-General Seeley, ex-Minister of War: "Chemical knowledge was now so far advanced that, with very little trouble and at very moderate cost, a hundred thousand people could be blotted out by lethal gas during an air raid. A great deal of nonsense had been spoken about wonderful discoveries. The truth was that the manufacture of the most deadly gases was easy and inexpensive. It was simple and horrible. The choice was really between disarmament and extermination."

Take another testimony by Thomas Edison: "There exists no means of preventing a flotilla of aeroplanes from flying over London to-morrow and spreading a gas that would poison its millions in three hours. One day science will invent a machine so terrible in its possibilities, so absolutely terrifying that man himself will be appalled and renounce war for ever."

Mr. Edison's science is probably better than his knowledge of human nature. The whole question is, whether that terrible and stupid animal, man, can in fact be frightened off war by the proof that it means his destruction in this bestial way. Perhaps he cannot. But in any case the facts are clear and indisputable.

In all the principal countries of the world, after the "war to end war," men of science are busy investigating methods of destroying by war men, women, children, factories, cities, countries, continents. In part they know how to do it already, in part they are perfecting their weapons; and there is no limit to their powers. This was not true in the past, but it is true in the present and it will be truer in the future. There is the new fact, that puts out of date all the ordinary discussion of war. War now means extermination, not of soldiers only, but of civilians and of civilisation.

II. WAR CANNOT BE REGULATED

But "No," someone perhaps will say, "we will not go so far. We will regulate war so that it shall be waged in the old gentlemanly way. Then we can have war without universal destruction."

But war was regulated before the last war, and the regulation made no difference. Every weapon that could be used for destruction was used. "That was the Germans' fault!" Well, if you like, it was. But we imitated them. We made poison gas, and made it better than they. We made liquid fire, and made it better than they. We made air raids, and made them better than they. And if we did not use the submarine to sink merchant ships, that was only because we could deal with them as easily without. Did not one of our most popular heroes, Lord Fisher, write to the German Admiral Tirpitz: "I don't blame you for the submarine business. I would have done the same myself, only our idiots in England wouldn't believe it when I told 'em"?

It is waste of time to argue about who began this scientific savagery. There has not been, and there will not be, any impartial inquiry. It is enough for us to know that someone will always begin it. And if you choose to believe that that someone will always be not the English, but their enemies, that belief does not alter the argument. Someone will do it, and then, by way of "reprisals," the others will imitate them. For "reprisals" mean doing what you think wrong on the plea that someone else did it first.

Did you notice, the other day, what happened at Washington? The Powers were discussing the use of the submarine in war. The British, to whom imports by sea are more important than they are to any other nation, who therefore fear the submarine more than any other nation, and who also expect always to command the sea, and thus to be able to cut off an enemy's trade without recourse to the submarine—the British, for those reasons, proposed the abolition of the submarine. What did the French reply? That the submarine is a weapon of "defence," not of "offence," and that they proposed to build an enormous fleet of them. The British then produced an article, written by a French Naval Officer, defending all that the Germans did with the submarine in war. The French thereupon repudiated the article, and a rule was solemnly drawn up prohibiting the use of submarines as commerce destroyers. Do you believe that rule will be kept? If so, you are credulous.

Similarly, a rule was adopted at Washington prohibiting the use of poison gas. Do you believe that rule will be kept? It would be interesting to know which of the nations who signed it—the Americans, the British, the French, the Italians, the Japanese—have, since, shut down their establishments for manufacturing poison gas. Have the English? Would you feel happy if they had? Probably not. Probably you think we ought to be "prepared" in case the other fellow breaks the rule. And so does everybody think. But I will go further. Suppose we were losing a war, and thought we could win it by breaking one of these rules. Would you stand for our losing the war rather than making the breach? And if you would, would the Press? Would the Music Halls? Would the War Office? Would the Admiralty? Would Parliament? You know very well, or, if you do not, you ought to know, that every nation considers everything right which may secure it from defeat. I do not know whether those who sign such conventions as were drawn up at Washington really believe

they will be observed. I should be surprised if they did. But
if they do, then they are not fit to take in hand the policy of
nations. For they are relying on a broken reed. No rules to
restrain the conduct of war will ever be observed if victory
seems to depend upon the breach of them.

In truth, the character of the next war must be judged not
from what governments say, but from what they do. Watch
their actual experimental work. Watch their constructive work.
And be sure that while war exists it will always be as destructive as it can be. For war is not now what once it was
in Italy—a game of professionals, in which both sides agree
that it is cheaper not to kill the combatants. We fight now to
kill, and to kill by every means.

This is so much a matter of course that it is never even
disputed, except when somebody remembers that the Public
must be deceived. Thus, to return to the debate to which I
have referred, the member who called attention to the menace involved by future war, also urged the necessity of
defence. And what was his proposal? That we should build
a stronger Air Force than the expected enemy (that enemy
being, by the bye, that very France which for four and a half
years has been our brother-in-arms). "Our Air Force," he
said, "was ludicrously weak. France was spending four times
as much money on the Air Service as we were." And observe, please, the moral of this. We must be stronger than
France; but also, and equally (say the French), France must
be stronger than we. Thus, every increase on the one side
must be met by a greater increase on the other. And so it
is with every arm, and with every nation. Preparing for war
means that every nation must continually spend more and
more income on making more and more destructive armaments. It means that armies become bigger, guns more powerful, gas more poisonous, germs more potent, and whatever
else may be in the heads of these patient men of science more
destructive, until the moment comes when all this preparation
explodes into action. And then? Then, I submit to you, without any belief that I am exaggerating, then—the end of
civilised man.

Every day you, whom I am addressing, go about your
work. You marry yourself, or you marry your son or your
daughter. You plan for the future. You look forward to life,
for yourself, for your children, for your country. The play,

he music hall, the concert occupy and amuse you. You read
books. You ride in motor-cars. You travel. You hope and
aspire. And all this time, side by side with you, in this laboratory, at that harbour, in those barracks, accompanied by
cheerful music, wooed by patriotic songs, the agents of destruction are at work. They are people, no doubt, much like
others. But their work is to destroy all that those others are
building up; to make mockery of all their purposes and
hopes; to kill, with incredible tortures, incredible numbers of
men. This they are doing as a matter of course, as a patriotic
duty. Surely there is something very strange about this! Is a
nation, after all, nothing but a crowd of homicidal lunatics?

III. WHAT SOLDIERS HAVE TO DO

It is worth while to pause for a moment at that question.
Perhaps the answer is "Yes." Perhaps, really, men exist to
destroy, not to build. I know young men who say so, or who
almost say so. And if it be so, the fact cannot be altered by
an odd person, like myself, who happens not to be homicidal.
I cannot answer my own question one way or the other. But
I can at least ask it. And choosing to suppose (absurdly no
doubt), that I have before me the men of whom I want to
ask it, I will ask it of them one by one.

You, I will suppose, are a sailor. You belong to the Navy
that boasts a tradition finer and cleaner than that of any
other service. Well, what were you doing in the Great War?
One gallant action was fought, so far as I remember. One
gallant landing attack was made. There may have been others.
You may have been present. You may be, legitimately
enough, proud of the fact. But this was not a war, as other
wars have been, of naval battles. What then were you really
doing, most of the time? Maintaining the blockade, by which,
we are sometimes told, the war was won. Well, what was the
blockade? An attempt to starve to death the population of
Germany, and, in particular (for, of course, the burden would
fall first on them), the old men, and women, and little children. Believe me, you were fairly successful in that. I have
been in Germany since the war. I have been at the hospitals,
I have seen the crowds of rickety children produced by our
blockade. The number of those who died of hunger, or of the

diseases caused by hunger, is estimated at hundreds of thousands. That is what you were doing during the war with Germany. Then, when that war was over, you did the same thing to Russia, to our late Ally, to the people who had perished by millions to gain our victory. Russians, too, you starved, so far as you could. Even medical stores you kept out, so that operations by the knife had to be performed without chloroform. That is what your proud service was really doing. Do you like it? Do you approve it? Is it what you want to give your life to? Yet, in every future war, that, more than anything else, will be what a navy will be doing. I am not reproaching you. I am asking you the question. It seems to me that you ought to answer it. And upon your answer, and that of thousands like you, will depend in part the future of mankind. You may, of course—you probably will—choose not to reply, and not to consider. But what you cannot choose is, that your acts shall not produce their consequences.

I turn next to the airmen. Of you, too, it is said that you maintain the tradition of chivalry in war. I daresay you do. You have courage, as almost all men have. You risk your lives, as all soldiers do, and also all doctors and all miners. You bear no malice to your enemy. You drop wreaths on his grave. Yes, all that, and much more, no doubt, of which I do not know. But also, and as your main work, the thing for which you exist, you drop bombs not only on troops but on cities. You were perhaps yourself one of those who dropped them on a circus of little children at Karlsruhe. That was not your object? Very likely. But what has that to do with it? It was your work, and it always will be, and always must be, your work. For you cannot, and will not, pick and choose where your bombs will fall. As I read these words I come across a little controversy about the action of our Air Force among primitive people. A Flight-Lieutenant writes correcting a statement that the population of a certain village had been destroyed by bombs. The population, he says (no doubt with truth), were first removed. And then he adds: "It is not the custom of the Royal Air Force to murder women and children, or even inflict casualties upon natives, *unless absolutely necessary*." The italics are mine, and the words italicised contain the gist of the matter. It will not always be possible to remove the inhabitants, even though it be desired, any more than the inhabitants of Amritsar were removed before General Dyer shot into them. Our Flight-Lieutenant, I suspect, would not profess that it was his duty to refrain from bombing unless the inhabitants had been removed. Whatever the intention, and whatever the feelings of the Royal Air Force, that Force is, in fact, a women-and-children-bombing Force, and cannot help being so.

But, leaving aside this question about "policing," what about the next great war? Everyone knows, and everyone admits, that it will be fought largely in the air, and that the first objective will be the capital cities of the enemy countries. Our Flight-Lieutenant, if he should live to see that day, will be sent to bomb Berlin, or Paris, or Petrograd, or New York, according to the direction which politicians, uncontrolled and unnoticed by him, may have given to our policy. Or again, he will be bombing food-ships in order to starve the whole civil population of the enemy country. Plans for this performance are being worked out elaborately in America. I read to-day of "a fast-cruising sea ship which will carry a super-giant airship, which will contain a swarm of aeroplanes which can be rapidly put together in the air and started on a mission of destruction. Not only will it be possible to enforce an air blockade at the other side of the world, if necessary, but by employing what is to be called this new 'sea-airplane' on an extensive scale, it would be possible to keep on bombing and harrying, night as well as day, food-ships bringing vital cargoes to any country which was the object of this insidious and terrible form of air attrition." And so on. Now please do not ride off on idle speculations as to whether, as yet, this particular thing is possible. You know very well that, if it is not, it will be. You know that there is no limit to the powers of destruction. The point I want you to attend to is different. During the late war, all the flood-gates of rhetoric were opened to condemn the German submarine warfare, because it destroyed merchant ships without warning. Now, in the country which went to war because of that "crime," the experts are working out the means of destroying merchant-ships from the air, without warning or possibility of defence. Well? What about all these moral transports? They were mere talk, expressing anger at an enemy country. Every country engaged in the next war will do things much worse than that, and do it with a clear conscience—if conscience be a word to use in connexion with war. And you? Are you going to do that too? You are, of course, if you are told to. But what do you think of the thing called war that puts you on that kind of job? Are you going to wait passively till you are called upon so to act? Or are you going to join those who intend to stop war? Which is it to be? The question has been asked. The responsibility henceforth is yours. Which is it to be?

And you next, the artilleryman. Perhaps, by the next war your occupation may be gone—I do not know. But, supposing it is not, what do you think of it? Your shells fall a mile or two away. You do not see what happens when they fall. You do not see the limbs blown to pieces. You do not hear the cries and groans. You are cheerful when you hit your mark and depressed when you do not. I know. I have talked to you, and have found you a sensitive, humane man. And, you said, you did not at all mind what you did. No! But was your not minding a result of your not seeing and, therefore, not feeling? I do not know. Once more I ask the question. Have you the right to evade it?

And you, the infantryman, you on whom fell the main brunt of the war. As you crouched in your lousy trenches, as you went over the top, as you trampled on the faces of wounded men, as you tossed bombs into dug-outs, as you bayoneted men who were stretching hands of surrender, did you really like doing it? Do you want to return to doing it? Do you feel that life would be unbearably flat if there were no chance of your doing it? Perhaps you will say, yes. And if you do, then, of course, you will try to maintain war, and to oppose those who wish to abolish it. All I am asking for is candour. And does not one man owe candour to another, or at least to himself?

Alan Dugan

HOW WE HEARD THE NAME

The river brought down
dead horses, dead men
and military debris,
indicative of war
or official acts upstream,
but it went by, it all
goes by, that is the thing
about the river. Then
a soldier on a log
went by. He seemed drunk
and we asked him why
had he and this junk
come down to us so
from the past upstream.
"Friends," he said, "the great
Battle of Granicus
has just been won
by all of the Greeks except
the Lacedaemonians and
myself: this is a joke
between me and a man
named Alexander, whom
all of you ba-bas
will hear of as a god."

Jane Elliot

LAMENT FOR FLODDEN

I've heard them lilting at the ewe-milking,
  Lasses a' lilting before dawn of day;
But now they are moaning on ilka green loaning—
  The Flowers of the Forest are a' wede away.

At bughts, in the morning, nae blythe lads are scorning,
  Lasses are lonely and dowie and wae;
Nae daffing, nae gabbing, but sighing and sabbing,
  Ilk ane lifts her leglin and hies her away.

In har'st, at the shearing, nae youths now are jeering,
  Bandsters are runkled, and lyart, or grey;
At fair or at preaching, nae wooing, nae fleeching—
  The Flowers of the Forest are a' wede away.

At e'en, in the gloaming, nae younkers are roaming
  'Bout stacks with the lasses at bogle to play;
But ilk maid sits dreary, lamenting her dearie—
  The Flowers of the Forest are weded away.

Dool and wae for the order, sent our lads to the Border!
  The English, for ance, by guile wan the day;
The Flowers of the Forest, that fought aye the foremost,
  The prime of our land, are cauld in the clay.

We'll hear nae mair lilting at the ewe-milking;
  Women and bairns are heartless and wae;
Sighing and moaning on ilka green loaning—
  The Flowers of the Forest are a' wede away.

D. J. Enright

APOCALYPSE

> *"After the New Apocalypse, very few members were still in possession of their instruments. Hardly a musician could call a decent suit his own. Yet by the early summer of 1945, strains of sweet music floated on the air again. While the town still reeked of smoke, charred buildings and the stench of corpses, the Philharmonic Orchestra bestowed the everlasting and imperishable joy which music never fails to give."*
>
> —from The Muses on the Banks of the Spree,
> a Berlin tourist brochure

It soothes the savage doubts.
One Bach outweighs ten Belsens. If 200,000 people
Were remaindered at Hiroshima, the sales of So-and-So's
new novel reached a higher figure in as short a time.
So, imperishable paintings reappeared:
Texts were reprinted:
Public buildings reconstructed:
Human beings reproduced.

After the Newer Apocalypse, very few members
Were still in possession of their instruments
(Very few were still in possession of their members),
And their suits were chiefly indecent.
Yet, while the town still reeked of smoke, etc.,
The Philharmonic Trio bestowed, etc.

A civilization vindicated,
A race with three legs still to stand on!
True, the violin was shortly silenced by leukaemia,
And the pianoforte crumbled softly into dust.
But the flute was left. And one is enough.
All, in a sense, goes on. All is in order.

And the ten-tongued mammoth larks,
The forty-foot crickets and the elephantine frogs
Decided that the little chap was harmless,
At least he made no noise, on the banks of whatever river it
    used to be.

One day, a reed-warbler stepped on him by accident.
However, all, in a sense, goes on. Still the everlasting and
    imperishable joy
Which music never fails to give is being given.

PARLIAMENT OF CATS

The cats caught a Yellow-vented Bulbul.
Snatched from them, for three days it uttered
Its gentle gospel, enthroned above their heads.
Became loved and respected of all the cats.
Then succumbed to internal injuries.
The cats regretted it all profoundly,
They would never forget the evil they had done.

Later the cats caught a Daurian Starling.
And ate it. For a Daurian Starling is not
A Yellow-vented Bulbul. (Genuflection.)
Its colouring is altogether different.
It walks in a different, quite unnatural fashion.
The case is not the same at all as that of
The Yellow-vented Bulbul. (Genuflection.)

The kittens caught a Yellow-vented Bulbul.
And ate it. What difference, they ask, between
A Yellow-vented Bulbul and that known criminal
The Daurian Starling? Both move through the air
In a quite unnatural fashion. This is not
The Yellow-vented Bulbul of our parents' day,
Who was a Saint of course! (Genuflection.)

Desiderius Erasmus

LETTER TO ANTHONY A BERGIS

*Erasmus Roterodamus to Anthony a Bergis,
Abbot of St Bertin, sendeth health.*

Most accomplished Father,

From the conversation of the bishop of Durham, and from
my friend Andrew Ammonius the king's secretary, I have
learned that you profess a warmth of affection for me which
I may call paternal. It is this circumstance which makes me
rejoice the more at the idea of returning to my country. I
wish I possessed there an independent income, just enough
to support me in a humble state of literary leisure. Not that
I dislike England, or have any reason to be dissatisfied with
the patronage of the Maecenas's, whom I have found in it.
I have a great many intimate friends, and experience uncommon instances of kindness from many of the bishops.
The archbishop of Canterbury fosters me with such peculiar
affection, and embraces me with such cordiality, that he could
not shew a greater love towards me if he were my brother or
my father. I enjoy a little pension issuing from a living which
he gave me, and allowed me to resign with an annuity out
of it. My other Maecenas adds an equal sum out of his own
purse; and many of the nobility contribute no inconsiderable
addition to my income. I might have a great deal more, if
I chose servilely to solicit or pay my court to great men,
which I can by no means prevail upon myself to do.

But the war which is preparing, has altered the very
temper and genius of this island. The price of every necessary of life increases every day, and the generosity of the
people of course decreases. Indeed how can it be otherwise?
People that are so often fleeced, must retrench in the liberal-
ity of their bounty. I assure you, I lately contracted a severe
fit of the gravel, by being under the necessity of drinking

bad beverage through the scarcity of good. Add to this, that as the whole island may be said, from the circumstance of its being surrounded by the sea, to be a place of confinement; so we are likely to be shut up still more closely by the wars. I see great commotions arising: whither they will tend, or how they will terminate, it is impossible to say. I only wish, God in his mercy would vouchsafe to still the raging sea which is agitating all Christendom.

I am often struck with astonishment and at a loss to account for the cause which can impel, I do not say Christians, but human creatures to such an extremity of madness and folly, as that they should rush headlong, with such ardour, at so great an expence of treasure, and with such dangers of every kind, to mutual destruction. For what is the business and chief concern of our whole lives, but to wage war with one another?

In the irrational part of the creation it is observable, that only those among the beasts who are called wild ever engage in war; and those not with one another, but with brutes of a different species; and they fight only with their own arms, the instruments of offence and defence supplied by nature. They do not attack with engines of destruction, invented by diabolical contrivance, nor on trifling causes and occasions, but either in defence of their young or for food. Our wars, for the most part, proceed either from ambition, from anger and malice, from the mere wantonness of unbridled power, or from some other mental distemper. The beasts of the forest meet not in battle array, with thousands assembled together and disciplined for murder.

To us, glorying as we do in the name of Christ, who taught nothing by his precept, and exhibited nothing in his example, but mildness and gentleness; who are members of one body, all of us one flesh, who grow in grace by one and the same spirit; who are fed by the same sacrament; who adhere to the same head; who are called to the same immortality; who hope for a sublime communion with God, that as Christ and the Father are one, so also we may be one with him; can any thing in this world be of such value as to provoke us to war? A state so destructive, so hideous, and so base, that even when it is founded on a just cause, it can never be pleasing to a good man. Do consider a moment, by what sort of persons it is actually carried into execution; by a herd of cutthroats, debauchees, gamesters, profligate wretches from the stews, the meanest and most sordid of mankind, hireling mankillers, to whom a little paltry pay is dearer than life. These are your fine fellows in war, who commit the very same villainies, with reward and with glory in the field of battle, which in society they formerly perpetrated, at the peril of the gallows. This filthy rabble of wretches must be admitted into your fields and your towns, in order that you may be enabled to carry on war: to these you must yourselves be in a state of subjection, that you may have it in your power to take vengeance of others in war.

Besides all this, consider what crimes are committed under the pretence of war, while the voice of salutary laws is compelled to be silent amidst the din of arms; what plunder, what sacrilege, what ravages, what other indecent transactions, which cannot for shame be enumerated. Such a taint of men's morals cannot but continue its influence long after a war is terminated. Compute also the expence, which is so enormous, that even if you come off conqueror, you sit down with more loss than gain: though indeed, by what standard can you appreciate the lives and the blood of so many thousand human creatures?

But the greatest share of the calamities inseparable from a state of war, falls to those persons who have no interest, no concern whatever, either in the cause, or the success of the war: whereas the advantages of peace reach all men of every rank and degree. In war, he who conquers weeps over his triumphs. War draws such a troop of evils in its train, that the poets find reason for the fiction which relates, that war was brought from hell to earth by a deputation of devils.

I will not now dwell upon the picking of the people's pockets, the intrigues and collusion of the leading men, the vicissitudes of public affairs, which never can undergo violent revolutions without consequences of a most calamitous nature.

But if it is a desire of glory which drags us to war, be assured that the glory which is eagerly sought after, is no glory; that it is impossible to derive real honour from doing mischief; and that, if we must point out something glorious, it is infinitely more glorious to build and establish, than to ruin and lay waste a flourishing community. Now what will you say, when you reflect, that it is the people, yes, the lowest of the people, who build and establish by industry and wisdom, that which kings claim a privilege to subvert and destroy by their folly. If gain rather than glory is the object in view, be it remembered, that no war whatever did, at any time, succeed so fortunately as not to produce more loss than gain, more evil than good: and that no man ever injured his enemy in war, but previously he did many and great injuries to his own people. In short, when I see all human affairs rapidly ebbing and flowing, like the tide of the Euripus, what avails it to establish or extend empire with such vast exertions, when it must very soon, and on very slight occasions, devolve to some other possessor? With how much blood was the Roman empire raised to its exalted pitch of grandeur, and how soon did it decline and fall?

But you will say, the rights of kings must of necessity be prosecuted at all events. It is not for me to speak rashly of the rights of kings; but one thing I know, the strictest right is often the greatest wrong, and that some kings first determine upon a measure, because it accords with their inclination, and then go in quest of some colourable pretence, under which they may cloak their unjustifiable conduct; and amidst so many changes and chances in human affairs, amidst so many treaties made and unmade, what man alive can ever be long at a loss for a colourable pretence? But if it were a nice point in dispute, to whom the right of dominion belonged, what need, in settling a question which requires reason and argument only, what need can there be of spilling human blood? The welfare and happiness of the people have nothing at all to do in the dispute; it is merely a question whether they shall have the privilege of calling this man or that man their king, 'and paying taxes to Thomas instead of John, or to John instead of Thomas'.

There are pontiffs and bishops, there are wise and honest men, who could settle such a trifling and contemptible business as this, without going to war about it, and confounding all things divine as well as human. The pope, the bishops, the cardinals, the abbots, could not employ themselves in any way more consistently with their characters and stations, than in composing the differences of kings: here they ought to exert their authority, and to shew how much the sanctity of their characters and their religion can actually avail.

Pope Julius, a pontiff not of the very best repute in the world, was able to excite the storm of war; and shall Leo, a man of real learning, integrity, and piety, be unable to appease it? The pretext for undertaking the war was, that Pope Julius was in imminent danger. The cause is confessedly removed, but the war does not yet cease.

We ought also to remember, that all men are free, especially all Christian men. Now, when they have been flourishing a long time under any prince, and by this time acknowledge him as their lawful sovereign, what justifiable occasion can there be for disturbing the world, in attempting a revolution? Long consent of the people constituted a lawful sovereign among the heathens, and much more among Christians, with whom the kingly office is a ministerial trust, a chief magistracy, an administration of delegated power, and not a property or absolute dominion; so that if some part of the territory subject to a Christian king were taken away, he is relieved from an onus, a burthensome task, rather than robbed or injured.

But suppose one of the litigant parties will not agree to abide by the arbitration of good men chosen as referees? In this case how would you wish me to act? In the first place, if you are verily and truly a Christian, I would have you bear the injury patiently, sit down with your heart at ease, and give up your right, be it what it will—Such would be the conduct of a Christian hero.

In the next place, if, waiving your pretensions of Christianity, you are only a prudent, sensible man of the world; weigh well how much the prosecution of your right will cost you. If it will cost you too dearly, and it certainly will cost you too dearly, if you prosecute it by the sword; then never consent to assert a claim, which perhaps after all is a groundless one, by bringing so much certain mischief to the human race, by so many murders, by making so many childless parents and fatherless children, and by causing the sighs and tears of your own people, who have no concern in your right.

What do you suppose the Turks think, when they hear of Christian kings raging against each other, with all the madness of so many evils let loose? And raging for what? merely on account of a claim set up for power, for empire, and dominion.

Italy is now rescued from the French. And what is the great matter gained by so much blood spilt? what but that, where a Frenchman lately administered the powers of government, there some other man now administers the same powers? And to say the truth, the country flourished more before, than it flourishes now. But I will not enter farther into this part of the subject.

Now, if there are any systems which admit of war, I must maintain that they are founded on a gross principle, and favour of a Christianity degenerating, and likely to be overlaid by worldly influence. I do not know whether these systems, such as they are, justify war in the eyes of some men; but I observe, that whenever, through a zeal for defending the faith, the Christian peace is to be defended against the attack of barbarians, war is not at all opposed by men of acknowledged piety. But why, on these occasions, do a few maxims handed down from one to another by mere men, suggest themselves to our minds, rather than many positive precepts uttered by Christ himself, by the Apostles, by orthodox and approved fathers, concerning peace, and patience under all evil?

As to the usual arguments and means of justifying war, what is there that may not admit of defence in some mode or other; especially when they who have the management of the thing to be defended, are those, whose very villainies are always bepraised by the adulation of great numbers, and whose errors no man dares openly to reprehend? But in the mean time, it is very clear what all good-hearted men pray for, wish for, sigh for.

If you look narrowly into the case, you will find that they are, chiefly, the private, sinister, and selfish motives of princes, which operate as the real causes of all war.

But pray do you think it a conduct worthy of a rational creature, and not fitter for brutes or devils, to put the world in confusion, whenever one prince takes it into his head to be angry with another prince, or to pretend to be angry?

You and I may wish every thing that would be best, and most conducive to the happiness of the human race, but we can do no more than wish it. For my own part, all the little property I have in the world, I have among the English; and I will resign the whole of it with the greatest pleasure, on condition, that among Christian princes there may be established a Christian peace. Your influence may have considerable weight in accomplishing this end, since you have great interest with one potentate, Charles; a great deal with Maximilian; and stand very well with all the nobility and aristocracy of England. I do not doubt but by this time you have experienced what losses one's own friends may procure one in war; and must be sensible, that it will be doing your own business, and serving your own interest, if you endeavour to prevail with the great ones to put an end to the present war. I mention this, to hint to you that your labour will not be without its reward. I shall make all the haste I can to shake hands with you, as soon as I shall have it in my power to take my flight from this country. In the mean time, most respectable Father, farewell. My best wishes attend Ghilbert the physician, and Anthony Lutzenburg,

London.
Pridie Id. Mart. 1513.

> *Translated into English by*
> *Vicesimus Knox, 1795*

Senator J. W. Fulbright

THE PRICE OF EMPIRE

Standing in the smoke and rubble of Detroit, a Negro veteran said: "I just got back from Vietnam a few months ago, but you know, I think the war is here."

There are in fact two wars going on. One is the war of power politics which our soldiers are fighting in the jungles of southeast Asia. The other is a war for America's soul which is being fought in the streets of Newark and Detroit and in the halls of Congress, in churches and protest meetings and on college campuses, and in the hearts and minds of silent Americans from Maine to Hawaii. I believe that the two wars have something to do with each other, not in the direct, tangibly causal way that bureaucrats require as proof of a connection between two things, but in a subtler, moral and qualitative way that is no less real for being intangible. Each of these wars might well be going on in the absence of the other, but neither, I suspect, standing alone, would seem so hopeless and demoralizing.

The connection between Vietnam and Detroit is in their conflicting and incompatible demands upon traditional American values. The one demands that they be set aside, the other that they be fulfilled. The one demands the acceptance by America of an imperial role in the world, or of what our policy makers like to call the "responsibilities of power," or of what I have called the "arrogance of power." The other demands freedom and social justice at home, an end to poverty, the fulfillment of our flawed democracy, and an effort to create a role for ourselves in the world which is compatible with our traditional values. The question, it should be emphasized, is not whether it is *possible* to engage in traditional power politics abroad and at the same time to perfect democracy at home, but whether it is possible for *us Americans,* with our particular history and national character, to combine morally incompatible roles.

Administration officials tell us that we can indeed afford both Vietnam and the Great Society, and they produce impressive statistics of the gross national product to prove it. The statistics show financial capacity but they do not show moral and psychological capacity. They do not show how a President preoccupied with bombing missions over North and South Vietnam can provide strong and consistent leadership for the renewal of our cities. They do not show how a Congress burdened with war costs and war measures, with emergency briefings and an endless series of dramatic appeals, with anxious constituents and a mounting anxiety of their own, can tend to the workaday business of studying social problems and legislating programs to meet them. Nor do the statistics tell how an anxious and puzzled people, bombarded by press and television with the bad news of American deaths in Vietnam, the "good news" of enemy deaths—and with vividly horrifying pictures to illustrate them—can be expected to support neighborhood anti-poverty projects and national programs for urban renewal, employment and education. Anxiety about war does not breed compassion for one's neighbors; nor do constant reminders of the cheapness of life abroad strengthen our faith in its sanctity at home. In these ways the war in Vietnam is poisoning and brutalizing our domestic life. Psychological incompatibility has proven to be more controlling than financial feasibility; and the Great Society has become a sick society.

I. IMPERIAL DESTINY AND THE AMERICAN DREAM

When he visited America a hundred years ago, Thomas Huxley wrote: "I cannot say that I am in the slightest degree impressed by your bigness, or your material resources, as such. Size is not grandeur, and territory does not make a nation. The great issue, about which hangs the terror of overhanging fate, is what are you going to do with all these things?"

The question is still with us and we seem to have come to a time of historical crisis when its answer can no longer be deferred. Before the Second World War our world role was a *potential* role; we were important in the world for what we *could* do with our power, for the leadership we *might* provide, for the example we *might* set. Now the choices are almost gone: we are *almost* the world's self-appointed policeman; we are *almost* the world defender of the *status quo*. We are well on our way to becoming a traditional great power—an imperial nation if you will—engaged in the exercise of power for its own sake, exercising it to the limit of our capacity and beyond, filling every vacuum and extending the American "presence" to the farthest reaches of the earth. And, as with the great empires of the past, as the power grows, it is becoming an end in itself, separated except by ritual incantation from its initial motives, governed, it would seem, by its own mystique, power without philosophy or purpose.

That describes what we have *almost* become, but we have not become a traditional empire yet. The old values remain —the populism and the optimism, the individualism and the rough-hewn equality, the friendliness and the good humor, the inventiveness and the zest for life, the caring about people and the sympathy for the underdog, and the idea, which goes back to the American revolution, that maybe—just maybe—we can set an example of democracy and human dignity for the world.

That is something which none of the great empires of the past has ever done—or tried to do—or wanted to do—but we were bold enough—or presumptuous enough—to think that we might be able to do it. And there are a great many Americans who still think we can do it—or at least they want to try.

That, I believe, is what all the hue and cry is about—the dissent in the Senate and the protest marches in the cities, the letters to the President from student leaders and former Peace Corps volunteers, the lonely searching of conscience by a student facing the draft and the letter to a Senator from a soldier in the field who can no longer accept the official explanations of why he has been sent to fight in the jungles of Vietnam. All believe that their country was cut out for something more ennobling than an imperial destiny. Our youth are showing that they still believe in the American dream, and their protests attest to its continuing vitality.

There appeared in a recent issue of the journal *Foreign Affairs* a curious little article complaining about the failure of many American intellectuals to support what the author regards as America's unavoidable "imperial role" in the world. The article took my attention because it seems a faithful statement of the governing philosophy of American foreign policy while also suggesting how little the makers of that policy appreciate the significance of the issue between themselves and their critics. It is taken for granted—not set forth as an hypothesis to be proved—that, any great power, in the author's words, "is entangled in a web of responsibilities from which there is no hope of escape," and that "there is no way the United States, as the world's mightiest power, can avoid such an imperial role. . . ."[1] The author's displeasure with the "intellectuals"—he uses the word more or less to describe people who disagree with the Administration's policy—is that, in the face of this alleged historical inevitability, they are putting up a disruptive, irritating and futile resistance. They are doing this, he believes, because they are believers in "ideology"—the better word would be "values" or "ideals"—and this causes their thinking to be "irrelevant" to foreign policy.

Here, inadvertently, the writer puts his finger on the nub of the current crisis. The students and churchmen and professors who are protesting the Vietnam war do not accept the notion that foreign policy is a matter of expedients to which values are irrelevant. They reject this notion because they understand, as some of our policy makers do not understand, that it is ultimately self-defeating to "fight fire with fire," that you cannot defend your values in a manner that does violence to those values without destroying the very thing you are trying to defend. They understand, as our policy makers do not, that when American soldiers are sent, in the name of freedom, to sustain corrupt dictators in a civil war, that when the CIA subverts student organizations to engage in propaganda activities abroad, or when the Export-Import Bank is used by the Pentagon to finance secret arms sales abroad, damage—perhaps irreparable damage—is being done to the very values that are meant to be defended. The critics understand, as our policy makers do not, that, through the undemocratic ex-

---

[1] Irving Kristol, "American Intellectuals and Foreign Policy," *Foreign Affairs*, July, 1967, pp. 602, 605.

pedients we have adopted for the defense of American democracy, we are weakening it to a degree that is beyond the resources of our bitterest enemies.

Nor do the dissenters accept the romantic view that nation is powerless to choose the role it will play in the world, that some mystic force of history or destiny requires a powerful nation to be an imperial nation, dedicated to what Paul Goodman calls the "empty system of power," to the pursuit of power without purpose, philosophy or compassion. They do not accept the Hegelian concept of history as something out of control, as something that happens to us rather than something that we make. They do not accept the view that, because other great nations have pursued power for its own sake—a pursuit which invariably has ended in decline or disaster—America must do the same. They think we have some choice about our own future and that the best basis for exercising that choice is the values on which this republic was founded.

The critics of our current course also challenge the contention that the traditional methods of foreign policy are safe and prudent and realistic. They are understandably skeptical of their wise and experienced elders who, in the name of prudence, caution against any departure from the tried and true methods that have led in this century to Sarajevo, Munich and Dien Bien Phu. They think that the methods of the past have been tried and found wanting, and two world wars attest powerfully to their belief. Most of all, they think that, in this first era of human history in which man has acquired weapons which threaten his entire species with destruction, safety and prudence and realism require us to change the rules of a dangerous and discredited game, to try as we have never tried before to civilize and humanize international relations, not only for the sake of civilization and humanity but for the sake of survival.

Even the most ardent advocates of an imperial role for the United States would probably agree that the proper objective of our foreign policy is the fostering of a world environment in which we can, with reasonable security, devote our main energies to the realization of the values of

2 *Like a Conquered Province, The Moral Ambiguity of America* (New York: Random House, 1967), p. 73.

ur own society. This does not require the adoption or im-
osition of these values on anybody, but it does require
us so to conduct ourselves that our society does not seem
hateful and repugnant to others.

At present much of the world is repelled by America and
what America seems to stand for in the world. Both in our
foreign affairs and in our domestic life we convey an image
of violence; I do not care very much about images as distinguished from the things they reflect, but this image is
rooted in reality. Abroad we are engaged in a savage and
unsuccessful war against poor people in a small and backward nation. At home—largely because of the neglect result-
ing from twenty-five years of preoccupation with foreign
involvements—our cities are exploding in violent protest
against generations of social injustice. America, which only
a few years ago seemed to the world to be a model of
democracy and social justice, has become a symbol of
violence and undisciplined power.

"It is excellent," wrote Shakespeare, "to have a giant's
strength; but it is tyrannous to use it like a giant."[3] By
using our power like a giant we are fostering a world environment which is, to put it mildly, uncongenial to our
society. By our undisciplined use of physical power we have
divested ourselves of a greater power: the power of example. How, for example, can we commend peaceful compromise to the Arabs and the Israelis when we are unwilling
to suspend our relentless bombing of North Vietnam? How
can we commend democratic social reform to Latin America when Newark, Detroit, and Milwaukee are providing
explosive evidence of our own inadequate efforts at democratic social reforms? How can we commend the free enterprise system to Asians and Africans when in our own country
it has produced vast, chaotic, noisy, dangerous and dirty
urban complexes while poisoning the very air and land and
water? There may come a time when Americans will again
be able to commend their country as an example to the
world and, more in hope than confidence, I retain my faith
that there will; but to do so right at this moment would
take more gall than I have.

Far from building a safe world environment for Amer-

---

[3] *Measure for Measure*, III, ii, 107.

ican values, our war in Vietnam and the domestic deterioration which it has aggravated are creating a most uncongenial world atmosphere for American ideas and values. The world has no need, in this age of nationalism and nuclear weapons, for a new imperial power, but there is a great need of moral leadership—by which I mean the leadership of decent example. That role could be ours but we have vacated the field and all that has kept the Russians from filling it is their own lack of imagination.

At the same time, as we have noted, and of even greater fundamental importance, our purposeless and undisciplined use of power is causing a profound controversy in our own society. This in a way is something to be proud of. We have sickened but not succumbed and, just as a healthy body fights disease, we are fighting the alien concept which is being thrust upon us, not by history but by our policy makers in the Department of State and the Pentagon. We are proving the strength of the American dream by resisting the dream of an imperial destiny. We are demonstrating the validity of our traditional values by the difficulty we are having in betraying them.

The principal defenders of these values are our remarkable younger generation, something of whose spirit is expressed in a letter which I received from an American soldier in Vietnam. Speaking of the phony propaganda on both sides, and then of the savagery of the war, or the people he describes as the "real casualties"—"the farmers and their families in the Delta mangled by air strikes, and the villagers here killed and burned out by our friendly Korean mercenaries"—this young soldier then asks ". . . whatever has become of our dream? Where is that America that opposed tyrannies at every turn, without inquiring first whether some particular forms of tyranny might be of use to us? Of the three rights which men have, the first, as I recall, was the right to life. How then have we come to be killing so many in such a dubious cause?"

II. THE SICK SOCIETY

While the death toll mounts in Vietnam, it is mounting too in the war at home. During a single week of July 1967,

164 Americans were killed and 1,442 wounded in Vietnam, while 65 Americans were killed and 2,100 were wounded in city riots in the United States. We are truly fighting a two-front war and doing badly in both. Each war feeds on the other and, although the President assures us that we have the resources to win both wars, in fact we are not winning either.

Together the two wars have set in motion a process of deterioration in American society and there is no question that each of the two crises is heightened by the impact of the other. Not only does the Vietnam war divert human and material resources from our festering cities; not only does it foster the conviction on the part of slum Negroes that their country is indifferent to their plight. In addition the war feeds the idea of violence as a way of solving problems. If, as Mr. Rusk tells us, only the rain of bombs can bring Ho Chi Minh to reason, why should not the same principle apply at home? Why should not riots and snipers' bullets bring the white man to an awareness of the Negro's plight when peaceful programs for housing and jobs and training have been more rhetoric than reality? Ugly and shocking thoughts are in the American air and they were forged in the Vietnam crucible. Black power extremists talk of "wars of liberation" in the urban ghettoes of America. A cartoon in a London newspaper showed two Negro soldiers in battle in Vietnam with one saying to the other: "This is going to be great training for civilian life."

The effect of domestic violence on the chances for peace in Vietnam may turn out to be no less damaging than the impact of the war on events at home. With their limited knowledge of the United States, the Vietcong and the North Vietnamese may regard the urban riots as a harbinger of impending breakdown and eventual American withdrawal from Vietnam, warranting stepped up warfare and an uncompromising position on negotiations. It is possible that the several opportunities to negotiate which our government has let pass, most recently last winter, could not now be retrieved. Some eighteen months ago General Maxwell Taylor said in testimony before the Senate Foreign Relations Committee that the war was being prolonged by domestic dissent. That dissent was based in part on apprehension as to the effects of the war on our domestic life. Now the war is being prolonged by the domestic deterioration which ha in fact occurred and it is doubtful that all of the dissenters in America, even if they wanted to, as they certainly do no could give the enemy a fraction of the aid and comfor that has been given him by Newark, Detroit and Milwaukee

An unnecessary and immoral war deserves in its own right to be liquidated; when its effect in addition is th aggravation of grave problems and the corrosion of value in our own society, its liquidation under terms of reasonable and honorable compromise is doubly imperative. Our coun try is being weakened by a grotesque inversion of priorities the effects of which are becoming clear to more and more Americans—in the Congress, in the press and in the coun try at large. Even the *Washington Post,* a newspaper which has obsequiously supported the Administration's policy in Vietnam, took note in a recent editorial of the "ugly image of a world policeman incapable of policing itself" as against the "absolute necessity of a sound domestic base for an effective foreign policy," and then commented: "We are confronted simultaneously with an urgent domestic crisis and an urgent foreign crisis and our commitments to both are clear. We should deal with both with all the energy and time and resources that may be required. But if the moment ever arises when we cannot deal adequately and effectively with both, there is no shame—and some considerable logic —in making it plain beyond a doubt that our first con sideration and our first priority rests with the security of the stockade."[4]

Commenting on the same problem of priorities, Mayor Cavanaugh of Detroit said:

"What will it profit this country if we, say, put our man on the moon by 1970 and at the same time you can't walk down Woodward Avenue in this city without some fear of violence?

"And we may be able to pacify every village in Vietnam, over a period of years, but what good does it do if we can't pacify the American cities?

"What I am saying . . . is that our priorities in this coun try are all out of balance. . . . Maybe Detroit was a water- shed this week in American history and it might well be

---

[4] *Washington Post,* July 27, 1967.

at out of the ashes of this city comes the national resolve
do far more than anything we have done in the past."[5]

Priorities are reflected in the things we spend money on.
ar from being a dry accounting of bookkeepers, a nation's
udget is full of moral implications; it tells what a society
ares about and what it does not care about; it tells what its
alues are.

Here are a few statistics on America's values: Since 1946
e have spent over $1,578 billion through our regular na-
onal budget. Of this amount over $904 billion, or 57.29
ercent of the total, have gone for military power. By con-
ast, less than $96 billion, or 6.08 percent, were spent on
social functions" including education, health, labor and
elfare programs, housing and community development. The
dministration's budget for fiscal year 1968 calls for almost
76 billion to be spent on the military and only $15 billion
or "social functions."

I would not say that we have shown ourselves to value
eapons five or ten times as much as we value domestic
ocial needs, as the figures suggest; certainly much of our
ilitary spending has been necessitated by genuine require-
ents of national security. I think, however, that we have
mbraced the necessity with excessive enthusiasm, that the
Congress has been all too willing to provide unlimited sums
or the military and not really very reluctant at all to offset
hese costs to a very small degree by cutting away funds
or the poverty program and urban renewal, for rent sup-
lements for the poor and even for a program to help
rotect slum children from being bitten by rats. Twenty
illion dollars a year to eliminate rats—about one one-hun-
redth of the monthly cost of the war in Vietnam—would
ot eliminate slum riots but, as Tom Wicker has written,
It would only suggest that somebody cared."[6] The discrep-
ncy of attitudes tells at least as much about our national
alues as the discrepancy of dollars.

---

[5] Comments on "Meet the Press," reported in *Washington Post*,
uly 31, 1967.

[6] *The New York Times*, July 23, 1967.

III. THE REGENERATIVE POWER OF YOUTH

While the country sickens for lack of moral leadersh[ip], a most remarkable younger generation has taken up t[he] standard of American idealism. Unlike so many of th[eir] elders, they have perceived the fraud and sham in Americ[an] life and are unequivocally rejecting it. Some, the hippi[es] have simply withdrawn, and while we may regret the l[oss] of their energies and their sense of decency, we can har[dly] gainsay their evaluation of the state of society. Others [of] our youth are sardonic and skeptical, not, I think, beca[use] they do not want ideals but because they want the genui[ne] article and will not tolerate fraud. Others—students w[ho] wrestle with their consciences about the draft, soldiers w[ho] wrestle with their consciences about the war, Peace Cor[ps] volunteers who strive to light the spark of human dign[ity] among the poor of India or Brazil, and VISTA voluntee[rs] who try to do the same for our own poor in Harlem [or] Appalachia—are striving to keep alive the traditional valu[es] of American democracy.

They are not really radical, these young idealists, no mo[re] radical, that is, than Jefferson's idea of freedom, Lincol[n's] idea of equality, or Wilson's idea of a peaceful commun[ity] of nations. Some of them, it is true, are taking what ma[ny] regard as radical action, but they are doing it in defense [of] traditional values and in protest against the radical depa[r]ture from those values embodied in the idea of an imper[ial] destiny for America.

The focus of their protest is the war in Vietnam and t[he] measure of their integrity is the fortitude with which th[ey] refuse to be deceived about it. By striking contrast w[ith] the young Germans who accepted the Nazi evil because t[he] values of their society had disintegrated and they had [no] normal frame of reference, these young Americans are demo[n]strating the vitality of American values. They are demonstr[at]ing that, while their country is capable of acting false[ly] to itself, it cannot do so without internal disruption, witho[ut] calling forth the regenerative counterforce of protest fro[m] Americans who are willing to act in defense of the pri[n]ciples they were brought up to believe in.

The spirit of this regenerative generation has been ric[h]

y demonstrated to me in letters from student leaders, from
ormer Peace Corps volunteers and from soldiers fighting
n Vietnam. I quoted from one earlier in my remarks. Another letter that is both striking and representative was
written by an officer still in Vietnam. He wrote:

"For eleven years I was, before this war, a Regular commissioned officer—a professional military man in name and
spirit; now—in name only. To fight well (as do the VC),
a soldier must believe in his leadership. I, and many I have
met, have lost faith in ours. Since I hold that duty to conscience is higher than duty to the administration (not 'country' as cry the nationalists), I declined a promotion and
have resigned my commission. I am to be discharged on
my return, at which time I hope to contribute in some way
to the search for peace in Vietnam."

Some years ago Archibald MacLeish characterized the
American people as follows:

"Races didn't bother the Americans. They were something a lot better than any race. They were a People. They
were the first self-constituted, self-declared, self-created People in the history of the world. And their manners were their
own business. And so were their politics. And so, but ten
times so, were their souls."[7]

Now the possession of their souls is being challenged by
the false and dangerous dream of an imperial destiny. It
may be that the challenge will succeed, that America will
succumb to becoming a traditional empire and will reign
for a time over what must surely be a moral if not a physical wasteland, and then, like the great empires of the past,
will decline or fall. Or it may be that the effort to create
so grotesque an anachronism will go up in flames of nuclear
holocaust. But if I had to bet my money on what is going
to happen, I would bet it on this younger generation—
this generation who reject the inhumanity of war in a poor
and distant land, who reject the poverty and sham in their
own country, this generation who are telling their elders
what their elders ought to have known, that the price of
empire is America's soul and that price is too high.

---

[7] Archibald MacLeish, *A Time to Act* (Boston: Houghton Mifflin
Co., 1943), p. 115.

Roy Fuller

EPITAPH ON A BOMBING VICTIM

Reader, could his limbs be found
Here would lie a common man:
History inflicts no wound
But explodes what it began,
And with its enormous lust
For division splits the dust.
Do not ask his nation; that
Was History's confederate.

Oliver Goldsmith

THE DISABLED SOLDIER

No observation is more common, and at the same time
more true, than that one half of the world are ignorant how
the other half lives. The misfortunes of the great are held
up to engage our attention; are enlarged upon in tones of
declamation; and the world is called upon to gaze at the
noble sufferers: the great, under the pressure of calamity,
are conscious of several others sympathizing with their distress; and have, at once, the comfort of admiration and pity.

There is nothing magnanimous in bearing misfortunes
with fortitude, when the whole world is looking on: men in
such circumstances will act bravely even from motives of
vanity: but he who, in the vale of obscurity, can brave ad-
versity; who without friends to encourage, acquaintances to
pity, or even without hope to alleviate his misfortunes, can
behave with tranquillity and indifference, is truly great:
whether peasant or courtier, he deserves admiration, and
should be held up for our imitation and respect.

While the slightest inconveniences of the great are mag-
nified into calamities; while tragedy mouths out their sufferings in all the strains of eloquence, the miseries of the poor
are entirely disregarded; and yet some of the lower ranks
of people undergo more real hardships in one day, than
those of a more exalted station suffer in their whole lives.
It is inconceivable what difficulties the meanest of our common sailors and soldiers endure without murmuring or
regret; without passionately declaiming against providence,
or calling their fellows to be gazers on their intrepidity.
Every day is to them a day of misery, and yet they enter-
tain their hard fate without repining.

With what indignation do I hear an Ovid, a Cicero, or a
Rabutin complain of their misfortunes and hardships, whose
greatest calamity was that of being unable to visit a certain

spot of earth, to which they had foolishly attached an ide
of happiness. Their distresses were pleasures, compared t
what many of the adventuring poor every day endure with
out murmuring. They ate, drank, and slept; they had slave
to attend them, and were sure of subsistence for life; whil
many of their fellow creatures are obliged to wander with
out a friend to comfort or assist them, and even withou
shelter from the severity of the season.

I have been led into these reflections from accidentall
meeting, some days ago, a poor fellow, whom I knew whe
a boy, dressed in a sailor's jacket, and begging at one c
the outlets of the town, with a wooden leg. I knew him t
have been honest and industrious when in the country, an
was curious to learn what had reduced him to his presen
situation. Wherefore, after giving him what I thought prope
I desired to know the history of his life and misfortune
and the manner in which he was reduced to his presen
distress. The disabled soldier, for such he was, thoug
dressed in a sailor's habit, scratching his head, and leanin
on his crutch, put himself into an attitude to comply wit
my request, and gave me his history as follows:

"As for my misfortunes, master, I can't pretend to hav
gone through any more than other folks; for, except th
loss of my limb, and my being obliged to beg, I don't knov
any reason, thank Heaven, that I have to complain. Ther
is Bill Tibbs, of our regiment, he has lost both his legs
and an eye to boot; but, thank Heaven, it is not so bad wit
me yet.

"I was born in Shropshire; my father was a laborer, and
died when I was five years old, so I was put upon the
parish. As he had been a wandering sort of man, the parish
ioners were not able to tell to what parish I belonged, o
where I was born, so they sent me to another parish, and
that parish sent me to a third. I thought in my heart, they
kept sending me about so long, that they would not let me
be born in any parish at all; but at last, however, they fixec
me. I had some disposition to be a scholar, and was resolvec
at least to know my letters: but the master of the work
house put me to business as soon as I was able to handle
a mallet; and here I lived an easy kind of life for five years
I only wrought ten hours in the day, and had my meat and
drink provided for my labor. It is true, I was not suffered

o stir out of the house, for fear, as they said, I should
un away; but what of that? I had the liberty of the whole
house, and the yard before the door, and that was enough
or me. I was then bound out to a farmer, where I was up
both early and late; but I ate and drank well; and liked
my business well enough, till he died, when I was obliged
o provide for myself; so I resolved to go seek my fortune.

"In this manner I went from town to town, worked when
I could get employment, and starved when I could get
none; when, happening one day to go through a field be-
onging to a justice of peace, I spied a hare crossing the
path just before me; and I believe the devil put it into my
head to fling my stick at it. Well, what will you have on't?
I killed the hare, and was bringing it away, when the justice himself met me; he called me a poacher and a villain,
and collaring me, desired I would give an account of myself. I fell upon my knees, begged his worship's pardon,
and began to give a full account of all that I knew of my
breed, seed, and generation; but though I gave a very true
account, the justice said I could give no account; so I was
indicted at the sessions, found guilty of being poor, and
sent up to London to Newgate, in order to be transported
as a vagabond.

"People may say this and that of being in jail, but, for
my part, I found Newgate as agreeable a place as ever I
was in in all my life. I had my belly full to eat and drink, and
did no work at all. This kind of life was too good to last
forever; so I was taken out of prison, after five months,
put on board of ship, and sent off, with two hundred more,
to the plantations. We had but an indifferent passage, for
being all confined in the hold, more than a hundred of our
people died for want of sweet air; and those that remained
were sickly enough, God knows. When we came ashore
we were sold to the planters, and I was bound for seven
years more. As I was no scholar, for I did not know my
letters, I was obliged to work among the negroes; and I
served out my time, as in duty bound to do.

"When my time was expired, I worked my passage home,
and glad I was to see old England again, because I loved
my country. I was afraid, however, that I should be indicted
for a vagabond once more, so did not much care to go down

into the country, but kept about the town, and did littl[e]
jobs when I could get them.

"I was very happy in this manner for some time till on[e]
evening, coming home from work, two men knocked m[e]
down, and then desired me to stand. They belonged to [a]
press-gang. I was carried before the justice, and as I coul[d]
give no account of myself, I had my choice left, wheth[er]
to go on board a man-of-war, or list for a soldier. I chos[e]
the latter, and in this post of a gentleman, I served tw[o]
campaigns in Flanders, was at the battles of Val and Fo[n]-
tenoy, and received but one wound through the breast her[e]
but the doctor of our regiment soon made me well again.

"When the peace came on I was discharged; and as [I]
could not work, because my wound was sometimes troubl[e]-
some, I listed for a landman in the East India Company['s]
service. I have fought the French in six pitched battles; an[d]
I verily believe that if I could read or write, our captai[n]
would have made me a corporal. But it was not my goo[d]
fortune to have any promotion, for I soon fell sick, an[d]
so got leave to return home again with forty pounds i[n]
my pocket. This was at the beginning of the present wa[r]
and I hoped to be set on shore, and to have the pleasur[e]
of spending my money; but the Government wanted me[n]
and so I was pressed for a sailor, before ever I could se[t]
a foot on shore.

"The boatswain found me, as he said, an obstinate fel[-]
low: he swore he knew that I understood my business wel[l]
but that I shammed Abraham, to be idle; but God know[s]
I knew nothing of sea-business, and he beat me withou[t]
considering what he was about. I had still, however, m[y]
forty pounds, and that was some comfort to me unde[r]
every beating; and the money I might have had to this da[y]
but that our ship was taken by the French, and so I los[t]
all.

"Our crew was carried into Brest, and many of the[m]
died, because they were not used to live in a jail; but, fo[r]
my part, it was nothing to me, for I was seasoned. On[e]
night, as I was asleep on the bed of boards, with a war[m]
blanket about me, for I always loved to lie well, I wa[s]
awakened by the boatswain, who had a dark lantern in hi[s]
hand. 'Jack,' says he to me, 'will you knock out the French
sentry's brains?' 'I don't care,' says I, striving to keep my-

self awake, 'if I lend a hand.' 'Then, follow me,' says he, 'and I hope we shall do business.' So up I got, and tied my blanket, which was all the clothes I had, about my middle, and went with him to fight the Frenchman. I hate the French, because they are all slaves, and wear wooden shoes.

"Though we had no arms, one Englishman is able to beat five French at any time; so we went down to the door where both the sentries were posted, and rushing upon them, seized their arms in a moment, and knocked them down. From thence nine of us ran together to the quay, and seizing the first boat we met, got out of the harbor and put to sea. We had not been here three days before we were taken up by the Dorset privateer, who were glad of so many good hands; and we consented to run our chance. However, we had not as much luck as we expected. In three days we fell in with the *Pompadour* privateer of forty guns, while we had but twenty-three, so to it we went, yard-arm and yard-arm. The fight lasted three hours, and I verily believe we should have taken the Frenchman, had we but had some more men left behind; but unfortunately we lost all our men just as we were going to get the victory.

"I was once more in the power of the French, and I believe it would have gone hard with me had I been brought back to Brest; but by good fortune we were retaken by the *Viper.* I had almost forgotten to tell you that in that engagement I was wounded in two places: I lost four fingers off the left hand, and my leg was shot off. If I had had the good fortune to have lost my leg and use of my hand on board a king's ship, and not aboard a privateer, I should have been entitled to clothing and maintenance during the rest of my life; but that was not my chance: one man is born with a silver spoon in his mouth, and another with a wooden ladle. However, blessed be God, I enjoy good health, and will forever love liberty and old England. Liberty, property, and old England, forever, huzza!"

Thus saying, he limped off, leaving me in admiration at his intrepidity and content; nor could I avoid acknowledging that an habitual acquaintance with misery serves better than philosophy to teach us to despise it.

Don Gordon

THE KIMONO

Celebrate the season of the death of the city.
Celebrate the woman in the newsreel, the print of her ki-
    mono
Burned in her back. Celebrate the bamboo leaves, the folded
    fans.

Exhibit A, formerly a person, was born as the white plant
    bloomed;
She is the night dream of the spectator, incised on the lid-
    less eye;
Woman without face or name that is known lives in my
    house.

Weigh her, measure her, peer for children
in her clouded history; check with Geiger counters
the click of the doomed leaves and fans.

Lost in events the beauty and the grace of women;
Ended the age of natural love as the bomb bay opened
On the burned shoulders: she is now the memorable one.

From the nightmare to the eye
from the eye to the house
from the house to the heart
enter the dimension of love:

woman of Hiroshima
be merciful to the merciless!

Leo Hamalian

NURSERY RHYME

I am the shell that awaits the word.

I am the gun that fires the shell
That shocks the solid flesh so well.

I am the hand that pulls the cord
(Now more potent than the sword)
When that certain word is roared.

I am the voice that roars the word
That touches off the deadly bird
When ordered by the one who's heard
From those who say it's time to gird.

I am the one who teaches to read
Those who spread the ancient creed
To aid the ones who feed the need
Of the hand that's forced to heed
The word that fathers forth the deed.

I am the one who works the drill,
Who tills the soil, who takes his pill,
Who backs with tax the shell he makes
To feed the hand of him who takes
The word that comes from certain men
Who give the word to fire when.

Who is this one who gives the word
To lift aloft the deadly bird?

I am the one behind the shell.

Edith Hamilton

A PACIFIST IN PERICLEAN ATHENS

The greatest piece of anti-war literature there is in the world was written 2,350 years ago. This is a statement worth a thought or two. Nothing since, no description or denunciation of war's terrors and futilities, ranks with *The Trojan Women,* which was put upon the Athenian stage by Euripides in the year 416 B.C. In that faraway age a man saw with perfect clarity what war was, and wrote what he saw in a play of surpassing power, and then—nothing happened. No one was won over to his side—no band of eager disciples took up his idea and went preaching it to a war-ridden world. That superlatively efficient war-machine, Rome, described by one of her own historians as having fought continuously for eight hundred years, went on to greater and greater efficiency, with never a glimmer from Euripides to disturb her complacency. In the long annals of literature no writer is recorded who took over his point of view. A few objectors to war are known to us. They crop out sporadically through the ages, but rarely and never with Euripides' deliberate intention of showing war up for what it is. And except for Christ, to whom non-resistance was fundamental, we do not know of anyone else who disbelieved in violence as a means of doing good. None of Christ's followers seem to have followed Him there until comparatively modern times. Not one medieval saint stands out to oppose the thousands of saintly believers in the holiness of this war or that. One soldier there was in the early days of Christianity, a simple, uneducated man, who refused to fight when he was converted, because, as he explained, Christ did not approve of men killing each other. But he was easily silenced —and the Church never denounced his executioners. He never came near to being made a saint. His very name, Marcellus, is known only to the curious. That was doctrine too dangerous for the Fathers of the Church. Christians refuse to fight? Rather, set up a cross as the banner of a triumphant army, conquering under that standard, killing in His name.

The men of religion, along with the men of letters, passed by, unseeing, the road Euripides had opened, and each usually vied with the other in glorifying and magnifying noble, heroic and holy war.

Consider the greatest of all, Shakespeare. He never bothered to think war through. Of course, that was not his way with anything. He had another method. Did he believe in "Contumelious, beastly, mad-brain'd war"? Or in "Pride, pomp and circumstance of glorious war"? He says as much on the one side as on the other.

"We few, we happy few, we band of brothers," King Henry cries before Agincourt:

> This day is called the feast of Crispian;
> And gentlemen of England now abed
> Shall think themselves accursed they were not here,
> And hold their manhoods cheap whiles any speaks
> That fought with us upon Saint Crispin's day.

And then a few pages on:

>   If impious war
> Array'd in flames like to the Prince of fiends,
> Do, with his smirched complexion, all fell feats
> Enlink'd to waste and desolation—

It is not possible to know what Shakespeare really thought about war, if he really thought about it at all. Always that disconcerting power of imagination blocks the way to our knowledge of him. He saw eye to eye with Henry on one page and with the citizens of Harfleur on the next, and what he saw when he looked only for himself, he did not care to record.

In our Western world Euripides stands alone. He understood what the world has only begun today to understand.

"The burden of the valley of vision," wrote Isaiah, when he alone knew what could save his world from ruin. To perceive an overwhelmingly important truth of which no one else sees a glimmer, is loneliness such as few even in the long history of the world can have had to suffer. But Euripides suffered it for the greater part of his long life. The valley of vision was his abiding place.

He was the youngest of the three Greek tragic poets, but only a few years younger than Sophocles, who, indeed, survived him. Each had the keen discernment and the profound spiritual perception of the supreme artist. Each lived and suffered through the long-drawn-out war, which ended in the crushing defeat of Athens, and together they watched the human deterioration brought about during those years. But what they saw was not the same. Sophocles never dreamed of a world in which such things could not be. To him the way to be enabled to endure what was happening, the only way for a man to put life through no matter what happened, was to face facts unwaveringly and accept them, to perceive clearly and bear steadfastly the burden of the human lot, which is as it is and never will be different. To look at the world thus, with profundity, but in tranquility of spirit, without bitterness, has been given to few, and to no other writer so completely as to Sophocles.

But Euripides saw clearest of all not what is, but what might be. So rebels are made. Great rebels all know the valley of vision. They see possibilities: this evil and that ended; human life transformed; people good and happy. "And there shall be neither sorrow nor crying, nor any more pain: for the former things are passed away." The clarity with which they see brings them anguish; they have a passion of longing to make their vision a reality. They feel, like a personal experience, the giant agony of the world. Not many among the greatest stand higher than Euripides in this aristocracy of humanity.

Sophocles said, "Nothing is wrong which gods command." Euripides said, "If gods do evil, then they are not gods." Two different worlds are outlined in those two ideas. Submission is the rule of the first. Not ours to pass judgment upon the divine. "There are thoughts too great for mortal men," was ever Sophocles' idea, or, in the words of another great Greek writer, "To long for the impossible is a disease of the soul." Keep then within the rational limit; "Sail not beyond the pillars of Heracles." But in the second world, Euripides' world, there can be no submission, because what reigns there is a passion for justice and a passion of pity for suffering. People who feel in that way do not submit to the inevitable, or even really perceive it. But they perceive intolerably what is wrong and under that tremendous impetus they are ready to throw all security aside, to call everything into question, to tear off the veils that hide ugly things, and often, certainly in Euripides' case, to give up forever peace of mind.

Two years before the end of the war Euripides died, not in Athens, but away up north in savage Thrace, lonelier in his death even than in his life. The reason he left his city is not recorded, but it was a compelling one. Men did not give up their home in Greek and Roman days unless they must. All we are told is a single sentence in the ancient *Life of Euripides* that he had to go away because of "the malicious exultation" aroused against him in the city. It is not hard to discover why.

Athens was fighting a life-and-death war. She did not want to think about anything. Soldiers must not think. If they begin to reason why, it is very bad for the army. Above all, they must not think about the rights and wrongs of the war. Athens called that being unpatriotic, not to say traitorous, just as emphatically as the most Aryan Nazi today could. And Euripides kept making her think. He put play after play on the stage which showed the hideousness of cruelty and the pitifulness of human weakness and human pain. The Athenians took their theater very seriously, and they were as keen and as sensitive an audience as has ever been in the world. It was unheard of in Athens to forbid a play because it was not in accordance with the ruling policy, but many a politician must have felt very uneasy as he listened to what Euripides had to say.

The war lasted twenty-seven years. Thucydides, the great historian of the time, remarks that "War, teaching men by violence, fits their characters to their conditions," and two of his austere black-laid-on-white pictures illustrate with startling clarity how quickly the Athenians went downhill under that teaching.

They had been fighting for three years only when an important island in the Aegean revolted. Athens sent a big fleet against her and captured her, and in furious anger voted to put all the men to death and make slaves of the women and children. They dispatched a ship to carry the order to the general in command, and then, true to the spirit of the city that was still so great, they realized the shocking thing they had done, and they sent another boat to try to overtake the first and bring it back, or, if that was impossible, to get to the island in time to prevent the massacre. We are told how the rowers rowed as none ever before, and how they did arrive in time. And Athens felt that weight of guilt lifted, and rejoiced.

But as the war went on men did not feel guilty when terrible deeds were done. They grew used to them. Twelve years later, when the war had lasted fifteen years, another island offended Athens, not by revolting, only by trying to keep neutral. It was a tiny island, in itself of no importance, but by that time Athens was incapable of weighing pros and cons. She took the island, she killed all the men and enslaved all the women and children, and we hear of no one who protested. But a few months later one man showed what he thought, not only of this terrible deed but of the whole horrible business of war. Euripides brought out *The Trojan Women*.

There is no plot in *The Trojan Women* and almost no action. After a ten-year war a town has been taken by storm and the men in it killed. Except for two subordinate parts the characters are all women. Their husbands are dead, their children taken from them, and they are waiting to be shipped off to slavery. They talk about what has happened and how they feel, and this talk makes up the substance of the play. They are very unlike each other, so that we see the situation from different points of view. There is the wife of the king, an old woman, whose husband was cut down before her eyes in their home as he clung to the altar; her sons, too, are dead, and she, a queen, is to be a slave to the conquerors. There is her daughter, a holy virgin, dedicated to the service of the god of truth, now to be the concubine of the victorious commander-in-chief. Her daughter-in-law too, wife of her dearest and most heroic son, she is to belong to the son of the man who killed him and misused him after death. Helen, the beautiful, is there as well, maneuvering to regain her power over the husband she betrayed, but, in the play, unsuccessful and led away to die. And there are a number of other women, not great or impressive at all except through their sufferings, pitiful creatures weeping for the loss of home, husband, children, and everything sweet and pleasant gone forever.

That is the whole of it. Not one gleam of light anywhere. Euripides had asked himself what war is like when one looks straight at it, and this is his answer. He knew his Homer. It was the Greek Bible. And that theme of glorious poetry about the dauntless deeds of valiant men, heroically fighting for the most beautiful woman in the world, turns in his hands into a little group of broken-hearted women.

A soldier from the victorious army, who comes to bring them orders, is surprised and irritated to find himself moved to pity them; but he shrugs his shoulders and says, "Well—that's war."

The pomp and pride and glorious circumstance are all gone. When the play opens it is just before dawn, and the only light in the darkness comes fitfully from the burning city. Against that background two gods talk to each other and at once Euripides makes clear what he thinks about war as a method of improving life in any way for anyone.

In the old stories about what happened after Troy fell, told for hundreds of years before Euripides, curiously the conquering Greeks did not come off well. They had an exceedingly bad voyage back, and even those who escaped storm and shipwreck found terrible things waiting for them at home. In those faraway times, long before history began, it would seem that some men had learned what our world hardly yet perceives, that inevitably victors and vanquished must in the end suffer together. It was one of those strange prophetic insights which occasionally disturb the sluggish flow of the human spirit, but seem to accomplish nothing for centuries of time. Euripides, however, had discovered the meaning behind the stories.

He makes his two gods decide that the fall of Troy shall turn out no better for the Greeks than for the Trojans. "Give the Greek ships a bitter homecoming," Athena, once the ally of the Greeks, says fiercely to the god of the sea. He agrees that when they set sail for Greece he will "make the wild Aegean roar until shores and reefs and cliffs will hold dead men, bodies of many dead," and when she leaves him he

meditates for a moment on human folly: "The fools, who
lay a city waste, so soon to die themselves."

"Mother," the Trojan queen's daughter says, "I will show
you,

> "This town, now, yes, Mother,
> is happier than the Greeks—
> They came here to the banks of the Scamander,
> and tens of thousands died. For what?
> No man had moved their land-marks
> or laid siege to their high-walled towns.
> But those whom war took never saw their children.
> No wife with gentle hand shrouded them for their grave.
> They lie in a strange land. And in their homes
> are sorrows too, the very same.
> Lonely women who died. Old men who waited
> for sons that never came.
> This is the glorious victory they won.
> But we—we Trojans died to save our people.
> Oh, fly from war if you are wise. But if war comes,
> to die well is to win the victor's crown."

But many whom war kills cannot win that crown. The
women talk little about the heroes, much about the helpless.
They think of the children who are

> Crying, crying,
> calling to us with tears,
> Mother, I am all alone—

They see the capture of the city through their eyes; the
terrible moment of the Greeks' entry as childish ears heard it:

> A shout rang out in the town,
> a cry of blood through the houses,
> and a frightened child caught his mother's skirt
> and hid himself in her cloak,
> while War came forth from his hiding place.

A child's death is the chief action in this play about war. A
little boy, hardly grown beyond babyhood, is taken from

his mother by the Greeks to be killed. She holds him in her
arms and talks to him. She bids him:

> Go die, my best-beloved, my own, my treasure,
> in cruel hands.
> Weeping, my little one? There, there,
> you cannot know. You little thing
> curled in my arms, how sweet the fragrance of you—
> Kiss me. Never again. Come closer, closer—
> Your mother who bore you—put your arms around
> her neck.
> Now kiss me, lips to lips—

When the little dead body is brought back, the mother is
gone, hurried away to a Greek ship. Only the grandmother
is there to receive it. She holds his hands,

> Dear hands, the same dear shape your father's had,
> how loosely now you fall. And dear proud lips
> forever closed.

She remembers the small boy climbing on to her bed in the
morning and telling her what he would do when he was
grown up.

> Not you, but I, old, homeless, childless,
> must lay you in your grave, so young,
> so miserably dead.

"The poet of the world's grief," Euripides was called: in this
play about war he sounded the deepest depths of that grief.
How not, he would have said, since no other suffering approaches that which war inflicts.

E. Y. Harburg

FISSION FASHION

When nuclear dust has extinguished their betters,
Will the turtles surviving wear people-neck sweaters?

*GO TO THE LEXICON, THOU SLUGGARD

In World War I they said that we
Would save the world for Democracy.

In World War II they said that we
Would save the world for Humanity.

In World War III they say we may
Still save the world for the Blattidae.*

POX OR PAX

Will little drops of fallout
And dabs of radiations,
Finally unite us all
In the Ignited Nations?

Thomas Hardy

CHANNEL FIRING

That night your great guns, unawares,
Shook all our coffins as we lay,
And broke the chancel window-squares,
We thought it was the Judgment-day

And sat upright. While drearisome
Arose the howl of wakened hounds:
The mouse let fall the altar-crumb,
The worms drew back into the mounds,

The glebe cow drooled. Till God called, "No;
It's gunnery practice out at sea
Just as before you went below;
The world is as it used to be:

"All nations striving strong to make
Red war yet redder. Mad as hatters
They do no more for Christés sake
Than you who are helpless in such matters.

"That this is not the judgment-hour
For some of them's a blessed thing,
For if it were they'd have to scour
Hell's floor for so much threatening. . . .

"Ha, ha. It will be warmer when
I blow the trumpet (if indeed
I ever do; for you are men,
And rest eternal sorely need)."

So we lay down again. "I wonder,
Will the world ever saner be,"
Said one, "than when He sent us under
In our indifferent century!"

And many a skeleton shook his head.
"Instead of preaching forty year,"
My neighbor Parson Thirdly said,
"I wish I had stuck to pipes and beer."

Again the guns disturbed the hour,
Roaring their readiness to avenge,
As far inland as Stourton Tower,
And Camelot, and starlit Stonehenge.

THE MAN HE KILLED

"Had he and I but met
    By some old ancient inn,
We should have sat us down to wet
    Right many a nipperkin!

"But ranged as infantry,
    And staring face to face,
I shot at him as he at me,
    And killed him in his place.

"I shot him dead because—
    Because he was my foe,
Just so: my foe of course he was;
    That's clear enough; although

"He thought he'd 'list, perhaps,
    Off-hand like—just as I;
Was out of work, had sold his traps—
    No other reason why.

"Yes; quaint and curious war is!
    You shoot a fellow down
You'd treat if met where any bar is,
    Or help to half-a-crown."

Ernest Hemingway

JAY RAVEN FROM PITTSBURGH

From *The New York Times*, April 25, 1937

MADRID, APRIL 24—The window of the hotel is open and, as you lie in bed, you hear the firing in the front line seventeen blocks away. There is a rifle fire all night long. The rifles go "tacrong, carong, craang, tacrong," and then a machine gun opens up. It has a bigger caliber and is much louder—"rong, cararibong, rong, rong."

Then there is the incoming boom of a trench-mortar shell and a burst of machine-gun fire. You lie and listen to it, and it is a great thing to be in bed with your feet stretched out gradually warming the cold foot of the bed and not out there in University City or Carabanchel. A man is singing hard-voiced in the street below and three drunks are arguing when you fall asleep.

In the morning, before your call comes from the desk, the roaring burst of a high-explosive shell wakes you. You go to the window and look out to see a man, his head down, his coat collar up, sprinting desperately across the paved square. There is the acrid smell of high explosive you hoped you'll never smell again.

In a bathrobe and bathroom slippers, you hurry down to the marble stairs and almost into a middle-aged woman, wounded in the abdomen, who is being helped into the hotel entrance by two men in blue workmen's smocks.

On the corner, twenty yards away, is a heap of rubble, smashed cement, and thrown-up dirt, a single dead man, his torn clothes dusty, and a great hole in the sidewalk from which the gas from a broken main is rising, looking like a heat mirage in the cold morning air.

"How many dead?" you ask a policeman.

"Only one," he says. "It went through the sidewalk and

burst below. If it had burst on the solid stone of the road there might have been fifty."

A policeman covers the body; they send for someone to repair the gas main, and you go in to breakfast. A charwoman, her eyes red, is scrubbing the blood off the marble floor of the corridor. The dead man wasn't you nor anyone you know, and everyone is very hungry in the morning after a cold night and a long day the day before up at the Guadalajara front.

"Did you see him?" asked someone else at breakfast.

"Sure," you say.

"That's where we pass a dozen times a day—right on that corner." But everyone has the feeling that characterizes war. It wasn't me, see? It wasn't me.

The Italian dead up on the Guadalajara weren't you, although Italian dead, because of where you had spent your boyhood, always seemed, still, like our dead. No. You went to the front early in the morning in a miserable little car with a more miserable little chauffeur who suffered visibly the closer he came up to the fighting. But at night, sometimes late, without lights, with the big trucks roaring past, you came on back to sleep in a bed with sheets in a good hotel, paying a dollar a day for the best rooms on the front.

The smaller rooms in the back, on the side away from the shelling, were considerably more expensive. After the shell that lighted on the sidewalk in front of the hotel, you got a beautiful double corner room on that side, twice the size of the one you had had, for less than a dollar. It wasn't me they killed. See? No. Not me. It wasn't me any more.

Then, in a hospital given by the American Friends of Spanish Democracy, located out behind the Morata front along the road to Valencia, they said, "Raven wants to see you."

"Do I know him?"

"I don't think so," they said, "but he wants to see you."

"Where is he?"

"Upstairs."

In the room upstairs they were giving a blood transfusion to a man with a very gray face who lay on a cot with his arm out, looking away from the gurgling bottle and moaning in a very impersonal way. He moaned mechanically and at regular intervals, and it did not seem to be he that made the sound. His lips did not move.

"Where's Raven?" I asked.

"I'm here," said Raven.

The voice came from a high mound covered by a shoddy gray blanket. There were two arms crossed on the top of the mound with a wide blanket across the eyes.

"Who is it?" asked Raven.

"Hemingway," I said. "I came up to see how you were doing."

"My face was pretty bad," he said. "It got sort of burned from the grenade, but it's peeled a couple of times and it's doing better."

"It looks swell," I said. "It's doing fine."

I wasn't looking at it when I spoke.

"How are things in America?" he asked. "What do they think of us over there?"

"Sentiment's changed a lot," I said. "They're beginning to realize the government is going to win the war."

"Do you think so?"

"Sure," I said.

"I'm awfully glad," he said. "You know, I wouldn't mind any of this if I could just watch what was going on. I don't mind the pain, you know. It never seemed important really. But I was always awfully interested in things and I really wouldn't mind the pain at all if I could just sort of follow things intelligently. I could even be of some use. You know, I didn't mind the war at all. I did all right in the war. I got hit once before and I was back and rejoined the battalion in two weeks. I couldn't stand to be put away. Then I got this."

He had put his hand in mine. It was not a worker's hand. There were no calluses and the nails on the long, spatulate fingers were smooth and rounded.

"How did you get it?" I asked.

"Well, there were some troops that were routed and we went over to sort of re-form them, and we did; and then we had quite a fight with the Fascists, and we beat them. It was quite a bad fight, you know, but we beat them and then someone threw this grenade at me."

Holding his hand and hearing him tell it, I did not believe a word of it. What was left of him did not sound like the wreckage of a soldier, somehow. I did not know how he had been wounded, but the story did not sound right. It was the sort of way everyone would like to have been wounded. But I wanted him to think I believed it.

"Where did you come from?" I asked.

"From Pittsburgh. I went to the university there."

"What did you do before you joined up here?"

"I was a social worker," he said.

Then I knew it couldn't be true, and I wondered how he had really been so frightfully wounded; and I didn't care. In the war that I had known, men often lied about the manner of their wounding. Not at first; but later. I'd lied a little myself in my time, especially late in the evening. But I was glad he thought I believed it, and we talked about books. He wanted to be a writer, and I told him about what had happened north of Guadalajara and promised to bring some things from Madrid next time we got out that way. I hoped I could get a radio.

"They tell me John Dos Passos and Sinclair Lewis are coming over, too," he said.

"Yes," I said. "And when they come I'll bring them up to see you."

"Gee, that will be great," he said. "You don't know what that will mean to me."

"I'll bring them," I said.

"Will they be here pretty soon?"

"Just as soon as they come I'll bring them."

"Good boy, Ernest," he said. "You don't mind if I call you Ernest, do you?"

The voice came very clear and gentle.

"Hell, no," I said. "Please. Listen, old-timer, you're going to be fine. You'll be a lot of good, you know. You can talk on the radio."

"Maybe," he said. "You'll be back?"

"Sure," I said. "Absolutely."

"Good-bye, Ernest," he said.

"Good-bye," I told him.

Downstairs they told me he'd lost both eyes and was also badly wounded all through the legs and in the feet.

"He's lost some toes, too," the doctor said, "but he doesn't know that."

"I wonder if he'll ever know it."

"Oh, sure he will," the doctor said. "He's going to get well."

And it still isn't you that gets hit, but it is your countryman now. Your countryman from Pennsylvania, where once we fought at Gettysburg.

Then, walking along the road, with his left arm in an airplane splint, walking with the gamecock walk of the professional British soldier that neither ten years of militant party work nor the projecting metal wings of the splint could destroy, I met Raven's commanding officer, Jock Cunningham, who had three fresh rifle wounds through his upper left arm (I looked at them, one was septic) and another rifle bullet under his shoulder blade that had entered his left chest, passed through, and lodged there.

He told me, in military terms, the history of the attempt to rally retiring troops on his battalion's right flank, of his bombing raid down a trench which was held at one end by the Fascists and at the other end by the government troops, of the taking of this trench and, with six men and a Lewis gun, cutting off a group of some eighty Fascists from their own lines, and of the final desperate defense of their impossible position his six men put up until the government troops came up and, attacking, straightened out the line again.

He told it clearly, completely convincingly, and with a strong Glasgow accent. He had deep, piercing eyes, sheltered like an eagle's; and, hearing him talk, you could tell the sort of soldier he was. For what he had done he would have had a VC in the last war. In this war there are no decorations. Wounds are the only decorations, and they don't award wound stripes.

"Raven was in the same show," he said. "I didn't know he'd been hit. Ay, he's a good mon. He got his after I got mine. The Fascists we'd cut off were very good troops. They never fired a useless shot when we were in that bad spot. They waited in the dark there until they had us located and then opened with volley fire. That's how I got four in the same place."

We talked for a while, and he told me many things. They were all important, but nothing was as important as that what Jay Raven, the social worker from Pittsburgh with no military training, had told me was true. This is a strange new kind of war where you learn just as much as you are able to believe.

Victor Hugo

ADDRESS TO THE CONGRÈS DE LA PAIX, PARIS, 1851

Gentlemen, is this religious idea, universal peace—the linking of the nations together by a common bond, the Gospel to become the supreme law, mediation to be substituted for war—is this religious idea a practical idea? Is this holy thought one that can be realized? Many practical minds . . . many politicians grown old . . . in the administration of affairs, answer 'No.' I answer with you; I answer unhesitatingly; I answer 'Yes,' and I will make an attempt to prove my case later on.

But I will go farther and not only say that it is a realizable end, but that it is an unavoidable end. Its coming can be delayed or hastened; that is all.

The law of the world is not nor can it be different from the law of God. Now, the law of God is not war; it is peace. . . .

When one asserts these high truths, it is quite natural that the assertion should be met with incredulity; it is quite natural that in this hour of our trouble and anguish, the idea of a universal peace should be surprising and shocking, very much like the apparition of the impossible and the ideal. It is quite natural that one should shout 'Utopia'; as for me, modest and obscure worker in this great work of the nineteenth century, I accept this resistance of other minds without being either astonished or disheartened by it. Is it possible that men's minds should not be turned and their eyes blink in a kind of dizziness, when, in the midst of the darkness which still weighs upon us, the radiant door to the future is suddenly thrust open?

Gentlemen, if someone four centuries ago, at a time when war raged from parish to parish, from town to town, from province to province—if someone had said to Lorraine, to Picardy, to Normandy, to Brittany, to Auvergne, to Provence, to Dauphine, to Burgundy, 'A day will come when you will no longer wage war, when you will no longer raise men of arms against each other, when it will no longer be said that Normans have attacked the men of Picardy, and the men of Lorraine have driven back those of Burgundy; that you will still have differences to settle, interests to discuss, certainly disputes to solve, but do you know what you will have in place of men on foot and horseback, in place of guns, falconets, spears, pikes, and swords? You will have a small box made of wood, which you will call a ballot box. And do you know what this box will bring forth? An assembly, an assembly in which you will all feel you live, an assembly which will be like your own soul, a supreme and popular council which will decide, judge, and solve everything in law, which will cause the sword to fall from every hand and justice to rise in every heart. And this event will say to you, 'There ends your right, here begins your duty. Lay down your arms! Live in peace!' On that day you will be conscious of a common thought, common interests, and a common destiny. You will clasp each other's hands and you will acknowledge that you are sons of the same blood and the same race. On that day you will no longer be hostile tribes, but a nation. You will no longer be Burgundy, Normandy, Brittany, Provence, you will be France. On that day your name will no longer be war, but civilization.

Well, you say today—and I am one of those who say it with you—all of us here, we say to France, to England, to Prussia, to Austria, to Spain, to Italy, to Russia, we say to them, 'A day will come when your weapons will fall from your hands, a day when war will seem absurd and be as impossible between Paris and London, St Petersburg and Berlin, Vienna and Turin, as today it would seem impossible between Rouen and Amiens, Boston and Philadelphia. A day will come when you France, you Russia, you Italy, you England, you Germany, all you continental nations, without losing your characteristics, your glorious individuality, will intimately dissolve into a superior unity and you will constitute the European brotherhood just as Normandy, Brittany, Burgundy, Lorraine, Alsace, and all our provinces, have dissolved into France. A day will come when there will be no battlefields, but markets opening to commerce and minds opening to ideas. A day will come when the bullets and bombs are replaced by votes, by universal suffrage, by the venerable arbitration of a great supreme senate which will be to Europe what Parliament is to England, the Diet to Germany, and the Legislative Assembly to France. A day will come when a cannon will be a museum-piece, as instruments of torture are today. And we will be amazed to think that these things once existed! A day will come when we shall see those two immense groups, the United States of America and the United States of Europe, stretching out their hands across the sea, exchanging their products, their arts, their works of genius, clearing up the globe, making deserts fruitful, ameliorating creation under the eyes of the Creator, and joining together to reap the well-being of all. . . .

Henceforth the goal of great politics, of true politics, is this: the recognition of all the nationalities, the restoration of the historical unity of nations and the uniting of the latter to civilization by peace, the relentless enlargement of the civilized group, the setting of an example to the still-savage nations; in short, and this recapitulates all I have said, the assurance that justice will have the last word, spoken in the past by might.

Aldous Huxley

ETHICS AND WAR

Pacifism is the application of the principles of individual morality to the problems of politics and economics. In practice we have two systems of morality: one for individuals and another for communities. Behaviour which, in an individual, would be considered wrong is excused or even commended when indulged in by a national community. Men and women who would shrink from doing anything dishonourable in the sphere of personal relationships are ready to lie and swindle, to steal and even murder when they are representing their country. The community is regarded as a wholly immoral being and loyalty to the community serves to justify the individual in committing every kind of crime.

The wars of earlier days were relatively harmless affairs. Few conquerors were systematically destructive; Jinghiz Khan was an exceptional monster. To-day, scientific weapons have made possible indiscriminate and unintentional destruction. Most military experts are agreed that a large-scale war waged with such weapons will be the ruin of European civilization. War was always wrong, and war-makers have always been men of criminal intentions; science has now provided the war-makers with the power of putting their intentions into destructive action on a scale which was undreamt of even a quarter of a century ago. In the past, national communities could afford to behave like maniacs or criminals. To-day the costs of lunacy and wickedness are excessive; nations can no longer afford to behave except like the sanest and most moral of beings.

Randall Jarrell

THE DEATH OF THE BALL TURRET GUNNER

From my mother's sleep I fell into the State,
And I hunched in its belly till my wet fur froze.
Six miles from earth, loosed from its dream of life,
I woke to black flak and the nightmare fighters.
When I died they washed me out of the turret with a hose.

EIGHTH AIR FORCE

If, in an odd angle of the hutment
A puppy laps the water from a can
Of flowers, and the drunk sergeant shaving
Whistles *O Paradiso!*—shall I say that man
Is not as men have said: a wolf to man?

The other murderers troop in yawning;
Three of them play Pitch, one sleeps, and one
Lies counting missions, lies there sweating
Till even his heart beats: One; One; One.
O murderers! . . . Still, this is how it's done:

This is a war . . . But since these play, before they die,
Like puppies with their puppy; since, a man,
I did as these have done, but did not die—
I will content the people as I can
And give up these to them: Behold the man!

I have suffered, in a dream, because of him,
Many things; for this last savior, man,
I have lied as I lie now. But what is lying?
Men wash their hands, in blood, as best they can.
I find no fault in this just man.

Samuel Johnson

THE VULTURES

Many naturalists are of opinion that the animals which we commonly consider as mute have the power of imparting their thoughts to one another. That they can express general sensations is very certain; every being that can utter sounds has a different voice for pleasure and for pain. The hound informs his fellows when he scents his game; the hen calls her chickens to their food by her cluck, and drives them from danger by her scream.

Birds have the greatest variety of notes; they have indeed a variety which seems almost sufficient to make a speech adequate to the purposes of a life, which is regulated by instinct, and can admit little change or improvement. To the cries of birds, curiosity or superstition has been always attentive; many have studied the language of the feathered tribes, and some have boasted that they understood it.

The most skillful or most confident interpreters of the sylvan dialogues have been commonly found among the philosophers of the East, in a country where the calmness of the air and the mildness of the seasons allow the student to pass a great part of the year in groves and bowers. But what may be done in one place by peculiar opportunities may be performed in another by peculiar diligence. A shepherd of Bohemia has, by long abode in the forests, enabled himself to understand the voice of birds; at least he relates with great confidence a story, of which the credibility is left to be considered by the learned.

"As I was sitting," said he, "within a hollow rock, and watching my sheep that fed in the valley, I heard two vultures interchangeably crying on the summit of the cliff. Both voices were earnest and deliberate. My curiosity prevailed over my care of the flock; I climbed slowly and silently from crag to crag, concealed among the shrubs till I found a cavity where I might sit and listen without suffering, or giving disturbance.

"I soon perceived that my labor would be well repaid; for an old vulture was sitting on a naked prominence with her young about her, whom she was instructing in the arts of a vulture's life, and preparing by the last lecture for their final dismission to the mountains and the skies.

" 'My children,' said the old vulture, 'you will the less want my instructions because you have had my practice before your eyes; you have seen me snatch from the farm the household fowl; you have seen me seize the leveret in the bush, and the kid in the pasture; you know how to fix your talons, and how to balance your flight when you are laden with your prey. But you remember the taste of more delicious food; I have often regaled you with the flesh of man.' 'Tell us,' said the young vultures, 'where man may be found, and how he may be known; his flesh is surely the natural food of a vulture. Why have you never brought a man in your talons to the nest?' 'He is too bulky,' said the mother; 'when we find a man, we can only tear away his flesh and leave his bones upon the ground.' 'Since man is so big,' said the young ones, 'how do you kill him? You are afraid of the wolf and of the bear; by what power are vultures superior to man? Is man more defenseless than a sheep?' 'We have not the strength of man,' returned the mother; 'and I am sometimes in doubt whether we have the subtlety; and the vultures would seldom feast upon his flesh, had not nature, that devoted him to our uses, infused into him *a strange ferocity* which I have never observed in any other being that feeds upon the earth. Two herds of men will often meet and shake the earth with noise, and fill the air with fire. When you hear noise and see fire, with flashes along the ground, hasten to the place with your swiftest wing, for men are surely destroying one another; you will then find the ground smoking with blood, and covered with carcasses, of which many are dismembered and mangled for the convenience of the vulture.' 'But when men have killed their prey,' said the pupil, 'why do they not eat it? When the wolf has killed a sheep, he suffers not the vulture to touch it till he has satisfied himself. Is not man another kind of wolf?' 'Man,' said the mother, 'is the only beast who kills that which he does not devour, and this quality makes him so much a benefactor to our species.' 'If men kill our prey and lay it in our way,' said the young one, 'what need shall we have of laboring for ourselves?' 'Because man will, sometimes,' replied the mother, 'remain for a long time quiet in his den. The old vultures will tell you when you are to watch his motions. When you see men in great numbers moving close together like a flight of storks, you may conclude that they are hunting, and that you will soon revel in human blood.' 'But still,' said the young one, 'I would gladly know the reason of this mutual slaughter. I could never kill what I could not eat.' 'My child,' said the mother, 'this is a question which I cannot answer, though I am reckoned the most subtle bird of the mountain. When I was young, I used frequently to visit the aerie of an old vulture who dwelt upon the Carpathian rocks; he had made many observations; he knew the places that afforded prey round his habitation as far in every direction as the strongest wing can fly between the rising and setting of the summer sun; he had fed year after year on the entrails of men. His opinion was that men had only the appearance of animal life, being really *vegetables with a power of motion;* and that as the boughs of an oak are dashed together by the storm that swine may fatten upon the falling acorns, so men are by some unaccountable power driven one against another till they lose their motion that vultures may be fed. Others think they have observed something of contrivance and policy among these mischievous beings; and those that hover more closely round them, pretend that there is in every herd one that gives directions to the rest, and seems to be more eminently delighted with a wide carnage. What it is that entitles him to such preeminence we know not; he is seldom the biggest or the swiftest, but he shows by his eagerness and diligence that he is, more than any of the others, a friend to vultures.' "

Laurie Lee

THE LONG WAR

Less passionate the long war throws
its burning thorn about all men,
caught in one grief, we share one wound,
and cry one dialect of pain.

We have forgot who fired the house,
whose easy mischief spilt first blood,
under one raging roof we lie
the fault no longer understood.

But as our twisted arms embrace
the desert where our cities stood,
death's family likeness in each face
must show, at last, our brotherhood.

Denise Levertov

WHAT WERE THEY LIKE? (QUESTIONS AND ANSWERS)

1) Did the people of Viet Nam
   use lanterns of stone?
2) Did they hold ceremonies
   to reverence the opening of buds?
3) Were they inclined to rippling laughter?
4) Did they use bone and ivory,
   jade and silver, for ornament?
5) Had they an epic poem?
6) Did they distinguish between speech and singing?

1) Sir, their light hearts turned to stone.
   It is not remembered whether in gardens
   stone lanterns illumined pleasant ways.
2) Perhaps they gathered once to delight in blossom,
   but after the children were killed
   there were no more buds.
3) Sir, laughter is bitter to the burned mouth.
4) A dream ago, perhaps. Ornament is for joy.
   All the bones were charred.
5) It is not remembered. Remember,
   most were peasants; their life
   was in rice and bamboo.
   When peaceful clouds were reflected in the paddies
   and the water-buffalo stepped surely along terraces,
   maybe fathers told their sons old tales.
   When bombs smashed the mirrors
   there was time only to scream.
6) There is an echo yet, it is said,
   of their speech which was like a song.
   It is reported their singing resembled
   the flight of moths in moonlight.
   Who can say? It is silent now.

Alun Lewis

THE RAID

My platoon and I were on training that morning. We've been on training every morning for the last three years, for that matter. On this occasion it was Current Affairs, which always boils down to how long the war is going to last, and when the orderly told me the C. O. wanted me in his office I broke the lads off for a cup of tea from the charwallah and nipped over to the orderly room, tidying myself as I went. I didn't expect anything unusual until I took a cautionary peep through the straw window of his matting shed and saw a strange officer in there. So I did a real dapper salute and braced myself. Self-defence is always the first instinct, self-suspicion the second. But I hadn't been drunk since I came to India and I hadn't written anything except love in my letters. As for politics, as far as they're concerned I don't exist, I'm never in. The other chap was a major and had a red armband.

"Come in, Selden," the colonel said. "This is the D. A. P. M. Head of military police. Got a job for you. Got your map case?"

"No, sir. It's in company office."

"Hurry off and fetch it."

When I came back they were hard at it, bending over the inch map. The C. O. looked up. His face got very red when he bent.

"Here's your objective, Selden. This village here, Chaudanullah. Eighteen miles away. Route: track south of Morje, river-bed up to Pimpardi, turn south a mile before Pimpardi and strike across the watershed on a fixed bearing. Work it out with a protractor on the map and set your compass before you march off. Strike the secondary road below this group of huts here, 247568, cross the road and work up the canal to the village. Throw a cordon round the village with two sections of your platoon. Take the third yourself and search the houses methodically. Government has a paid agent in the village who will meet you at this canal bridge here—got it?—at 06.00 hours. The agent reported that your man arrived there last night after dark and is lying up in one of the hovels."

"What man, sir?" I asked.

"Christ, didn't I tell you? Why the devil didn't you stop me? This fellow, what's-his-name—it's all on that paper there—he's wanted. Remember the bomb in the cinema last Tuesday, killed three British other ranks? He's wanted for that. Read the description before you go. Any questions so far? Right. Well, you'll avoid all houses, make a detour round villages, keep off the road all the way. Understand? News travels faster than infantry in India. He'll be away before you're within ten miles if you show yourself. Let's see. Twenty miles by night. Give you ten hours. Leave here at 19.30 hours. Arrive an hour before first light. Go in at dawn, keep your eyes skinned. M. T. will R. V. outside the village at dawn. Drive the prisoner straight to jail. D. A. P. M. will be there."

"Very good, sir. Dress, sir?" I said.

"Dress? P.T. shoes, cloth caps, overalls, basic pouches, rifles, 50 rounds of .303 per man, and grenades. 69 grenades if he won't come out, 36 grenades if he makes a fight of it. Anything else?"

"No, sir."

"Good. Remember to avoid the villages. Stalk him good and proper. Keep up-wind of him. I'm picking you and your platoon because I think you're the best I've got. I want results, Selden."

"I'll give you a good show, sir."

"Bloody good shot with a point 22, Selden is," the C. O. said to the D. A. P. M. by way of light conversation. "Shot six mallard with me last Sunday."

"Of course we want the man alive, sir, if it's at all possible," the D. A. P. M. said, fiddling with his nervous pink moustache. "He's not proved guilty yet, you see, sir, and with public opinion in India what it is."

"Quite," said the colonel. "Quite. Make a note of that, Selden. Tell your men to shoot low."

"Very good, sir."

"Got the route marked on your talc?"

"Yes, sir." I'd marked the route in chinograph pencil and the Chaudanullah place in red as we do for enemy objectives. It was all thick.

"Rub it all off, then. Security. Read his description. Have you read it? What is it?"

"Dark eyes, sir. Scar on left knee. Prominent cheekbones. Left corner of mouth droops. Front incisor discoloured. Last seen wearing European suit, may be dressed in native dhoti, Mahratta style."

"And his ring?" said the C. O. He's as keen as mustard the old man is.

"Oh yes, sir. Plain gold wedding ring."

"Correct. Don't forget these details. Invaluable sometimes. Off with you."

I saluted and marched out.

"Damn good fellow, Selden," I heard the C. O. say. "Your man is in the bag."

I felt pretty pleased with that. Comes of shooting those six mallard.

The platoon was reassembling after their tea and I felt pretty important, going back with all that dope. After all, it was the first bit of action we'd seen in two and a half years. It would be good for morale. I knew they'd moan like hell, having to do a twenty-mile route march by night, but I could sell them that all right. So I fell them in in threes and called them to attention for disciplinary reasons and told them they'd been picked for a special job and this was it. . . .

They were very impressed by the time I'd finished.

"Any questions?" I said.

"Yes, sir," said Chalky White. He was an L. P. T. B. conductor and you won't find him forgetting a halfpenny. "Do we take haversack rations and will we be in time for breakfast?" He thinks the same way as Napoleon.

"Yes," I said. "Anything else?"

"What's this fellow done, sir?" Bottomley asked, then. Bottomley always was a bit Bolshie, and he's had his knife into me for two and a half years because I was a bank clerk in Civvy Street and played golf on Sundays.

"Killed three troops, I think," I said. "Is that good enough?"

I felt I'd scored pretty heavy over his Red stuff this time.

"Right," I said. "Break off till 19.00 hours. Keep your mouths shut. White will draw rations at the cookhouse. No cigarettes or matches will be taken."

I did that for disciplinary purposes. They didn't say a word. Pretty good.

We crossed the start line dead on 19.30 hours and everybody looked at us with some interest. I felt mighty "hush-hush." My security was first class. Hadn't told a soul, except Ken More and Ted Paynter.

"Bring 'em back alive," a soldier jeered outside the cookhouse.

Somebody's let the cat out of the bag. Damn them all. Can't trust a soul in the ranks with the skin of a sausage.

Anyway, we got going bang away. I knew the first stretch past Morje and Pimpardi and we did about three miles an hour there. The night was breathless and stuffy; we put hankies round our foreheads to keep the sweat out of our eyes. And the perpetual buzzing of the crickets got on my nerves like a motor horn when the points jam and all the pedestrians laugh. I suppose I was a bit worked up. Every time a mosquito or midge touched me I let out a blow fit to knacker a bull. But I settled down after a while and began to enjoy the sense of freedom and deep still peace that informs the night out in the tropics. You've read all about tropical stars; well, it's quite true. They're marvellous; and we use some of them for direction-finding at night too. The Plough, for instance, and one called Cassiopeia that you bisect for the Pole Star.

Then there was the tricky bit over the mountain by compass. I just hoped for the best on that leg. Luckily the moon came up and put the lads in a good mood. I allowed them to talk in whispers for one hour and they had to keep silent for the next hour for disciplinary reasons. We halted for half an hour on the crest of the watershed and ate our bully beef sandwiches with relish, though bully tastes like a hot poultice out here. It was a damn fine view from that crest. A broad valley a thousand feet below with clusters of fires in the villages and round a hill temple on the other side. Either a festival or a funeral, obviously. I could hear the drums beating there, too; it was very clear and echoing. made my flesh creep. You feel so out of it in India somehow. You just slink around in the wilds and you feel very white and different. I don't know. . . . You know, I'd have said that valley *hated* us that night, on those rocky crests. Queer.

I didn't know which group of huts was which, but I could see the canal glittering in the moonlight so I was near enough right, praise be. The jackals were howling too, and some creature came right up to us, it gave me a scare. I knew that bully had a pretty bad stench. Anyway we got on the move again, Chalky White saying next stop Hammersmiff Bridge, and we slithered down as quietly as we could, hanging on to each other's rifles on the steep bits. We made our way between the villages and the drums beat themselves into a frenzy that had something personal about it. Then we went up the canal for about four miles, keeping about a hundred yards off the path and pretty rough going it was. Then we came to what I felt must be our objective, a cluster of crumbled huts on the foothills, pretty poor show even for these parts, and the boys were blistered and beat so I scattered them under the bushes and told them to lie low. It was only 5.30 a.m. and the agent fellow wasn't due until six. I had a nap myself, matter of fact, though it's a shootable offence. I woke up with a start and it was five past six, and I peered round my tree and there wasn't a sound. No drums, no jackals, no pie dogs. It was singing in my ears, the silence, and I wished to God we'd got this job over. It could go wrong so easily. He might fight, or his pals might help him, or he might have got wind of us, or I might have come to the wrong place. I was like an old woman. I loaded my Colt and felt better. Then I went down the canal to look for the chow-key fellow. I took a pretty poor view of a traitor, but I took a poorer view of him not turning up. He wasn't there and I walked up the path and just when I was getting really scared he appeared out of nowhere and I damn near shot him on the spot.

"Officer sahib huzzoor," he said. "Mai Sarkar ko dost hai," something. And he said the name of the man I was after, which was the password.

"Achiba," I said, meaning good show. "Tairo a minute while I bolo my phaltan and then we'll jao jillo." He got the idea.

I nipped back and roused the lads quietly from under the trees and we moved up like ghosts on that village. I never want to see that village again. It was so still and fragile in the reluctant grey light. Even the pie dogs were asleep, and the bullocks lying on their sides. Once I travelled overnight from Dieppe to Paris and the countryside looked just as ghostly that morning. But this time it was dangerous. I had a feeling somebody was going to die and there'd be a hell of a shemozzle. And at the same time the houses looked so poor and harmless, almost timid somehow. And the chowkey bloke was like a ghost. It was seeing him so scared that put me steady again. He was afraid of being seen with us as far as I could make out, and said he'd show us where this fellow was lying up and then he'd disappear please. I said never mind about the peace, let's get the war over first, and I told Bottomley to watch the bloke in case he had anything up his sleeve.

We got to the ring of trees outside the village without a sound, and the two section leaders led their men round each side of the village in a pincer movement. All the boys were white and dirty and their eyes were like stones. I remember suddenly feeling very proud of them just then.

I gave them ten minutes to get into position and close the road at the rear of the village. And then a damned pie dog set up a yelp over on the right flank and another replied with a long shivering howl. I knew things would start going wrong if I didn't act quickly. We didn't want the village to find out until we'd gone if possible. For political reasons. And for reasons of health, I thought. So I gave the Follow-me sign and closed in on the huddled houses. There were a couple of outlying houses with a little shrine, and then the village proper with a crooked street running down it. The chowkey seemed to know where to go. I pointed to the single buildings and he said, "Nay, sahib," and pointed to the street. So I posted a man to picket the shrine and led the rest through the bush behind our scruffy guide. He moved like a beaten dog, crouching and limping, bare-foot. There was a dead ox in the bush and a pair of kites sleeping and gorged beside it. It stank like a bad death. Turned me. We hurried on. The bushes were in flower, sort of wisteria, the blossoms closed and drooping. We crept along under a tumbledown wall and paused, kneeling, at the street corner. I posted two men there, one on each side with fixed bayonets, to fire down the street if he bolted. The other two sections would be covering it from the other end. Then I nudged the chowkey man and signalled to my grenade man and rifleman to cover me in. I slipped round the corner and went gingerly down the street. Suddenly I felt quite cool and excited at the same time. The chowkey went about fifteen yards down the street and then slunk against the wall on his knees, pointing inwards to the house he was kneeling against. It was made of branches woven with straw and reed, a beggared place. He looked up at me and my revolver and he was sweating with fear. He had the pox all over his face, too. I took a breath to steady myself, took the first pressure on my trigger, kicked the door lattice aside and jumped in. Stand in the light in the doorway and you're a dead man.

I crouched in the dark corner. It was very dark in there still. There was a pile of straw on the floor and straw heaped in the corner. And some huge thing moved ponderously. I nearly yelped. Then I saw what it was. It was a cow. Honestly. A sleepy fawn cow with a soft mild face like somebody's dream woman.

"She never frew no bomb," Chalky said. He was my rifleman. Cool as ice. His voice must have broken the fellow's nerve. There was a huge rustle in the straw in the corner behind the cow and a man stood up, a man in a white dhoti, young, thin, sort of smiling. Discoloured teeth. Chalky lunged his bayonet. The chap still had plenty of nerve left. He just swayed a little.

"Please," he said. "Have you got a smoke upon you?"

"Watch him, White," I said. I searched him.

"Please," he said. "I have nothing." He was breathing quickly and smiling.

"Come on," I said. "Quietly."

"You know you are taking me to my death?" he said. "No doubt?"

"I'm taking you to Poona," I said. "You killed three of our men."

The smile sort of congealed on his face. Like a trick. His head nodded like an old doll. "Did I?" he said. "Three men died? Did I?"

"Come on," I said. "It's daylight."

"It's dreadful," he said. He looked sick. I felt sorry for him, nodding his head and sick, sallow. Looked like a student, I should say.

"Keep your hands up," Chalky said, prodding him in the back.

We went quietly down the street, no incident at all, and I signalled the two enveloping sections together and we got down the road out of sight. I was in a cold sweat and I wanted to laugh.

The trucks weren't there. God, I cursed them, waiting there. They might bitch the whole show. The villagers were going to the well quite close.

"What did you do it for, mate?" I heard Bottomley ask.

After a long silence the chap said very quietly, "For my country."

Chalky said, "Everybody says that. Beats me." Then we heard the trucks, and Chalky said, "We ought to be there in time for breakfast, boys."

Robert Lowell

CHRISTMAS EVE UNDER HOOKER'S STATUE

Tonight in a blackout. Twenty years ago
I hung my stocking on the tree, and hell's
Serpent entwined the apple in the toe
To sting the child with knowledge. Hooker's heels
Kicking at nothing in the shifting snow,
A cannon and a cairn of cannon balls
Rusting before the blackened Statehouse, know
How the long horn of plenty broke like glass
In Hooker's gauntlets. Once I came from Mass;

Now storm-clouds shelter Christmas, once again
Mars meets his fruitless star with open arms,
His heavy sabre flashes with the rime,
The war-god's bronzed and empty forehead forms
Anonymous machinery from raw men;
The cannon on the Common cannot stun
The blundering butcher as he rides on Time—
The barrel clinks with holly. I am cold:
I ask for bread, my father gives me mould;

His stocking is full of stones. Santa in red
Is crowned with wizened berries. Man of war,
Where is the summer's garden? In its bed
The ancient speckled serpent will appear,
And black-eyed susan with her frizzled head.
When Chancellorsville mowed down the volunteer,
"All wars are boyish," Herman Melville said;
But we are old, our fields are running wild:
Till Christ again turn wanderer and child.

ugh MacDiarmid

REFLECTIONS IN AN IRONWORKS

Would you resembled the metal you work with,
Would the iron entered into your souls,
Would you became like steel on your own behalf!
You are still only putty that tyranny rolls
Between its fingers! You makers of bayonets and guns
For your own destruction! No wonder that those
Weapons you make turn on you and mangle and murder—
You fools who equip your otherwise helpless foes!

IF I WAS NOT A SOLDIER

If I wasn't a soldier, a soldier said,
What would I be?—I wouldn't be,
It's hardly likely it seems to me,
A money lord or armament maker,
Territorial magnate or business chief.
I'd probably be just a working man,
   The slave of a licensed thief,—
One of the criminals I'm shielding now!

If I wasn't a soldier, a soldier said,
I'd be down and out as likely as not
And suffering the horrible starving lot
Of hundreds of thousands of my kind,
And that would make me a Red as well
Till I rose with the rest and was batoned or shot
By some cowardly brute—such as I am now!

Archibald MacLeish

THE END OF THE WORLD

Quite unexpectedly, as Vasserot
The armless ambidextrian was lighting
A match between his great and second toe,
And Ralph the lion was engaged in biting
The neck of Madame Sossman while the drum
Pointed, and Teeny was about to cough
In waltz-time swinging Jocko by the thumb—
Quite unexpectedly the top blew off:

And there, there overhead, there, there hung over
Those thousands of white faces, those dazed eyes,
There in the starless dark the poise, the hover,
There with vast wings across the cancelled skies,
There in the sudden blackness the black pall
Of nothing, nothing, nothing—nothing at all.

Louis MacNeice

THE CONSCRIPT

Being so young he feels the weight of history
Like clay around his boots; he would, if he could, fly
In search of a future like a sycamore seed
But is prevented by his own Necessity,
His own yet alien, which, whatever he may plead,
To every question gives the same reply.

Choiceless therefore, driven from pillar to post,
Expiating his pedigree, fulfilling
An oracle whose returns grow less and less,
Bandied from camp to camp to practise killing
He fails even so at times to remain engrossed
And is aware, at times, of life's largesse.

From camp to camp, from Eocene to chalk,
He lives a paradox, lives in a groove
That runs dead straight to an ordained disaster
So that in two dimensions he must move
Like an automaton, yet his inward stalk
Vertically aspires and makes him his own master.

Hence, though on the flat his life has no
Promise but of diminishing returns,
By feeling down and upwards he can divine
That dignity which far above him burns
In stars that yet are his and which below
Stands rooted like a dolmen in his spine.

Maurice Maeterlinck

THE MASSACRE OF THE INNOCENTS

Towards the hour of supper on Friday, the twenty-sixth day of the month of December, a little shepherd lad came into Nazareth, crying bitterly.

Some peasants, who were drinking ale in the Blue Lion, opened the shutters to look into the village orchard, and saw the child running over the snow. They recognized him as the son of Korneliz, and called from the window: "What is the matter? It's time you were abed!"

But, sobbing still and shaking with terror, the boy cried that the Spaniards had come, that they had set fire to the farm, had hanged his mother among the nut trees and bound his nine little sisters to the trunk of a big tree. At this the peasants rushed out of the inn. Surrounding the child, they stunned him with their questionings and outcries. Between his sobs, he added that the soldiers were on horseback and wore armor, that they had taken away the cattle of his uncle, Petrus Krayer, and would soon be in the forest with the sheep and cows. All now ran to the Golden Swan where, as they knew, Korneliz and his brother-in-law were also drinking their mug of ale. The moment the innkeeper heard these terrifying tidings, he hurried into the village, crying that the Spaniards were at hand.

What a stir, what an uproar there was then in Nazareth! Women opened windows, and peasants hurriedly left their houses carrying lights which were put out when they reached the orchard, where, because of the snow and the full moon, one could see as well as at midday.

Later, they gathered round Korneliz and Krayer, in the open space which faced the inns. Several of them had brought pitchforks and rakes, and consulted together, terror-stricken, under the trees.

But, as they did not know what to do, one of them ran to

fetch the curé, who owned Korneliz's farm. He came out of the house with the sacristan carrying the keys of the church. All followed him into the churchyard, whither his cry came to them from the top of the tower, that he beheld nothing either in the fields, or by the forest, but that around the farm he saw ominous red clouds, for all that the sky was of a deep blue and agleam with stars over the rest of the plain.

After taking counsel for a long time in the churchyard, they decided to hide in the wood through which the Spaniards must pass, and, if these were not too numerous, to attack them and recover Petrus Krayer's cattle and the plunder which had been taken from the farm.

Having armed themselves with pitchforks and spades, while the women remained outside the church with the curé, they sought a suitable ambuscade. Approaching a mill on a rising ground adjacent to the verge of the forest, they saw the light of the burning farm flaming against the stars. There they waited under enormous oaks, before a frozen mere.

A shepherd, known as Red Dwarf, climbed the hill to warn the miller, who had stopped his mill when he saw the flames on the horizon. He bade the peasant enter, and both men went to a window to stare out into the night.

Before them the moon shone over the burning farmstead, and in its light they saw a long procession winding athwart the snow. Having carefully scrutinized it, the Dwarf descended where his comrades waited under the trees, and, now, they too gradually distinguished four men on horseback behind a flock which moved grazing on the plain.

While the peasants in their blue breeches and red cloaks continued to search about the margins of the mere and under the snowlit trees, the sacristan pointed out to them a boxhedge, behind which they hid.

The Spaniards, driving before them the sheep and the cattle, advanced upon the ice. When the sheep reached the hedge they began to nibble at the green stuff, and now Korneliz broke from the shadows of the bushes, followed by the others with their pitchforks. Then in the midst of the huddled-up sheep and of the cows who stared affrighted, the savage strife was fought out beneath the moon, and ended in a massacre.

When they had slain not only the Spaniards, but also their horses, Korneliz rushed thence across the meadow in the direction of the flames, while the others plundered and stripped the dead. Thereafter all returned to the village with their flocks. The women, who were observing the dark forest from behind the churchyard walls, saw them coming through the trees and ran with the curé to meet them, and all returned dancing joyously amid the laughter of the children and the barking of the dogs.

But, while they made merry, under the pear trees of the orchard, where the Red Dwarf had hung lanterns in honor of the kermesse, they anxiously demanded of the curé what was to be done.

The outcome of this was the harnessing of a horse to a cart in order to fetch the bodies of the woman and the nine little girls to the village. The sisters and other relations of the dead woman got into the cart along with the curé, who, being old and very fat, could not walk so far.

In silence they entered the forest, and emerged upon the moonlit plain. There, in the white light, they descried the dead men, rigid and naked, among the slain horses. Then they moved onward towards the farm, which still burned in the midst of the plain.

When they came to the orchard of the flaming house, they stopped at the gate of the garden, dumb before the overwhelming misfortune of the peasant. For there, his wife hung, quite naked, on the branches of an enormous nut tree, among which he himself was now mounting on a ladder, and beneath which, on the frozen grass, lay his nine little daughters. Korneliz had already climbed along the vast boughs, when suddenly, by the light of the snow, he saw the crowd who horror-struck watched his every movement. With tears in his eyes, he made a sign to them to help him, whereat the innkeepers of the Blue Lion and the Golden Sun, the curé, with a lantern, and many others, climbed up in the moonshine amid the snow-laden branches, to unfasten the dead. The women of the village received the corpse in their arms at the foot of the tree; even as our Lord Jesus Christ was received by the women at the foot of the Cross.

On the morrow they buried her, and for the week thereafter nothing unusual happened in Nazareth.

But the following Sunday, hungry wolves ran through the village after high mass, and it snowed until midday. Then, suddenly, the sun shone brilliantly, and the peasants went to dine, as was their wont, and dressed for the benediction.

There was no one to be seen on the Place, for it froze bitterly. Only the dogs and chickens roamed about under the trees, or the sheep nibbled at a three-cornered bit of grass, while the curé's servant swept away the snow from his garden.

At that moment a troop of armed men crossed the stone bridge at the end of the village, and halted in the orchard. Peasants hurried from their houses, but, recognizing the new comers as Spaniards, they retreated terrified, and went to the windows to see what would happen.

About thirty soldiers, in full armor, surrounded an old man with a white beard. Behind them, on pillions, rode red and yellow lancers who jumped down and ran over the snow to shake off their stiffness, while several of the soldiers in armor dismounted likewise and fastened their horses to the trees.

Then they moved in the direction of the Golden Sun, and knocked at the door. It was opened reluctantly; the soldiers went in, warmed themselves near the fire, and called for ale.

Presently they came out of the inn, carrying pots, jugs, and rye-bread for their companions, who surrounded the man with the white beard, where he waited behind the hedge of lances.

As the street remained deserted the commander sent some horsemen to the back of the houses, to guard the village on the country side. He then ordered the lancers to bring him all the children of two years old and under, to be massacred, as is written in the Gospel of St. Matthew.

The soldiers first went to the little inn of the Green Cabbage, and to the barber's cottage, which stood side by side midway in the street.

One of them opened a sty and a litter of pigs wandered into the village. The innkeeper and the barber came out, and humbly asked the men what they wanted; but they did not understand Flemish, and went into the houses to look for the children.

The innkeeper had one child, who, in its little shift, was screaming on the table where they had just dined. A soldier took it in his arms, and carried it away under the apple trees, while the father and mother followed, crying.

Thereafter the lancers opened other stable doors,—those of the cooper, the blacksmith, the cobbler,—and calves, cows, asses, pigs, goats, and sheep roamed about the square. When they broke the carpenter's windows, several of the oldest and richest inhabitants of the village assembled in the street, and went to meet the Spaniards. Respectfully they took off their caps and hats to the leader in the velvet mantle, and asked him what he was going to do. He did not, however, understand their language; so some one ran to fetch the curé.

The priest was putting on a gold chasuble in the vestry, in readiness for the benediction. The peasant cried: "The Spaniards are in the orchard!" Horrified, the curé ran to the door of the church, and the choir-boys followed, carrying wax-tapers and censer.

As he stood there, he saw the animals from the pens and stables wandering on the snow and on the grass; the horsemen in the village, the soldiers before the doors, horses tied to trees all along the street; men and women entreating the man who held the child in its little shift.

The curé hastened into the churchyard, and the peasants turned anxiously towards him as he came through the pear trees, like the Divine Presence itself robed in white and gold. They crowded about him where he confronted the man with the white beard.

He spoke in Flemish and in Latin, but the commander merely shrugged his shoulders to show that he did not understand.

The villagers asked their priest in a low voice: "What does he say? What is he going to do?" Others, when they saw the curé in the orchard, came cautiously from their cottages, women hurried up and whispered in groups, while the soldiers, till that moment besieging an inn, ran back at sight of the crowd in the square.

Then the man who held the innkeeper's child by the leg cut off its head with his sword.

The people saw the head fall, and thereafter the body lie bleeding upon the grass. The mother picked it up, and carried it away, but forgot the head. She ran towards her home, but stumbling against a tree fell prone on the snow, where she lay in a swoon, while the father struggled between two soldiers.

Some young peasants cast stones and blocks of wood at the Spaniards, but the horsemen all lowered their lances; the women fled and the curé with his parishioners began to shriek with horror, amid the bleating of the sheep, the cackling of the geese, and the barking of the dogs.

But as the soldiers moved away again into the street, the crowd stood silent to see what would happen.

A troop entered the shop kept by the sacristan's sisters, but came out quietly, without harming the seven women, who knelt on the threshold praying.

From there they went to the inn of St. Nicholas, which belonged to the Hunchback. Here, too, so as to appease them, the door was opened at once; but, when the soldiers reappeared amid a great uproar, they carried three children in their arms. The marauders were surrounded by the Hunchback, his wife, and daughters, all, with clasped hands, imploring for mercy.

When the soldiers came to their white-bearded leader, they placed the children at the foot of an elm, where the little ones remained seated on the snow in their Sunday clothes. But one of them, in a yellow frock, got up and toddled unsteadily towards the sheep. A soldier followed, with bare sword; and the child died with his face in the grass, while the others were killed around the tree.

The peasants and the innkeeper's daughters all fled screaming, and shut themselves up in their houses. The curé, who was left alone in the orchard, threw himself on his knees, first before one horseman, then another, and with crossed arms, supplicated the Spaniards piteously, while the fathers and mothers seated on the snow beyond wept bitterly for the dead children whom they held upon their knees.

As the lancers passed along the street, they noticed a big blue farmstead. When they had tried, in vain, to force open the oaken door studded with nails, they clambered atop of some tubs, which were frozen over near the threshold, and by this means gained the house through the upper windows.

There had been a kermesse in this farm. At sound of the broken window-panes, the families who had assembled there to eat gaufres, custards, and hams, crowded together behind the table on which stood some empty jugs and dishes. The soldiers entered the kitchen, and after a savage struggle in which many were wounded, they seized all the little boys and girls; then, with these, and the servant who had bitten a lancer's thumb, they left the house and fastened the door behind them in such a way that the parents could not get out.

The villagers who had no children slowly left their houses and followed the soldiers at a distance. They saw them throw down their victims on the grass before the old man, and callously kill them with lance and sword. During this, men and women leaned out of all the windows of the blue house, and out of the barn, blaspheming and flinging their hands to heaven, when they saw the red, pink, and white frocks of their motionless little ones on the grass between the trees. The soldiers next hanged the farm servant at the sign of the Half Moon on the other side of the street, and there was a long silence in the village.

The massacre now became general. Mothers fled from their houses, and attempted to escape through the flower and vegetable gardens, and so into the country beyond, but the horsemen pursued them and drove them back into the street. Peasants with caps in their clasped hands knelt before the men who dragged away their children, while amid the confusion the dogs barked joyously. The curé, with hands upraised to heaven, rushed up and down in front of the houses and under the trees, praying desperately; here and there, soldiers, trembling with cold, blew on their fingers as they moved about the road, or waited with hands in their breeches pockets, and swords under their arms, before the windows of the houses which were being scaled.

Everywhere, as in small bands of twos and threes they moved along the streets where these scenes were being enacted, and entered the houses, they beheld the piteous grief of the peasants. The wife of a market-gardener, who occupied a red brick cottage near the church, pursued with a wooden stool the two men who carried off her children in a wheelbarrow. When she saw them die, a horrible sickness came upon her, and they thrust her down on the stool, under a tree by the roadside.

Other soldiers swarmed up the lime trees in front of a farmstead with its blank walls tinted mauve, and entered the house by removing the tiles. When they came back on to the roof, the father and mother, with outstretched arms, tried to follow them through the opening, but the soldiers repeatedly pushed them back, and had at last to strike them on the head with their swords, before they could disengage themselves and regain the street.

One family shut up in the cellar of a large cottage lamented near the grating, through which the father wildly brandished a pitchfork. Outside on a heap of manure, a bald old man sobbed all alone; in the square, a woman in a yellow dress had swooned, and her weeping husband now supported her under the arms, against a pear tree; another woman in red fondled her little girl, bereft of her hands, and lifted now one tiny arm, now the other, to see if the child would not move. Yet another woman fled towards the country; but the soldiers pursued her among the hayricks, which stood out in black relief against the fields of snow.

Beneath the inn of the Four Sons of Aymon a surging tumult reigned. The inhabitants had formed a barricade, and the soldiers went round and round the house without being able to enter. Then they were attempting to climb up to the signboard by the creepers, when they noticed a ladder behind the garden door. This they raised against the wall, and went up it in file. But the innkeeper and all his family hurled tables, stools, plates, and cradles down upon them from the windows; the ladder was overturned, and the soldiers fell.

In a wooden hut at the end of the village, another band found a peasant woman washing her children in a tub near the fire. Being old and very deaf, she did not hear them enter. Two men took the tub and carried it away, and the stupefied woman followed with the clothes in which she was about to dress the children. But when she saw traces of blood everywhere in the village, swords in the orchards, cradles overturned in the street, women on their knees, others who wrung their hands over the dead, she began to scream and beat the soldiers, who put down the tub to defend themselves. The curé hastened up also, and with hands clasped over his chasuble, entreated the Spaniards before the naked little ones howling in the water. Some soldiers came up, tied the mad peasant to a tree, and carried off the children.

The butcher, who had hidden his little girl, leaned against his shop, and looked on callously. A lancer and one of the men in armor entered the house and found the child in a copper boiler. Then the butcher in despair took one of his knives and rushed after them into the street, but soldiers who were passing disarmed him and hanged him by the hands to the hooks in the wall—there, among the flayed animals, he kicked and struggled, blaspheming, until the evening.

Near the churchyard, there was a great gathering before a long, low house, painted green. The owner, standing on his threshold, shed bitter tears; as he was very fat and jovial looking, he excited the pity of some soldiers who were seated in the sun against the wall, patting a dog. The one, too, who dragged away his child by the hand, gesticulated as if to say: "What can I do? It's not my fault!"

A peasant, who was pursued, jumped into a boat, moored near the stone bridge, and with his wife and children moved away across the unfrozen part of the narrow lagoon. Not daring to follow, the soldiers strode furiously through the reeds. They climbed up into the willows on the banks to try to reach the fugitives with their lances—as they did not succeed, they continued for a long time to threaten the terrified family adrift upon the black water.

The orchard was still full of people, for it was there, in front of the white-bearded man who directed the massacre, that most of the children were killed. Little tots who could just walk alone stood side by side munching their slices of bread and jam, and stared curiously at the slaying of their helpless playmates, or collected round the village fool who played his flute on the grass.

Then suddenly there was a uniform movement in the village. The peasants ran towards the castle which stood on the brown rising ground, at the end of the street. They had seen their seigneur leaning on the battlements of his tower and watching the massacre. Men, women, old people, with hands outstretched, supplicated to him, in his velvet mantle and his gold cap, as to a king in heaven. But he raised his arms and shrugged his shoulders to show his helplessness, and when they implored him more and more persistently, kneeling in the snow, with bared heads, and uttering piteous cries, he turned slowly into the tower and the peasants' last hope was gone.

When all the children were slain, the tired soldiers wiped their swords on the grass, and supped under the pear trees. Then they mounted one behind the other, and rode out of Nazareth across the stone bridge by which they had come.

The setting of the sun behind the forest made the woods aflame, and dyed the village blood-red. Exhausted with running and entreating, the curé had thrown himself upon the snow, in front of the church, and his servant stood near him. They stared upon the street and the orchard, both thronged with the peasants in their best clothes. Before many thresholds, parents with dead children on their knees bewailed with ever fresh amaze their bitter grief. Others still lamented over the children where they had died, near a barrel, under a barrow, or at the edge of a pool. Others carried away the dead in silence. There were some who began to wash the benches, the stools, the tables, the blood-stained shifts, and to pick up the cradles which had been thrown into the street. Mother by mother moaned under the trees over the dead bodies which lay upon the grass, little mutilated bodies which they recognized by their woollen frocks. Those who were childless moved aimlessly through the square, stopping at times in front of the bereaved, who wailed and sobbed in their sorrow. The men, who no longer wept, sullenly pursued their strayed animals, around which the barking dogs coursed; or, in silence, repaired so far their broken windows and rifled roofs. As the moon solemnly rose through the quietudes of the sky, deep silence as of sleep descended upon the village, where now not the shadow of a living thing stirred.

Translated by Edith Wingate Rinder

William March

THE UNKNOWN SOLDIER

We were returning from a wiring party that quiet night and the men were in high spirits. Then two Maxims opened a deadly enfilading fire, and one of my companions threw his hands up and fell without a sound. I stood there confused at the sudden attack, not knowing which way to turn. Then I heard some one shout: "Look out! Look out for the wire!" and I saw my companions, flat on their frightened bellies, scattering in all directions. I started to run, but at that moment something shoved me, and something took my breath away, and I toppled backward, and the wire caught me.

At first I did not realize that I was wounded. I lay there on the wire, breathing heavily. "I must keep perfectly calm," I thought. "If I move about, I'll entangle myself so badly that I'll never get out." Then a white flare went up and in the light that followed I saw my belly was ripped open and that my entrails hung down like a badly arranged bouquet of blue roses. The sight frightened me and I began to struggle, but the more I twisted about, the deeper the barbs sank in. Finally I could not move my legs any more and I knew, then, that I was going to die. So I lay stretched quietly, moaning and spitting blood.

I could not forget the faces of the men and the way they had scurried off when the machine guns opened up. I remembered a time when I was a little boy and had gone to visit my grandfather, who lived on a farm. Rabbits were eating his cabbages that year, so grandfather had closed all the entrances to his field except one, and he baited that one with lettuce leaves and young carrots. When the field was full of rabbits, the fun began. Grandfather opened the gate and let in the dog, and the hired man stood at the gap, a broomstick in his hand, breaking the necks of the rabbits as they leaped out. I had stood to one side, I remembered, pitying the rabbits and thinking how stupid they were to let themselves be caught in such an obvious trap.—And now as I lay on the wire, the scene came back to me vividly. . . . *I had pitied the rabbits!*—I, of all people . . .

I lay back, my eyes closed, thinking of that. Then I heard the mayor of our town making his annual address in the Soldiers' Cemetery at home. Fragments of his speech kept floating through my mind: "These men died gloriously on the Field of Honor! . . . Gave their lives gladly in a Noble Cause! . . . What a feeling of exaltation was theirs when Death kissed their mouths and closed their eyes for an Immortal Eternity! . . ." Suddenly I saw myself, too, a boy in the crowd, my throat tight to keep back the tears, listening enraptured to the speech and believing every word of it; and at that instant I understood clearly why I now lay dying on the wire. . . .

The first shock had passed and my wounds began to pain me. I had seen other men die on the wire and I had said if it happened to me, I would make no sound, but after a while I couldn't stand the pain any longer and I began to make a shrill, wavering noise. I cried like that for a long time. I couldn't help it. . . .

Towards daybreak a German sentry crawled out from his post and came to where I lay. "Hush!" he said in a soft voice. "Hush, please!"

He sat on his haunches and stared at me, a compassionate look in his eyes. Then I began to talk to him: "It's all a lie that people tell each other, and nobody really believes," I said. . . . "And I'm a part of it, whether I want to be or not.—I'm more a part of it now than ever before: In a few years, when war is over, they'll move my body back home to the Soldiers' Cemetery, just as they moved the bodies of the soldiers killed before I was born. There will be a brass band and speech making and a beautiful marble shaft with my name chiseled on its base. . . . The mayor will be there also, pointing to my name with his thick, trembling forefinger and shouting meaningless words about glorious deaths and fields of honor. . . . And there will be other little boys in that crowd to listen and believe him, just as I listened and believed!"

"Hush," said the German softly. "Hush! . . . Hush!"

I began to twist about on the wire and to cry again.

"I can't stand the thought of that! I can't stand it! . . . I never want to hear military music or high sounding words again: I want to be buried where nobody will ever find me. —I want to be wiped out completely . . ."

Then, suddenly, I became silent, for I had seen a way out. I took off my identification tags and threw them into the wire, as far as I could. I tore to pieces the letters and the photographs I carried and scattered the fragments. I threw my helmet away, so that no one could guess my identity from the serial number stamped on the sweatband. Then I lay back exultant!

The German had risen and stood looking at me, as if puzzled. . . . "I've beaten the orators and the wreath layers at their own game!" I said. . . . "I've beaten them all!—Nobody will ever use me as a symbol. Nobody will ever tell lies over my dead body now! . . ."

"Hush," said the German softly. "Hush! . . . Hush!"

Then my pain became so unbearable that I began to choke and bite at the wire with my teeth. The German came closer to me, touching my head with his hand. . . .

"Hush," he said. . . . "Hush, please. . . ."

But I could not stop. I thrashed about on the wire and cried in a shrill voice. The German took out his pistol and stood twisting it in his hand, not looking at me. Then he put his arm under my head, lifting me up, and kissed me softly on my cheek, repeating phrases which I could not understand. I saw, then, that he, too, had been crying for a long time. . . .

"Do it quickly!" I said. "Quickly! . . . Quickly!"

He stood with trembling hands for a moment before he placed the barrel of his pistol against my temple, turned his head away, and fired. My eyes fluttered twice and then closed; my hands clutched and relaxed slowly.

"I have broken the chain," I whispered. "I have defeated the inherent stupidity of life."

"Hush," he said. "Hush! . . . Hush! . . . Hush! . . ."

Herman Melville

THE APPARITION

A Retrospect

Convulsions came; and, where the field
    Long slept in pastoral green,
A goblin-mountain was upheaved
(Sure the scared sense was all deceived),
    Marl-glen and slag-ravine.

The unreserve of Ill was there,
    The clinkers in her last retreat;
But, ere the eye could take it in,
Or mind could comprehension win,
    It sunk!—and at our feet.

So, then, Solidity's a crust—
    The core of fire below;
All may go well for many a year,
But who can think without a fear
    Of horrors that happen so?

SHILOH

A Requiem
(April, 1862)

Skimming lightly, wheeling still,
    The swallows fly low
Over the field in clouded days,
    The forest-field of Shiloh—

Over the field where April rain
Solaced the parched ones stretched in pain
Through the pause of night
That followed the Sunday fight
    Around the church of Shiloh—
The church so lone, the log-built one,
That echoed to many a parting groan
    And natural prayer
  Of dying foemen mingled there—
Foemen at morn, but friends at eve—
  Fame or country least their care:
(What like a bullet can undeceive!)
    But now they lie low,
While over them the swallows skim,
    And all is hushed at Shiloh.

omas Merton

CHANT TO BE USED IN PROCESSIONS
AROUND A SITE WITH FURNACES

w we made them sleep and purified them

w we perfectly cleaned up the people and worked
ig heater

vas the commander I made improvements and installed
guaranteed system taking account of human weakness
urified and I remained decent

ow I commanded

made cleaning appointments and then I made the travelers
ep and after that I made soap

was born into a Catholic family but as these people were
t going to need a priest I did not become a priest
installed a perfectly good machine it gave
tisfaction to many

hen trains arrived the soiled passengers received
pointments for fun in the bathroom
ey did not guess

was a very big bathroom for two thousand people
awaited arrival and they arrived safely

here would be an orchestra of merry widows not all
e time much art

they arrived at all they would be given a greeting card
send home taken care of with good jobs
ishing you would come to our joke

Another improvement I made was I built the chambers fo
two thousand invitations at a time the naked votaries v
disinfected with Zyklon B

Children of tender age were always invited by reason of
their youth they were unable to work
they were marked out for play

They were washed like the others and more than the oth

Very frequently women would hide their children in the p
of clothing but of course when we came to find them we wo
send the children into the chamber to be bathed

How I often commanded and made improvements and sea
the door on top there were flowers the men came with crys
I guaranteed always the crystal parlor

I guaranteed the chamber and it was sealed you could
see through portholes

They waited for the shower it was not hot water that cam
through vents though efficient winds gave full satisfaction
portholes showed this

The satisfied all ran together to the doors awaiting arrival
it was guaranteed they made ends meet

How I could tell by their cries that love came to a full st
I found the ones I had made clean after about a half hou

Jewish male inmates then worked up nice they had rubber
boots in return for adequate food I could not guess
their appetite

Those at the door were taken apart out of a fully stopped
love for rubber made inmates strategic hair and teeth be
used later for defense

Then the males removed all clean rings and made away wi
happy gold

big new firm promoted steel forks operating on a cylinder
ey got the contract and with faultless workmanship
livered very fast goods

ow I commanded and made soap 12 lbs fat 10 quarts water
oz to a lb of caustic soda but it was hard to find any fat

or transporting the customers we suggest using light carts
wheels a drawing is submitted"

Ve acknowledge four steady furnaces and an emergency
arantee"

am a big new commander operating on a cylinder
elevate the purified materials boil for 2 to 3 hours
d then cool"

or putting them into a test fragrance I suggested an express
evator operated by the latest cylinder it was guaranteed

heir love was fully stopped by our perfected ovens but
e love rings were salvaged

hanks to the satisfaction of male inmates operating the
aters without need of compensation our guests were warmed

ll the while I had obeyed perfectly

I was hanged in a commanding position with a full view
the site plant and grounds

ou smile at my career but you would do as I did if
ou knew yourself and dared

my day we worked hard we saw what we did our
lf-sacrifice was conscientious and complete our work
as faultless and detailed

o not think yourself better because you burn up
iends and enemies with long-range missiles without
ver seeing what you have done

Charles C. Moskos, Jr.

A SOCIOLOGIST APPRAISES THE G.I.

SAIGON.

The absence of a national consensus on the war in Viet nam is obvious. Yet, in the midst of the domestic agony over the war, it is seldom asked how the American soldier who is actually fighting reacts. To try to answer such a question is a presumptuous undertaking. But some general impressions of the attitudes of men in combat, based on personal observation, can be offered. In the summers of 1965 and 1967 I was permitted to live with infantry units in Vietnam. During these periods, I became intimately acquainted with the enlisted men of two rifle squads as they engaged in combat operations. From these experiences it is possible to draw a sort of sociological profile of today's American fighting man.

In any large-scale military organization, even in the actual theater of war, only a fraction of the men under arms personally experience combat. The war in Vietnam is no exception. But figures on the proportion of men actually in combat are extremely difficult to obtain. The lack of combat statistics by unit designation, conflicting definitions of what constitutes combat, and changing numbers of men all preclude a final answer. However, press reports in mid-1967 have placed the proportion of American soldiers in the first echelon—that is directly engaging with the enemy—at 14 per cent. To this one can add about the same proportion of the total force who are in second-echelon or close combat support units.

In other words, approximately 70 per cent of the men in Vietnam cannot be considered combat soldiers except by the loosest of definitions. The notion that the conflict in Vietnam is a "no-front war" is, of course, one that is fostered by many rear-area personnel. There is also a certain amount of bureaucratic support for defining the war in such terms,

mbat pay is given to all military personnel in Vietnam
gardless of duties, and the one-year rotation cycle applies
ually to the supply clerk in Saigon as well as the rifleman
o has spent all his time in the field.

The distinction between combat and rear-echelon personnel
one that is too often overlooked in discussions of reforming
r abolishing) the draft and making entry into the armed
rces more equitable. The fact is that no matter how fair
e method of one's induction, once a man is in the service,
s assignment is very likely to reflect his civilian background.
rveys have shown that among active-duty personnel there
a strong likelihood for persons from lower socio-education-
levels and minority groups to end up in combat units.
ese findings are dramatically reflected in the social com-
sition of the two rifle squads I observed. The 24 mem-
rs of these squads had the following civilian backgrounds:
ve were high-school dropouts who had never been em-
oyed; six entered the service after high-school graduation;
ven had held blue-collar jobs; four had white-collar em-
oyment; two were college dropouts. None was a college
aduate.

As for other social background characteristics: Five were
egroes; one was an American Indian; another was from
uam; the other 17 were whites, including two Mexican-
mericans and one Puerto Rican. Only three of the squad
embers were married. Except for the sergeants, who were
their mid-20's, the men ranged in age from 18 to 21.
gain excepting the sergeants, all were on their initial en-
tments. Sixteen were Regular Army men and eight were
aftees. Significantly, except for sardonic comments directed
ward the regulars by the draftees, their behavior and their
titudes toward the war were very similar regardless of how
ey had entered the service.

To understand the way in which the soldier's attitudes are
aped, one must try to comprehend the physical conditions
der which he must manage. In combat, life is short, nasty
d brutish. The issues of national policy which brought him
to war are irrelevant to the combat soldier; he is con-
rned with his literal life chances. Conveying the immediacy
 the combat situation is hard enough for a novelist, much
ss a sociologist. There is not only the imminent danger

of the loss of one's own life or, more frightening for mc
limbs, but also the sight of one's comrades' wounds a
deaths. Moreover, there are the routine physical stresses
combat existence—e.g., the weight of the pack, tasteless foc
diarrhea, thirst, leeches, mosquitoes, rain, heat, mud and lo
of sleep.

In an actual firefight, the scene is generally one of cha
Acts of bravery and cowardice intermingle with momen
of terror and exhilaration and even comedy. Prisoners m
be subjected to atrocities in the rage of battle or its imme
ate aftermath. The soldier's distaste for endangering civilia
is overcome by his fear that Vietnamese of any age or sex c
be responsible for his own death.

Once the combat is over, there is still little idea in a str
tegic sense of what has been accomplished. The soldie
view of the war is limited to his own personal observatio
and his subsequent talks with others in the same platoo
or company. The often-noted reluctance of combat soldie
to discuss their experiences when back home is not the ca
in the field. Battles and skirmishes with the enemy are fr
quently recounted, not so much for their intrinsic interest
to specify tactical procedures which may save lives in futu
encounters.

Much has been made in war literature of the semimystic
bonds of comradeship which tie men together in combat. Y
it must also be kept in mind that there are self-serving mo
vations at work. Under the harsh circumstances of groun
warfare, the individual soldier must necessarily develop an
take part in small-group relationships. His own physical su
vival is directly dependent on the support—moral, physic
and technical—of fellow squad members. In turn, such su
port will be forthcoming largely to the degree with whic
he reciprocates. Ultimately, the soldier's overriding concer
is to stay alive. This is not to deny in any way the existenc
of strong interpersonal ties within combat squads, but onl
to understand them as outgrowths of the very private wa
each individual is fighting for his own survival.

In considering the nature of the bonds of social solidarit
formed within a combat squad it is instructive to note th
letters written and received. Letters from squad membe
who have returned to the United States to those remainin
behind are rare. In most cases, nothing more is heard from

soldier once he leaves the unit. Perhaps even more revealing, seldom is any attempt made to initiate mail contact with a departed person by those squad members still in the combat area. The rupture of communication is mutual despite protestations of lifelong friendship during the shared combat period.

Under current policy, enlisted men serve a 12-month tour of duty in Vietnam. Thus, barring his being severely wounded or killed, every soldier knows his exact departure date; he is aware of how much time—down to the day—he has remaining. (In the First and Second World Wars, men served for the duration; in the Korean war, a rotation policy was introduced, but men assigned to rear echelons served longer tours than those in combat units.)

During his year in Vietnam, the combat soldier undergoes definite changes in attitude toward his condition. Such attitudes vary, of course, depending on individual personality and combat exposure, but a more or less general picture of the soldier's changing responses to the combat situation would be as follows: Upon arrival at his unit and for several weeks following, the soldier is excited to be in the war zone and looks forward to engaging the enemy. After the first serious encounter, however, he loses his enthusiasm for combat. He becomes highly respectful of the enemy's fighting abilities, and also begins to develop anti-South Vietnamese sentiments. He is dubious of victory statements issued from headquarters and official reports of enemy casualties. During this period, the soldier performs well but avoids taking risks if at all possible.

By the eighth or ninth month, his *esprit* picks up and he begins to regard himself as an "old soldier." It is at this point that he is generally most combat-effective. As he approaches the end of his tour, however, his efficiency begins to decline. He becomes reluctant to engage in offensive combat operations. Stories are repeated of the men killed the day before they were to rotate back to the United States. "Short-timer's fever" is tacitly recognized by his comrades and demands on the soon-to-depart soldier are commensurately reduced. The final disengagement period of the combat soldier is considered a kind of earned prerogative which others in the rotation cycle hope eventually to enjoy.

The over-all impact of the rotation system on the combat soldier's attitude toward the war is to reinforce a perspective which is essentially private and self-concerned. The end of the war is seen as the individual's rotation date and not in terms of the war's eventual outcome—whether victory, defeat or stalemate. One frequently hears: *"My* war is over when I go home." When the soldier feels concern over the fate of others, it is for those he personally knows in his own outfit. His concern does not extend to those unknown persons who will eventually replace him. Rather, his attitude is, typically: "I've done my time; let them do theirs."

Although the American soldier has generally given a good account of himself in combat, he is extremely unlikely to voice patriotic rhetoric or overt political sentiments. Indeed, anti-ideology is itself an integral part of the soldier's belief system. Patriotic slogans and exhortations are dismissed or met by "What a crock," "Be serious, man," or "Who's kidding who?" He sees no relationship between his presence in Vietnam and the national policies which brought him there. As one soldier put it, "Maybe we're supposed to be here and maybe not. But you don't have time to think about things like that. You worry about getting zapped and dry socks tomorrow. The other stuff is a joke."

When the soldier is pressed as to why he is in Vietnam, his answers are couched in a quite individualistic frame of reference. For example: "I'm here because my unit was sent here," "I was fool enough to join this man's Army," "My own stupidity for listening to the recruiting sergeant," or "I happened to be at the wrong place at the wrong time." When asked specifically what the United States is doing in Vietnam, the soldier will usually say that it is there "to stop Communism." And "to stop Communism" is the only ideological slogan that the combat soldier can be brought to utter.

When further queried as to what is so bad about Communism that it must be stopped at the risk of his own life, the combat soldier is often perplexed. After thinking about it, he will generally express his distaste for Communism by stressing its authoritarian aspects. Typical descriptions of Communism are "That's when you can't do what you want to do," and "Somebody's always telling you what to do." As one man wryly put it: "Communism is something like the Army."

While the most frequently mentioned negative aspects of Communism concern the individual's relationship to higher authority, there are also occasional remarks expressing worry over Communism's antireligious aspects. Interestingly, the question of public versus private property ownership is rarely mentioned even after extensive discussion.

That the American combat soldier is not overtly ideological should not obscure the existence of salient values which need not be formally articulated. That is, despite the combat soldier's pronounced embarrassment in the face of patriotic rhetoric, he displays a kind of elemental nationalism in the belief that the United States is the best country in the world. Even though he hates being in the war, the combat soldier believes he is fighting for his American homeland. On those occasions when the soldier does articulate the purposes of the war, the view is expressed that if Communist aggression is not stopped in Southeast Asia, it will be only a matter of time before the United States itself is in jeopardy. The suasion of the so-called "domino theory" is powerful among combat soldiers as well as in the general public back home. But the soldier definitely does not see himself fighting for South Vietnam *per se*. Quite the contrary: He regards it as a country not worth the risk of anyone's life.

Indeed, the soldier's high evaluation of his American homeland has its reverse side in a widespread dislike of the Vietnamese. There are constant derogatory comments on the avarice of those who pander to G.I.'s, and the treachery of the Vietnamese people. Anti-Vietnamese sentiment is most glaringly apparent in the hostility toward the Army of the Republic of Vietnam or ARVN (pronounced "Arvin"), who are supposed military allies. Disparaging remarks about the hopelessness of the South Vietnamese forces are endemic.

In marked contrast is the respect given by American soldiers to enemy forces, whether Vietcong or North Vietnamese regulars. In particular, the Vietcong's ability to improvise tactically and make do with rudimentary weaponry is ruefully admired. There are frequent statements along the lines of: "If Arvin only had a couple of guys like the V.C., we could go home today." Yet, the American soldier is somewhat puzzled as to the reasons behind his opponents' excellent fighting abilities and valor in combat. One occasionally hears serious explanations attributing the bravery of the enemy to their using marijuana or narcotics.

A variety of factors underlie the soldier's fundamental pro-Americanism. Not the least of these is his immediate reliance on fellow Americans for mutual support in a country where virtually all indigenous people are seen as actual or potential threats to his physical safety.

On another level, however, a major element in the soldier's belief in the superiority of the American way of life is the creature comforts that life can offer. When the soldier talks about what he considers to be the good life in the United States, it is most frequently in terms of high-paying jobs, automobiles, self-owned homes, consumer goods and leisure activities. In other words, it is the materialistic—and the word is not used here pejoratively—aspects of life in America that are most salient to the soldier.

The soldier's belief in the merits of the American way of life are further reinforced by the contrast with the Vietnamese standard of living. He is hard-pressed not to make invidious comparisons between the life he knew and expects to live in the United States (even if he is of lower-class background) and that which he sees in Vietnamese society. Moreover, the combat soldier's somewhat romanticized view of life back home is buttressed by his own personal lower standard of living. As has often been noted, front-line soldiers bitterly contrast their plight with the physical comforts enjoyed by their fellow countrymen, both rear-echelon soldiers and civilians back home. While this is true on one level, the attitudes of American combat soldiers toward their civilian compatriots are somewhat more ambivalent. For at the same time the soldier is begrudging the civilian his physical comforts, it is these very comforts for which he is largely fighting. Similarly, the attitude toward certain rear-echelon personnel who engage in *sub rosa* profiteering is more one of envy than of disapproval.

Although it is more characteristic of rear-echelon personnel, even among combat soldiers one cannot help but be impressed by the plethora of individually owned gadgets. Transistor radios are practically *de rigueur*. Cameras are common, and tape recorders are increasingly used for letters to and from home. It seems more than coincidental that American soldiers refer to the United States as "The Land of the Big PX."

Another factor in maintaining combat motivation is the notion of masculinity and physical toughness which pervades much of the soldier's outlook toward warfare. Being a combat soldier is seen as a man's job. Front-line soldiers often make invidious comparisons with the virility of rear-echelon personnel. Likewise, paratroopers express disdain for "legs," or non-airborne soldiers.

In many ways the combat soldier's vision of manly endeavors is a carryover from the teenage subculture. It should be stressed, however, that an exaggerated masculine ethic is less evident among soldiers after their units have been bloodied. As the realities of combat are faced, more prosaic definitions of manly honor emerge. In other words, notions of masculinity serve to create initial motivation to enter combat, but recede once the life-and-death facts of warfare are experienced.

Moreover, once the unit is tempered by combat, definitions of manly honor are not seen to encompass individual heroics. Quite the contrary: The very word "hero" is used negatively to describe any soldier who recklessly jeopardizes the unit's welfare. Men try to avoid going out on patrols with individuals who are overly anxious to make contact with the enemy. Much like the slacker at the other end of the spectrum, the "hero" is seen as one who endangers the safety of others. As is the case with virtually all combat activities, the ultimate evaluative criterion rests on keeping alive.

Any discussion of combat soldiers in Vietnam must make reference to developments on the racial scene back home. Militant black leaders vehemently oppose the war and even Negro participation in the armed forces. Moreover, Negro over-representation in combat units has led to correspondingly high casualty rates. Yet the fact remains that the Negro re-enlistment rate is twice that of whites, and that Negro combat performance in Vietnam has been exceptional.

A tragic commentary on our country is that many Negro men by seeking to enter and stay in the armed forces are saying that even the risk of being killed is worthwhile in order to get away from a dead-end existence, and to become part of the only institution in this society which seems really to be integrated. Most likely, and somewhat paradoxically, we will witness more vocal antimilitary sentiment by black militant groups at the same time that the military is becoming an avenue of career opportunity for many Negro men.

In any event, from the combat soldier's viewpoint—white or black—the antiwar effort at home is not usually seen as part of the Negro revolution. Rather, he is more likely to see it as a movement of college draft-dodgers. Although the combat soldier fervently wishes to be out of the war, he nevertheless is strongly hostile toward peace demonstrations. In fact, the antiwar movement has probably had a boomerang effect on soldiers by engendering more support for hawklike attitudes than would otherwise exist. The typical reaction toward peace demonstrators is "Draft the son of a bitch so he can find what it's all about" rather than any disposition to weigh the merits of the antiwar arguments.

At the same time, the combat soldier has scarcely more affection for "support-the-boys" campaigns. Again, the they-don't-know-what-it's-all-about attitude applies. As one soldier succinctly put it—and his words spoke for many: "The only support I want is out."

Edwin Muir

THE INTERROGATION

We could have crossed the road but hesitated.
And then came the patrol;
The leader conscientious and intent,
The men surly, indifferent.
While we stood by and waited
The interrogation began. He says the whole
Must come out now, who, what we are,
Where we have come from, with what purpose, whose
Country or camp we plot for or betray.
Question on question.
We have stood and answered through the standing day
And watched across the road beyond the hedge
The careless lovers in pairs go by.
Hand linked in hand, wandering another star,
So near we could shout to them. We cannot choose
Answer or action here,
Though still the careless lovers saunter by
And the thoughtless field is near.
We are on the very edge,
Endurance almost done,
And still the interrogation is going on.

THE COMBAT

It was not meant for human eyes,
That combat on the shabby patch
Of clods and trampled turf that lies
Somewhere beneath the sodden skies
For eye of toad or adder to catch.

And having seen it I accuse
The crested animal in his pride,
Arrayed in all the royal hues
Which hide the claws he well can use
To tear the heart out of the side.

Body of leopard, eagle's head
And whetted beak, and lion's mane,
And frost-grey hedge of feathers spread
Behind—he seemed of all things bred.
I shall not see his like again.

As for his enemy, there came in
A soft round beast as brown as clay;
All rent and patched his wretched skin;
A battered bag he might have been,
Some old used thing to throw away.

Yet he awaited face to face
The furious beast and the swift attack.
Soon over and done. That was no place
Or time for chivalry or for grace.
The fury had him on his back.

And two small paws like hands flew out
To right and left as the trees stood by.
One would have said beyond a doubt
This was the very end of the bout,
But that the creature would not die.

For ere the death-stroke he was gone,
Writhed, whirled, huddled into his den,
Safe somehow there. The fight was done,
And he had lost who had all but won.
But oh his deadly fury then.

A while the place lay blank, forlorn,
Drowsing as in relief from pain.
The cricket chirped, the grating thorn
Stirred, and a little sound was born.
The champions took their posts again.

And all began. The stealthy paw
Slashed out and in. Could nothing save
These rags and tatters from the claw?
Nothing. And yet I never saw
A beast so helpless and so brave.

And now, while the trees stand watching, still
The unequal battle rages there.
The killing beast that cannot kill
Swells and swells in his fury till
You'd almost think it was despair.

THE HORSES

Barely a twelvemonth after
The seven days war that put the world to sleep,
Late in the evening the strange horses came.
By then we had made our covenant with silence,
But in the first few days it was so still
We listened to our breathing and were afraid.
On the second day
The radios failed; we turned the knobs; no answer.
On the third day a warship passed us, heading north,
Dead bodies piled on the deck. On the sixth day
A plane plunged over us into the sea. Thereafter
Nothing. The radios dumb;
And still they stand in corners of our kitchens,
And stand, perhaps, turned on, in a million rooms
All over the world. But now if they should speak,
If on a sudden they should speak again,
If on the stroke of noon a voice should speak,
We would not listen, we would not let it bring
That old bad world that swallowed its children quick
At one great gulp. We would not have it again.
Sometimes we think of the nations lying asleep,
Curled blindly in impenetrable sorrow,
And then the thought confounds us with its strangeness.
The tractors lie about our fields; at evening
They look like dank sea-monsters couched and waiting.
We leave them where they are and let them rust:

'They'll moulder away and be like other loam.'
We make our oxen drag our rusty ploughs,
Long laid aside. We have gone back
Far past our fathers' land.

                      And then, that evening
Late in the summer the strange horses came.
We heard a distant tapping on the road,
A deepening drumming; it stopped, went on again
And at the corner changed to hollow thunder.
We saw the heads
Like a wild wave charging and were afraid.
We had sold our horses in our fathers' time
To buy new tractors. Now they were strange to us
As fabulous steeds set on an ancient shield
Or illustrations in a book of knights.
We did not dare go near them. Yet they waited,
Stubborn and shy, as if they had been sent
By an old command to find our whereabouts
And that long-lost archaic companionship.
In the first moment we had never a thought
That they were creatures to be owned and used.
Among them were some half-a-dozen colts
Dropped in some wilderness of the broken world,
Yet new as if they had come from their own Eden.
Since then they have pulled our ploughs and borne our loads
But that free servitude still can pierce our hearts.
Our life is changed; their coming our beginning.

rank O'Connor

GUESTS OF THE NATION

I

At dusk the big Englishman Belcher would shift his long
gs out of the ashes and ask, 'Well, chums, what about it?'
d Noble or me would say, 'As you please, chum' (for we
ad picked up some of their curious expressions), and the
tle Englishman 'Awkins would light the lamp and produce
e cards. Sometimes Jeremiah Donovan would come up of
evening and supervise the play, and grow excited over
Awkins's cards (which he always played badly), and shout
him as if he was one of our own, 'Ach, you divil you, why
dn't you play the tray?' But, ordinarily, Jeremiah was a
ber and contented poor devil like the big Englishman Bel-
er, and was looked up to at all only because he was a fair
and at documents, though slow enough at these, I vow.
e wore a small cloth hat and big gaiters over his long pants,
d seldom did I perceive his hands outside the pockets of
at pants. He reddened when you talked to him, tilting from
e to heel and back and looking down all the while at his
g farmer's feet. His uncommon broad accent was a great
urce of jest to me, I being from the town as you may recog-
se.

I couldn't at the time see the point of me and Noble being
ith Belcher and 'Awkins at all, for it was and is my fixed
lief you could have planted that pair in any untended spot
om this to Claregalway and they'd have stayed put and
ourished like a native weed. I never seen in my short ex-
erience two men that took to the country as they did.

They were handed on to us by the Second Battalion to keep
hen the search for them became too hot, and Noble and
yself, being young, took charge with a natural feeling of re-
onsibility. But little 'Awkins made us look right fools when

he displayed he knew the countryside as well as we did an something more. 'You're the bloke they calls Bonaparte?' I said to me. 'Well, Bonaparte, Mary Brigid Ho'Connell w arskin abaout you and said 'ow you'd a pair of socks belong ing to 'er young brother.' For it seemed, as they explained that the Second used to have little evenings of their own, an some of the girls of the neighbourhood would turn in, an seeing they were such decent fellows, our lads couldn't wo ignore the two Englishmen, but invited them in and were ha fellow-well-met with them. 'Awkins told me he learned dance 'The Walls of Limerick' and 'The Siege of Ennis' an 'The Waves of Tory' in a night or two, though naturally I could not return the compliment, because our lads at th time did not dance foreign dances on principle.

So whatever privileges and favours Belcher and 'Awkin had with the Second they duly took with us, and after th first evening we gave up all pretence of keeping a close ey on their behaviour. Not that they could have got far, for the had a notable accent and wore khaki tunics and overcoa with civilian pants and boots. But it's my belief they neve had an idea of escaping and were quite contented with the lot.

Now, it was a treat to see how Belcher got off with the ol woman of the house we were staying in. She was a great war rant to scold, and crotchety even with us, but before ever sh had a chance of giving our guests, as I call them, a lick o her tongue, Belcher had made her his friend for life. She wa breaking sticks at the time, and Belcher, who hadn't bee in the house for more than ten minutes, jumped up out o his seat and went across to her.

'Allow me, madam,' he says, smiling his queer little smile 'please allow me,' and takes the hatchet from her hand. Sh was struck too parlatic to speak, and ever after Belche would be at her heels carrying a bucket, or basket, or load o turf, as the case might be. As Noble wittily remarked, he go into looking before she lept, and hot water or any little thin she wanted Belcher would have it ready for her. For such a huge man (and though I am five foot ten myself I had to look up to him) he had an uncommon shortness—or should I say lack—of speech. It took us some time to get used to him walking in and out like a ghost, without a syllable out o him. Especially because 'Awkins talked enough for a platoon

was strange to hear big Belcher with his toes in the ashes
me out with a solitary 'Excuse me, chum,' or 'That's right,
um.' His one and only abiding passion was cards, and I
ll say for him he was a good card-player. He could have
eced me and Noble many a time; only if we lost to him,
wkins lost to us, and 'Awkins played with the money
lcher gave him.

'Awkins lost to us because he talked too much, and I think
w we lost to Belcher for the same reason. 'Awkins and
ble would spit at one another about religion into the early
urs of the morning; the little Englishman as you could see
orrying the soul out of young Noble (whose brother was a
est) with a string of questions that would puzzle a cardi-
l. And to make it worse, even in treating of these holy sub-
ts, 'Awkins had a deplorable tongue; I never in all my
reer struck across a man who could mix such a variety of
rsing and bad language into the simplest topic. Oh, a
rible man was little 'Awkins, and a fright to argue! He nev-
did a stroke of work, and when he had no one else to talk
he fixed his claws into the old woman.

I am glad to say that in her he met his match, for one day
en he tried to get her to complain profanely of the drought
e gave him a great comedown by blaming the drought upon
piter Pluvius (a deity neither 'Awkins nor I had ever
ard of, though Noble said among the pagans he was held
have something to do with rain). And another day the
me 'Awkins was swearing at the capitalists for starting the
erman war, when the old dame laid down her iron, puck-
ed up her little crab's mouth and said, 'Mr. 'Awkins, you
n say what you please about the war, thinking to deceive
e because I'm an ignorant old woman, but I know well
hat started the war. It was that Italian count that stole the
athen divinity out of the temple in Japan, for believe me,
r. 'Awkins, nothing but sorrow and want follows them
at disturbs the hidden powers!' Oh, a queer old dame, as
ou remark!

II

So one evening we had our tea together, and 'Awkins lit
e lamp and we all sat in to cards. Jeremiah Donovan came

in too, and sat down and watched us for a while. Though ┃
was a shy man and didn't speak much, it was easy to see ┃
had no great love for the two Englishmen, and I was su
prised it hadn't struck me so clearly before. Well, like that
the story, a terrible dispute blew up late in the evening b
tween 'Awkins and Noble, about capitalists and priests a▸
love for your own country.

'The capitalists,' says 'Awkins, with an angry gulp, 't▸
capitalists pays the priests to tell you all abaout the ne
world, so's you waon't notice what they do in this!'

'Nonsense, man,' says Noble, losing his temper, 'befo
ever a capitalist was thought of people believed in the ne
world.'

'Awkins stood up as if he was preaching a sermon. 'O
they did, did they?' he says with a sneer. 'They believed a
the things you believe, that's what you mean? And you b
lieve that God created Hadam and Hadam created Shem ar
Shem created Jehoshophat? You believe all the silly ho
fairy-tale abaout Heve and Heden and the happle? Well, liste
to me, chum. If you're entitled to 'old to a silly belief lil▸
that, I'm entitled to 'old to my own silly belief—which i▸
that the fust thing your God created was a bleedin' cap
talist with mirality and Rolls Royce complete. Am I righ▸
chum?' he says then to Belcher.

'You're right, chum,' says Belcher, with his queer smil◂
and gets up from the table to stretch his long legs into the fi▸
and stroke his moustache. So, seeing that Jeremiah Donova▸
was going, and there was no knowing when the conversatio
about religion would be over, I took my hat and went ou
with him. We strolled down towards the village together, an
then he suddenly stopped, and blushing and mumbling, an
shifting, as his way was, from toe to heel, he said I ought t▸
be behind keeping guard on the prisoners. And I, having i▸
put to me so suddenly, asked him what the hell he wanted
guard on the prisoners at all for, and said that so far a▸
Noble and me were concerned we had talked it over an◂
would rather be out with a column. 'What use is that pair t◂
us?' I asked him.

He looked at me for a spell and said, 'I thought you knev
we were keeping them as hostages.' 'Hostages——?' says ┃
not quite understanding. 'The enemy,' he says in his heav▸
way, 'have prisoners belong to us, and now they talk o

oting them. If they shoot our prisoners we'll shoot theirs,
d serve them right.' 'Shoot them?' said I, the possibility
t beginning to dawn on me. 'Shoot them, exactly,' said he.
ow,' said I, 'wasn't it very unforeseen of you not to tell me
d Noble that?' 'How so?' he asks. 'Seeing that we were act-
g as guards upon them, of course.' 'And hadn't you reason
ough to guess that much?' 'We had not, Jeremiah Dono-
n, we had not. How were we to know when the men were
our hands so long?' 'And what difference does it make?
e enemy have our prisoners as long or longer, haven't
ey?' 'It makes a great difference,' said I. 'How so?' said he
arply; but I couldn't tell him the difference it made, for I
as struck too silly to speak. 'And when may we expect to be
leased from this anyway?' said I. 'You may expect it to-
ght,' says he. 'Or to-morrow or the next day at latest. So if
s hanging around here that worries you, you'll be free soon
ough.'

I cannot explain it even now, how sad I felt, but I went
ck to the cottage, a miserable man. When I arrived the dis-
ussion was still on, 'Awkins holding forth to all and sundry
at there was no next world at all and Noble answering in
s best canonical style that there was. But I saw 'Awkins was
ter having the best of it. 'Do you know what, chum?' he
as saying, with his saucy smile, 'I think you're jest as big a
eedin' hunbeliever as I am. You say you believe in the next
orld and you know jest as much abaout the next world as I
, which is sweet damn-all. What's 'Eaven? You dunno.
here's 'Eaven? You dunno. Who's in 'Eaven? You dunno.
ou know sweet damn-all! I arsk you again, do they wear
ings?'

'Very well then,' says Noble, 'they do; is that enough for
ou? They do wear wings.' 'Where do they get them? Who
akes them? 'Ave they a fact'ry for wings? 'Ave they a sort
f store where you 'ands in your chit and tikes your bleedin'
ings? Answer me that.'

'Oh, you're an impossible man to argue with,' says Noble.
Now listen to me——'. And off the pair of them went again.
It was long after midnight when we locked up the English-
en and went to bed ourselves. As I blew out the candle I
ld Noble what Jeremiah Donovan had told me. Noble took
very quietly. After we had been in bed about an hour he

asked me did I think we ought to tell the Englishmen. I ha[d]
ing thought of the same thing myself (among many other[s])
said no, because it was more than likely the English would[n't]
shoot our men, and anyhow it wasn't to be supposed the B[ri]
gade who were always up and down with the second battali[on]
and knew the Englishmen well would be likely to want the[m]
bumped off. 'I think so,' says Noble. 'It would be sort [of]
cruelty to put the wind up them now.' 'It was very unforese[en]
of Jeremiah Donovan anyhow,' says I, and by Noble's silen[ce]
I realised he took my meaning.

So I lay there half the night, and thought and thought, an[d]
picturing myself and young Noble trying to prevent the B[ri]
gade from shooting 'Awkins and Belcher sent a cold swe[at]
out through me. Because there were men on the Brigade yo[u]
daren't let nor hinder without a gun in your hand, and at an[y]
rate, in those days disunion between brothers seemed to m[e]
an awful crime. I knew better after.

It was next morning we found it so hard to face Belch[er]
and 'Awkins with a smile. We went about the house all da[y]
scarcely saying a word. Belcher didn't mind us much; h[e]
was stretched into the ashes as usual with his usual look [of]
waiting in quietness for something unforeseen to happen, b[ut]
little 'Awkins gave us a bad time with his audacious gibin[g]
and questioning. He was disgusted at Noble's not answerin[g]
him back. 'Why can't you tike your beating like a ma[n]
chum?' he says. 'You with your Hadam and Heve! I'm [a]
Communist—or an Anarchist. An Anarchist, that's what [I]
am.' And for hours after he went round the house, mumblin[g]
when the fit took him 'Hadam and Heve! Hadam and Heve[!]

III

I don't know clearly how we got over that day, but g[ot]
over it we did, and a great relief it was when the tea-thing[s]
were cleared away and Belcher said in his peaceable manne[r]
'Well, chums, what about it?' So we all sat round the tab[le]
and 'Awkins produced the cards, and at that moment I hear[d]
Jeremiah Donovan's footsteps up the path, and a dark pre[-]
sentiment crossed my mind. I rose quietly from the table an[d]
laid my hand on him before he reached the door. 'What d[o]

you want?' I asked him. 'I want those two soldier friends of yours,' he says reddening. 'Is that the way it is, Jeremiah Donovan?' I ask. 'That's the way. There were four of our lads went west this morning, one of them a boy of sixteen.' 'That's bad, Jeremiah,' says I.

At that moment Noble came out, and we walked down the path together talking in whispers. Feeney, the local intelligence officer, was standing by the gate. 'What are you going to do about it?' I asked Jeremiah Donovan. 'I want you and Noble to bring them out: you can tell them they're being shifted again; that'll be the quietest way.' 'Leave me out of that,' says Noble suddenly. Jeremiah Donovan looked at him hard for a minute or two. 'All right so,' he said peaceably. 'You and Feeney collect a few tools from the shed and dig a hole by the far end of the bog. Bonaparte and I'll be after you in about twenty minutes. But whatever else you do, don't let anyone see you with the tools. No one must know but the four of ourselves.'

We saw Feeney and Noble go round to the houseen where the tools were kept, and sidled in. Everything if I can so express myself was tottering before my eyes, and I left Jeremiah Donovan to do the explaining as best he could, while I took a seat and said nothing. He told them they were to go back to the Second. 'Awkins let a mouthful of curses out of him at that, and it was plain that Belcher, though he said nothing, was duly perturbed. The old woman was for having them stay in spite of us, and she did not shut her mouth until Jeremiah Donovan lost his temper and said some nasty things to her. Within the house by this time it was pitch dark, but no one thought of lighting the lamp, and in the darkness the two Englishmen fetched their khaki topcoats and said goodbye to the woman of the house. 'Just as a man mikes a 'ome of a bleedin' place,' mumbles 'Awkins shaking her by the hand, 'some bastard at headquarters thinks you're too cushy and shunts you off.' Belcher shakes her hand very hearty. 'A thousand thanks, madam,' he says, 'a thousand thanks for everything . . .' as though he'd made it all up.

We go round to the back of the house and down towards the fatal bog. Then Jeremiah Donovan comes out with what is in his mind. 'There were four of our lads shot by your fellows this morning so now you're to be bumped off.' 'Cut that stuff out,' says 'Awkins flaring up. 'It's bad enough to be mucked about such as we are without you plying at soldiers.' 'It's true,' says Jeremiah Donovan, 'I'm sorry, 'Awkins, but 'tis true,' and comes out with the usual rigmarole about doing our duty and obeying our superiors. 'Cut it out,' says 'Awkins irritably. 'Cut it out!'

Then, when Donovan sees he is not being believed he turns to me. 'Ask Bonaparte here,' he says. 'I don't need to arsk Bonaparte. Me and Bonaparte are chums.' 'Isn't it true, Bonaparte?' says Jeremiah Donovan solemnly to me. 'It is,' I say sadly, 'it is.' 'Awkins stops. 'Now, for Christ's sike. . . .' 'I mean it, chum,' I say. 'You daon't saound as if you mean it. You knaow well you don't mean it.' 'Well, if he don't I do,' says Jeremiah Donovan. 'Why the 'ell sh'd you want to shoot me, Jeremiah Donovan?' 'Why the hell should your people take out four prisoners and shoot them in cold blood upon a barrack square?' I perceive Jeremiah Donovan is trying to encourage himself with hot words.

Anyway, he took little 'Awkins by the arm and dragged him on, but it was impossible to make him understand that we were in earnest. From which you will perceive how difficult it was for me, as I kept feeling my Smith and Wesson and thinking what I would do if they happened to put up a fight or ran for it, and wishing in my heart they would. I knew if only they ran I would never fire on them. 'Was Noble in this?' 'Awkins wanted to know, and we said yes. He laughed. But why should Noble want to shoot him? Why should we want to shoot him? What had he done to us? Weren't we chums (the word lingers painfully in my memory)? Weren't we? Didn't we understand him and didn't he understand us? Did either of us imagine for an instant that he'd shoot us for all the so-and-so brigadiers in the so-and-so British Army? By this time I began to perceive in the dusk the desolate edges of the bog that was to be their last earthly bed, and, so great a sadness overtook my mind, I could not answer him. We walked along the edge of it in the darkness, and every now and then 'Awkins would call a halt and begin again, just as if he was wound up, about us being chums, and I was in despair that nothing but the cold and open grave made ready for his presence would convince him that we meant it all. But all the same, if you can understand, I didn't want him to be bumped off.

IV

At last we saw the unsteady glint of a lantern in the distance and made towards it. Noble was carrying it, and Feeney stood somewhere in the darkness behind, and somehow the picture of the two of them so silent in the boglands was like the pain of death in my heart. Belcher, on recognising Noble, said ' 'Allo, chum' in his usual peaceable way, but 'Awkins flew at the poor boy immediately, and the dispute began all over again, only that Noble hadn't a word to say for himself, and stood there with the swaying lantern between his gaitered legs.

It was Jeremiah Donovan who did the answering. 'Awkins asked for the twentieth time (for it seemed to haunt his mind) if anybody thought he'd shoot Noble. 'You would,' says Jeremiah Donovan shortly. 'I wouldn't, damn you!' 'You would if you knew you'd be shot for not doing it.' 'I wouldn't, not if I was to be shot twenty times over; he's my chum. And Belcher wouldn't—isn't that right, Belcher?' 'That's right, chum,' says Belcher peaceably. 'Damned if I would. Anyway, who says Noble'd be shot if I wasn't bumped off? What d'you think I'd do if I was in Noble's place and we were out in the middle of a blasted bog?' 'What would you do?' 'I'd go with him wherever he was going. I'd share my last bob with him and stick by 'im through thick and thin.'

'We've had enough of this,' says Jeremiah Donovan, cocking his revolver. 'Is there any message you want to send before I fire?' 'No, there isn't, but . . .' 'Do you want to say your prayers?' 'Awkins came out with a cold-blooded remark that shocked even me and turned to Noble again. 'Listen to me, Noble,' he said. 'You and me are chums. You won't come over to my side, so I'll come over to your side. Is that fair? Just you give me a rifle and I'll go with you wherever you want.'

Nobody answered him.

'Do you understand?' he said. 'I'm through with it all. I'm a deserter or anything else you like, but from this on I'm one of you. Does that prove to you that I mean what I say?' Noble raised his head, but as Donovan began to speak he lowered it again without answering. 'For the last time have you any messages to send?' says Donovan in a cold and excited voice.

'Ah, shut up, you, Donovan; you don't understand me, but these fellows do. They're my chums; they stand by me and I stand by them. We're not the capitalist tools you seem to think us.'

I alone of the crowd saw Donovan raise his Webley to the back of 'Awkins's neck, and as he did so I shut my eyes and tried to say a prayer. 'Awkins had begun to say something else when Donovan let fly, and, as I opened my eyes at the bang, I saw him stagger at the knees and lie out flat at Noble's feet, slowly, and as quiet as a child, with the lantern-light falling sadly upon his lean legs and bright farmer's boots. We all stood very still for a while watching him settle out in the last agony.

Then Belcher quietly takes out a handkerchief, and begins to tie it about his own eyes (for in our excitement we had forgotten to offer the same to 'Awkins), and, seeing it is not big enough, turns and asks for a loan of mine. I give it to him and as he knots the two together he points with his foot at 'Awkins. ' 'E's not quite dead,' he says, 'better give 'im another.' Sure enough 'Awkins's left knee as we see it under the lantern is rising again. I bend down and put my gun to his ear; then, recollecting myself and the company of Belcher, I stand up again with a few hasty words. Belcher understands what is in my mind. 'Give 'im 'is first,' he says. 'I don't mind. Poor bastard, we dunno what's 'appening to 'im now.' As by this time I am beyond all feeling I kneel down again and skilfully give 'Awkins the last shot so as to put him for ever out of pain.

Belcher who is fumbling a bit awkwardly with the handkerchiefs comes out with a laugh when he hears the shot. It is the first time I have heard him laugh, and it sends a shiver down my spine, coming as it does so inappropriately upon the tragic death of his old friend. 'Poor blighter,' he says quietly, 'and last night he was so curious abaout it all. It's very queer, chums, I always think. Naow, 'e knows as much abaout it as they'll ever let 'im know, and last night 'e was all in the dark.'

Donovan helps him to tie the handkerchief about his eyes. 'Thanks, chum,' he says. Donovan asks him if there are any messages he would like to send. 'Naow, chum,' he says, 'none

for me. If any of you likes to write to 'Awkins's mother you'll
find a letter from 'er in 'is pocket. But my missus left me eight
years ago. Went away with another fellow and took the kid
with her. I likes the feelin' of a 'ome (as you may 'ave
noticed) but I couldn't start again after that.'

We stand around like fools now that he can no longer see
us. Donovan looks at Noble and Noble shakes his head. Then
Donovan raises his Webley again and just at that moment
Belcher laughs his queer nervous laugh again. He must think
we are talking of him; anyway, Donovan lowers his gun.
' 'Scuse me, chums,' says Belcher, 'I feel I'm talking the 'ell
of a lot . . . and so silly . . . abaout me being so 'andy
about a 'ouse. But this thing come on me so sudden. You'll
forgive me, I'm sure.' 'You don't want to say a prayer?' asks
Jeremiah Donovan. 'No, chum,' he replies, 'I don't think
that'd 'elp. I'm ready if you want to get it over.' 'You understand,' says Jeremiah Donovan, 'it's not so much our doing.
It's our duty, so to speak.' Belcher's head is raised like a real
blind man's, so that you can only see his nose and chin in the
lamplight. 'I never could make out what duty was myself,' he
said, 'but I think you're all good lads, if that's what you
mean. I'm not complaining.' Noble, with a look of despera-
tion, signals to Donovan, and in a flash Donovan raises his
gun and fires. The big man goes over like a sack of meal, and
this time there is no need of a second shot.

I don't remember much about the burying, but that it was
worse than all the rest, because we had to carry the warm
corpses a few yards before we sunk them in the windy bog. It
was all mad lonely, with only a bit of lantern between ourselves and the pitch-blackness, and birds hooting and screech-
ing all round disturbed by the guns. Noble had to search
'Awkins first to get the letter from his mother. Then having
smoothed all signs of the grave away, Noble and I collected
our tools, said good-bye to the others, and went back along
the desolate edge of the treacherous bog without a word. We
put the tools in the houseen and went into the house. The
kitchen was pitch-black and cold, just as we left it, and the
old woman was sitting over the hearth telling her beads. We
walked past her into the room, and Noble struck a match to
light the lamp. Just then she rose quietly and came to the
doorway, being not at all so bold or crabbed as usual.

'What did ye do with them?' she says in a sort of whisper,

and Noble took such a mortal start the match quenched in his trembling hand. 'What's that?' he asks without turning round. 'I heard ye,' she said. 'What did you hear?' asks Noble, but sure he wouldn't deceive a child the way he said it. 'I heard ye. Do you think I wasn't listening to ye putting the things back in the houseen?' Noble struck another match and this time the lamp lit for him. 'Was that what ye did with them?' she said, and Noble said nothing—after all what could he say?

So then, by God, she fell on her two knees by the door, and began telling her beads, and after a minute or two Noble went on his knees by the fireplace, so I pushed my way out past her, and stood at the door, watching the stars and listening to the damned shrieking of the birds. It is so strange what you feel at such moments, and not to be written afterwards. Noble says he felt he seen everything ten times as big, perceiving nothing around him but the little patch of black bog with the two Englishmen stiffening into it; but with me it was the other way, as though the patch of bog where the two Englishmen were was a thousand miles away from me, and even Noble mumbling just behind me and the old woman and the birds and the bloody stars were all far away, and I was somehow very small and very lonely. And anything that ever happened me after I never felt the same about again.

Wilfred Owen

ANTHEM FOR DOOMED YOUTH

What passing-bells for these who die as cattle?
Only the monstrous anger of the guns.
Only the stuttering rifles' rapid rattle
Can patter out their hasty orisons.
No mockeries for them; no prayers nor bells,
Nor any voice of mourning save the choirs,—
The shrill, demented choirs of wailing shells;
And bugles calling for them from sad shires.
What candles may be held to speed them all?
Not in the hands of boys, but in their eyes
Shall shine the holy glimmers of good-byes.
The pallor of girls' brows shall be their pall;
Their flowers the tenderness of patient minds,
And each slow dusk a drawing-down of blinds.

DULCE ET DECORUM EST

Bent double, like old beggars under sacks,
Knock-kneed, coughing like hags, we cursed through sludge,
Till on the haunting flares we turned our backs,
And towards our distant rest began to trudge.
Men marched asleep. Many had lost their boots,
But limped on, blood-shod. All went lame, all blind;
Drunk with fatigue; deaf even to the hoots
Of gas-shells dropping softly behind.

Gas! Gas! Quick, boys!—An ecstasy of fumbling,
Fitting the clumsy helmets just in time,
But someone still was yelling out and stumbling
And floundering like a man in fire or lime.—

Dim through the misty panes and thick green light,
As under a green sea, I saw him drowning.

In all my dreams before my helpless sight
He plunges at me, guttering, choking, drowning.

If in some smothering dreams, you too could pace
Behind the wagon that we flung him in,
And watch the white eyes writhing in his face,
His hanging face, like a devil's sick of sin;
If you could hear, at every jolt, the blood
Come gargling from the froth-corrupted lungs,
Bitter as the cud
Of vile, incurable sores on innocent tongues,—
My friend, you would not tell with such high zest
To children ardent for some desperate glory,
The old Lie: *Dulce et decorum est*
Pro patria mori.

STRANGE MEETING

It seemed that out of the battle I escaped
Down some profound dull tunnel, long since scooped
Through granites which Titanic wars had groined.
Yet also there encumbered sleepers groaned,
Too fast in thought or death to be bestirred.
Then, as I probed them, one sprang up, and stared
With piteous recognition in fixed eyes,
Lifting distressful hands as if to bless.
And by his smile, I knew that sullen hall;
By his dead smile I knew we stood in Hell.
With a thousand pains that vision's face was grained;
Yet no blood reached there from the upper ground,
And no guns thumped, or down the flues made moan.
"Strange, friend," I said, "here is no cause to mourn."
"None," said the other, "save the undone years,
The hopelessness. Whatever hope is yours,
Was my life also; I went hunting wild
After the wildest beauty in the world,
Which lies not calm in eyes, or braided hair,

But mocks the steady running of the hour,
And if it grieves, grieves richlier than here.
For by my glee might many men have laughed,
And of my weeping something has been left,
Which must die now. I mean the truth untold,
The pity of war, the pity war distilled.
Now men will go content with what we spoiled,
Or, discontent, boil bloody, and be spilled.
They will be swift with swiftness of the tigress,
None will break ranks, though nations trek from progress.
Courage was mine, and I had mystery,
Wisdom was mine, and I had mastery;
To miss the march of this retreating world
Into vain citadels that are not walled.
Then when much blood had clogged their chariot-wheels
I would go up and wash them from sweet wells,
Even with truths that lie too deep for taint.
I would have poured my spirit without stint
But not through wounds; not on the cess of war.
Foreheads of men have bled where no wounds were.
I am the enemy you killed, my friend.
I knew you in this dark; for so you frowned
Yesterday through me as you jabbed and killed.
I parried; but my hands were loath and cold.
Let us sleep now. . . ."

Dorothy Parker

SOLDIERS OF THE REPUBLIC

That Sunday afternoon we sat with the Swedish girl in the big café in Valencia. We had vermouth in thick goblets, each with a cube of honeycombed gray ice in it. The waiter was so proud of that ice he could hardly bear to leave the glasses on the table, and thus part from it forever. He went to his duty—all over the room they were clapping their hands and hissing to draw his attention—but he looked back over his shoulder.

It was dark outside, the quick, new dark that leaps down without dusk on the day; but, because there were no lights in the streets, it seemed as set and as old as midnight. So you wondered that all the babies were still up. There were babies everywhere in the café, babies serious without solemnity and interested in a tolerant way in their surroundings.

At the table next ours, there was a notably small one; maybe six months old. Its father, a little man in a big uniform that dragged his shoulders down, held it carefully on his knee. It was doing nothing whatever, yet he and his thin young wife, whose belly was already big again under her sleazy dress, sat watching it in a sort of ecstasy of admiration, while their coffee cooled in front of them. The baby was in Sunday white; its dress was patched so delicately that you would have thought the fabric whole had not the patches varied in their shades of whiteness. In its hair was a bow of new blue ribbon, tied with absolute balance of loops and ends. The ribbon was of no use; there was not enough hair to require restraint. The bow was sheerly an adornment, a calculated bit of dash.

"Oh, for God's sake, stop that!" I said to myself. "All right, so it's got a piece of blue ribbon on its hair. All right, so its mother went without eating so it could look pretty when its father came home on leave. All right, so it's her business, and none of yours. All right, so what have you got to cry about?"

The big, dim room was crowded and lively. That morning there had been a bombing from the air, the more horrible for broad daylight. But nobody in the café sat tense and strained, nobody desperately forced forgetfulness. They drank coffee or bottled lemonade, in the pleasant, earned ease of Sunday afternoon, chatting of small, gay matters, all talking at once, all hearing and answering.

There were many soldiers in the room, in what appeared to be the uniforms of twenty different armies until you saw that the variety lay in the different ways the cloth had worn or faded. Only a few of them had been wounded; here and there you saw one stepping gingerly, leaning on a crutch or two canes, but so far on toward recovery that his face had color. There were many men, too, in civilian clothes—some of them soldiers home on leave, some of them governmental workers, some of them anybody's guess. There were plump, comfortable wives, active with paper fans, and old women as quiet as their grandchildren. There were many pretty girls and some beauties, of whom you did not remark, "There's a charming Spanish type," but said, "What a beautiful girl!" The women's clothes were not new, and their material was too humble ever to have warranted skillful cutting.

"It's funny," I said to the Swedish girl, "how when nobody in a place is best-dressed, you don't notice that everybody isn't."

"Please?" the Swedish girl said.

No one, save an occasional soldier, wore a hat. When we had first come to Valencia, I lived in a state of puzzled pain as to why everybody on the streets laughed at me. It was not because "West End Avenue" was writ across my face as if left there by a customs officer's chalked scrawl. They like Americans in Valencia, where they have seen good ones— the doctors who left their practices and came to help, the calm young nurses, the men of the International Brigade. But when I walked forth men and women courteously laid their hands across their splitting faces and little children, too innocent for dissembling, doubled with glee and pointed and cried, *"Olé!"* Then, pretty late, I made my discovery, and left my hat off; and there was laughter no longer. It was not one of those comic hats, either; it was just a hat.

The café filled to overflow, and I left our table to speak to a friend across the room. When I came back to the table, six soldiers were sitting there. They were crowded in, and I scraped past them to my chair. They looked tired and dusty and little, the way that the newly dead look little, and the first things you saw about them were the tendons in their necks. I felt like a prize sow.

They were all in conversation with the Swedish girl. She has Spanish, French, German, anything in Scandinavian, Italian, and English. When she has a moment for regret, she sighs that her Dutch is so rusty she can no longer speak it, only read it, and the same is true of her Rumanian.

They had told her, she told us, that they were at the end of forty-eight hours' leave from the trenches, and, for their holiday, they had all pooled their money for cigarettes, and something had gone wrong, and the cigarettes had never come through to them. I had a pack of American cigarettes—in Spain rubies are as nothing to them—and I brought it out, and by nods and smiles and a sort of breast stroke, made it understood that I was offering it to those six men yearning for tobacco. When they saw what I meant, each one of them rose and shook my hand. Darling of me to share my cigarettes with the men on their way back to the trenches. Little Lady Bountiful. The prize sow.

Each one lit his cigarette with a contrivance of yellow rope that stank when afire and was also used, the Swedish girl translated, for igniting grenades. Each one received what he had ordered, a glass of coffee, and each one murmured appreciatively over the tiny cornucopia of coarse sugar that accompanied it. Then they talked.

They talked through the Swedish girl, but they did to us that thing we all do when we speak our own language to one who has no knowledge of it. They looked us square in the face, and spoke slowly, and pronounced their words with elaborate movements of their lips. Then, as their stories came, they poured them at us so vehemently, so emphatically that they were sure we must understand. They were so convinced we would understand that we were ashamed for not understanding.

But the Swedish girl told us. They were all farmers and farmers' sons, from a district so poor that you try not to remember there is that kind of poverty. Their village was next that one where the old men and the sick men and the women and children had gone, on a holiday, to the bullring; and the planes had come over and dropped bombs on the bullring, and the old men and the sick men and the women were more than two hundred.

They had all, the six of them, been in the war for over a year, and most of that time they had been in the trenches. Four of them were married. One had one child, two had three children, one had five. They had not had word from their families since they had left for the front. There had been no communication; two of them had learned to write from men fighting next them in the trench, but they had not dared to write home. They belonged to a union, and union men, of course, are put to death if taken. The village where their families lived had been captured, and if your wife gets a letter from a union man, who knows but they'll shoot her for the connection?

They told about how they had not heard from their families for more than a year. They did not tell it gallantly or whimsically or stoically. They told it as if— Well, look. You have been in the trenches, fighting, for a year. You have heard nothing of your wife and your children. They do not know if you are dead or alive or blinded. You do not know where they are, or if they are. You must talk to somebody. That is the way they told about it.

One of them, some six months before, had heard of his wife and his three children—they had such beautiful eyes, he said—from a brother-in-law in France. They were all alive then, he was told, and had a bowl of beans a day. But his wife had not complained of the food, he heard. What had troubled her was that she had no thread to mend the children's ragged clothes. So that troubled him, too.

"She has no thread," he kept telling us. "My wife has no thread to mend with. No thread."

We sat there, and listened to what the Swedish girl told us they were saying. Suddenly one of them looked at the clock, and then there was excitement. They jumped up, as a man, and there were calls for the waiter and rapid talk with him, and each of them shook the hand of each of us. We went through more swimming motions to explain to them that they were to take the rest of the cigarettes—fourteen cigarettes for six soldiers to take to war—and then they shook our hands again. Then all of us said *"Salud!"* as many times as could be for six of them and three of us, and then they filed out of the café, the six of them, tired and dusty and little, as men of a mighty horde are little.

Only the Swedish girl talked, after they had gone. The Swedish girl has been in Spain since the start of the war. She has nursed splintered men, and she has carried stretchers into the trenches and, heavier laden, back to the hospital. She has seen and heard too much to be knocked into silence.

Presently it was time to go, and the Swedish girl raised her hands above her head and clapped them twice together to summon the waiter. He came, but he only shook his head and his hand, and moved away.

The soldiers had paid for our drinks.

Kenneth Patchen

IN ORDER TO

Apply for the position (I've forgotten now for what) I had to marry the Second Mayor's daughter by twelve noon. The order arrived three minutes of.

I already had a wife; the Second Mayor was childless: but I did it.

Next they told me to shave off my father's beard. All right. No matter that he'd been a eunuch, and had succumbed in early childhood: I did it, I shaved him.

Then they told me to burn a village; next, a fair-sized town; then, a city; a bigger city; a small, down-at-heels country; then one of "the great powers"; then another (another, another)—In fact, they went right on until they'd told me to burn up every man-made thing on the face of the earth! And I did it, I burned away every last trace, I left nothing, nothing of any kind whatever.

Then they told me to blow it all to hell and gone! And I blew it all to hell and gone (oh, didn't I). . .

Now, they said, put it back together again; put it all back the way it was when you started.

Well . . . it was my turn then to tell *them* something! Shucks, I didn't want any job that bad.

Thomas Love Peacock

THE WAR-SONG OF DINAS VAWR

The mountain sheep are sweeter,
But the valley sheep are fatter;
We therefore deemed it meeter
To carry off the latter.
We made an expedition;
We met a host, and quelled it;
We forced a strong position,
And killed the men who held it.

On Dyfed's richest valley,
Where herds of kine were browsing,
We made a mighty sally,
To furnish our carousing.
Fierce warriors rushed to meet us;
We met them, and o'erthrew them:
They struggled hard to beat us;
But we conquered them, and slew them.

As we drove our prize at leisure,
The king marched forth to catch us:
His rage surpassed all measure,
But his people could not match us.
He fled to his hall-pillars;
And, ere our force we led off,
Some sacked his house and cellars,
While others cut his head off.

We there, in strife bewild'ring,
Spilt blood enough to swim in:
We orphaned many children,
And widowed many women.

The eagles and the ravens
We glutted with our foemen;
The heroes and the cravens,
The spearmen and the bowmen.

We brought away from battle,
And much their land bemoaned them,
Two thousand head of cattle,
And the head of him who owned them:
Ednyfed, king of Dyfed,
His head was borne before us;
His wine and beasts supplied our feasts,
And his overthrow, our chorus.

Henry Reed

NAMING OF PARTS

Today we have naming of parts. Yesterday,
We had daily cleaning. And tomorrow morning,
We shall have what to do after firing. But today,
Today we have naming of parts. Japonica
Glistens like coral in all of the neighboring gardens,
    And today we have naming of parts.

This is the lower sling swivel. And this
Is the upper sling swivel, whose use you will see,
When you are given your slings. And this is the piling swivel,
Which in your case you have not got. The branches
Hold in the gardens their silent, eloquent gestures,
    Which in our case we have not got.

This is the safety catch, which is always released
With an easy flick of the thumb. And please do not let me
See anyone using his finger. You can do it quite easy
If you have any strength in your thumb. The blossoms
Are fragile and motionless, never letting anyone see
    Any of them using their fingers.

And this you can see is the bolt. The purpose of this
Is to open the breech, as you see. We can slide it
Rapidly backwards and forwards: we call this
Easing the spring. And rapidly backwards and forwards
The early bees are assaulting and fumbling the flowers:
    They call it easing the Spring.

They call it easing the Spring: it is perfectly easy
If you have any strength in your thumb: like the bolt,
And the breech, and the cocking-piece, and the point of bal-
    ance,

'hich in our case we have not got; and the almond blossom
lent in all of the gardens and the bees going backwards and
forwards,
For today we have naming of parts.

Isaac Rosenberg

BREAK OF DAY IN THE TRENCHES

The darkness crumbles away—
It is the same old druid Time as ever.
Only a live thing leaps my hand—
A queer sardonic rat—
As I pull the parapet's poppy
To stick behind my ear.
Droll rat, they would shoot you if they knew
Your cosmopolitan sympathies.
Now you have touched this English hand
You will do the same to a German—
Soon, no doubt, if it be your pleasure
To cross the sleeping green between.
It seems you inwardly grin as you pass
Strong eyes, fine limbs, haughty athletes
Less chanced than you for life,
Bonds to the whims of murder,
Sprawled in the bowels of the earth,
The torn fields of France.
What do you see in our eyes
At the shrieking iron and flame
Hurled through still heavens?
What quaver—what heart aghast?
Poppies whose roots are in man's veins
Drop, and are ever dropping;
But mine in my ear is safe,
Just a little white with the dust.

Thomas Sackville, Earl of Dorset

LASTLY STOOD WAR

Lastly stood War, in glittering arms y-clad,
With visage grim, stern looks, and blackly hued;
In his right hand a naked sword he had,
That to the hilts was all with blood embrued,
And in his left (that kings and kingdoms rued)
    Famine and fire he held, and therewithal
    He razed towns, and threw down towers and all.

Cities he sacked, and realms that whilom flowered
In honor, glory, and rule above the best
He overwhelmed, and all their fame devoured,
Consumed, destroyed, wasted, and never ceased
Till he their wealth, their name, and all oppressed;
    His face forehewed with wounds, and by his side
    There hung his targe, with gashes deep and wide.

Sagittarius

NOW WE ARE SIX

My daddy's dressing up as Father Christmas
    With presents for the stocking and the tree—
I know he is, because he's always Santa Claus,
    And it used to take me in, when I was three.
I did believe in fairies, and in Santa,
    But definitely stopped when I was four;
It isn't that I won't, but simply that I don't
      Any more.

When mummies shop to make a merry Christmas
    It's up to kiddies all to play the game—
I wouldn't be the one to spoil the parents' fun,
    And my little baby sister says the same.
The parents think we still believe in fairies,
    But we have heard and seen an awful lot.
They think that games and holly and things will make us
      jolly—
      Well, we're not.

It's clear to me the whole world situation
    Has gone from bad to worse since I was five—
We kiddies are agreed, from all we hear and read,
    Next Christmas we mayn't even be alive.
I've talked it over with my baby sister,
    It sometimes makes us feel a little blue—
We want to go to heaven, but not before we're seven,
      Well, would you?

When I was one, a bomb came down the chimney,
    When I was two, they said war clouds had passed—
Now veterans in the nursery this Christmas anniversary
    Expect it may be probably their last.

With all the nations of the earth rearming
  We feel it's the beginning of the end.
We're really not neurotic, but I think it idiotic
    To pretend.

When Daddy's dressing up as Father Christmas,
  When grown-ups are enjoying Christmas fun,
It makes the children glad to think that mum and dad
  Have not the least idea what's going on.
We want to be good democratic kiddies,
  My baby sister loves the common cause—
But sometimes she and I confess we wonder why
  Grown-ups can still believe in Santa Claus.

PROLOGUE TO A MURDER IN THE CATHEDRAL

*The speakers are imaginary and any resemblance to living
personages is accidental.*

PREMIER   A word, my Lord Archbishop. I deplore
           Your fulminations on atomic war.
           Necessity knows neither right nor wrong;
           Prayers to the Church, arms to the State belong.

PRIMATE   I stand rebuked; but you must understand
           It was the scientists who forced my hand.
           When physicists talk morals out of turn
           It must the Church most seriously concern,
           For she alone can speak for Christendom,
           Touching the ethics of the atom-bomb.

PREMIER   Agreed; but take a realistic line.

PRIMATE   Can I equate it with the law divine?

PREMIER   To righteous war the Church gives countenance,
           And, though the atom supersedes the lance,
           Her benediction should not be denied—
           The weapon by the cause is sanctified.

PRIMATE   The broadsword I would bless, and never flinch—
           Small-arms, and even cannon, at a pinch . . .

PREMIER   Bless one, bless all!

PRIMATE   Do not suggest, I beg,
           I hallow that abominable egg.

PREMIER   A-bombs, like curates' eggs, are good in parts,
Striking cold terror to aggressors' hearts,
While Christian scruples guard against abuse.
They are but stockpiled for deterrent use.

PRIMATE   The hell-bomb in the womb of hell once hatched,
Trust me, will ultimately be despatched.

PREMIER   But not by us; you know, as well as I,
It rests the secret of our great ally.

PRIMATE   A miserable quibble! His the act,
But you, accessory before the fact,
Must share responsibility for guilt.

PREMIER   So be it. I back our ally to the hilt,
And find no sin when I my conscience search.

PRIMATE   The keeper of your conscience is the Church.

PREMIER   Your province is ecclesiastical;
Speak for the State, or do not speak at all.
The Church does not exist *in vacuo,*
Your elevation to the State you owe;
The priest is none the less a citizen.
Ends warrant means.

PRIMATE   I will not say amen.

PREMIER   Our foes you comfort and our friends alarm
If you withdraw the spiritual arm.
And, if high heaven resort to war ordain,
The deadliest weapon may be most humane.

PRIMATE   So atom-bombs are mercy weapons now!

PREMIER   All to the logic of events must bow.
The Church herself mass-bombing justified.

PRIMATE   I shudder at absolving genocide.

PREMIER   The State can no such fine distinctions draw.

PRIMATE   I owe obedience to a higher law.
Whatever past complaisance you may quote,
The atom-bomb sticks in the Church's throat.
I am no spiritual satellite,
But charge the State to ban the bomb outright.

PREMIER   I ban the bomb? I neither will, nor can,
While enemies support the atom-ban!

PRIMATE   I bless the bomb? I'd rather lose my See
Than preach atomic Christianity!

PREMIER   At this grave juncture I will tolerate
No fatal fission splitting Church and State,
Nor let the Church subversive doctrines screen.

PRIMATE   I am, sir, the Archbishop, *not* the Dean.
And I hereby revoke, with conscience clear,
My homage as a spiritual peer.
Do what you will, I shall the Christian case
Cry from the rooftops and the market-place,
Henceforward from the temporal yoke released.

Exit.

PREMIER   Will no man free me from this pacifist priest?

Carl Sandburg

BUTTONS

I have been watching the war map slammed up for adver-
tising in front of the newspaper office.
Buttons—red and yellow buttons—black and blue buttons—
are shoved back and forth across the map.

A laughing young man, sunny with freckles,
Climbs a ladder, yells a joke to somebody in the crowd,
And then fixes a yellow button one inch west
And follows the yellow button with a black button one inch
west.

(Ten thousand men and boys twist on their bodies in a red
soak along a river edge,
Gasping of wounds, calling for water, some rattling death in
their throats.)
Who by Christ would guess what it cost to move two buttons
one inch west on the war map here in front of the newspaper office where the freckle-faced young man is laughing at us?

William Sansom

HOW CLAEYS DIED

In Germany, two months after the capitulation, tall green
grass and corn had grown up round every remnant of battle, so that the war seemed to have happened many years
ago. A tank, nosing up from the corn like a pale grey toad,
would already be rusted, ancient; the underside of an overturned carrier exposed intricacies red-brown and clogged
like an agricultural machine abandoned for years. Such objects were no longer the contemporary traffic, they were
exceptional carcasses; one expected their armour to melt like
the armour of crushed beetles, to enter the earth and help
fertilise further the green growth in which they were already
drowned.

Claeys and his party—two officers and a driver—drove
past many of these histories, through miles of such fertile
green growth stretching flatly to either side of the straight
and endless grey avenues. Presently they entered the out-
skirts of a town. This was a cathedral town, not large, not
known much—until by virtue of a battle its name now
resounded in black letters the size of the capital letters on
the maps of whole countries. This name would now ring
huge for generations, it would take its part in the hymn of
national glory; such a name had already become sacred,
stony, a symbol of valour. Claeys looked about him with
interest—he had never seen the town before, only heard of
the battle and suffered with the soldiers who had taken it
and held it for four hopeful days with the hope dying each
hour until nearly all were dead, hope and soldiers. Now as
they entered the main street, where already the white tram-
trains were hooting, where the pale walls were chipped and
bullet-chopped, where nevertheless there had never been the
broad damage of heavy bombs and where therefore the pave-
ments and shop-fronts were already washed and civil—as

they entered these streets decked with summer dresses an
flecked with leaf patterns, Claeys looked in vain for the tow
of big letters, and smelled only perfume; a wall of perfum
they seemed to have entered a scent-burg, a sissy-burg,
town of female essences, Grasse—but it was only that th
town happened to be planted with lime-trees, lime-trees ever
where, and these limes were all in flower, their shaded greer
ery alive with the golden powdery flower, whose essenc
drifted down to the streets and filled them. The blood wa
gone, the effort of blood had evaporated. Only scent, flower
trams, sunlight, white dresses.

"A nice memorial," Claeys thought. "Keep it in the geogra
phy book." Then the car stopped outside a barracks. Th
officers got out. Claeys said he would wait in the car. H
was not in uniform, he was on a civil mission, attache
temporarily to the army. It does not matter what missior
It was never fulfilled. All that need be said is that Claey
was a teacher, engaged then on relief measures, a voluntee
for this work of rehabilitation of the enemy, perhaps a sor
of half-brother-of-mercy as during the occupation he ha
been a sort of half-killer. Now he wanted to construc
quickly the world of which he had dreamed during th
shadow years; now he was often as impatient of inaction a
he had learned to be patient before. Patience bends befor
promise: perhaps this curiosity for spheres of action quick
ened his interest as now a lorry-load of soldiers drew u
and jumped down at the barrack-gate. One of the soldier
said: "They're using mortars." Another was saying: "An
do you blame 'em?"

There had been trouble, they told Claeys, up at the camp
for expatriates—the camp where forced labourers importee
from all over Europe waited for shipment home. A group o
these had heard that a released German prisoner-of-war wa
returning to work his farm in the vicinity of the camp. They
had decided to raid the farm at nightfall, grab as much food
as possible, teach the German a trick or two. But the Germar
had somehow got hold of a grenade—from the fields, or
perhaps hidden in the farmhouse. At any rate, he had throw
it and killed two of the expatriates. The others had retreated
the story had spat round, before long the expatriates were
coming back on the farm in full strength. They had rifle
and even mortars. The news got back to the occupationa

military and a piquet had been sent over. The mortars were opening fire as it arrived: but they were stopped, the expatriates respected the British. Yet to maintain this respect they had to keep a piquet out there for the night. Not all the polskis or czechskis or whoever they were had gone home. A few had hung about, grumbling. The air was by no means clear.

When the officers returned, Claeys told them that he had altered his plans, he wanted to go up and take a look at this expatriates' camp. He gave no reason, and it is doubtful whether he had then a special reason; he felt only that he ought to see these expatriates and talk to them. He had no idea of what to say, but something of the circumstances might suggest a line later.

So they drove out into the country again, into the green. Rich lucent corn stretched endlessly to either side of the straight and endless road. Regularly, in perfect order, precisely intervalled beeches flashed by: a rich, easy, discreet roof of leaves shaded their passage as the foliage met high above. Occasionally a notice at the roadside reminded them of mines uncleared beyond the verges, occasionally a tree bore an orderly white notice addressed to civil traffic. And occasionally a unit of civil traffic passed—a family wheeling a handcart, a cyclist and his passenger, and once a slow-trudging German soldier making his grey way back along the long road to his farm. But there was nothing about this figure in grey-green to suggest more than a farmer dressed as a soldier; he walked slowly, he seemed to be thinking slowly, secure in his destination and free of time as any countryman walking slowly home on an empty road.

All was order. Birds, of course, sang. A green land, unbelievably quiet and rich, sunned its moisture. Each square yard lay unconcerned with the next, just as each measure of the road lay back as they passed, unconcerned with their passing, contented, remaining where it had always been under its own beech, a piece of land. And when at last the beech-rows stopped, the whole of that flat country seemed to spread itself suddenly open. The sky appeared, blue and sailing small white clouds to give it air. Those who deny the flatlands forget the sky—over flat country the sky approaches closer than anywhere else, it takes shape, it becomes the blue-domed lid on a flat plate of earth. Here is a greater intimacy between the elements; and for once, for a little, the world appears finite.

The carload of four travelled like a speck over this flat space. And Claeys was thinking: "Such a summer, such still air—something like a mother presiding heavily and quietly while down in her young the little vigours boil and breed . . air almost solid, a sort of unseen fruit fibre . . . a husk guarding the orderly chaos of the breeding ground. . . ."

Such a strict order seemed indeed to preside within the intricate anarchy—success and failure, vigorous saplings from the seeds of good fortune, a pennyworth of gas from the seeds that fall on stony ground: yet a sum total of what might appear to be complete achievement, and what on the human level appears to be peace. And on that level, the only real level, there appeared—over by the poplar plumes? Or by the windmill? Or at some flat point among the converged hedges?—there appeared one scar, a scar of purely human disorder: over somewhere lay this camp of ten thousand displaced souls, newly freed but imprisoned still by their strange environment and by their great expectations born and then as instantly barred. On the face of it, these seemed to represent disorder, or at most a residue of disorder. But was this really so? Would such disorder not have appeared elsewhere, in similar quantity and under conditions of apparent order? Were they, perhaps, not anything more than stony-grounders—the disfavoured residue of an anarchic nature never governed directly, only impalpably guided by more general and less concerned governments? Was it right to rationalise, to impose order upon such seed, was it right—or at least, was it sensible? It was right, obviously—for a brain made to reason is itself a part of nature and it would be wrong to divert it from its necessitous reasoning. But right though reason may be, there was no more reason to put one's faith in the impeccable work of the reasoning brain than to imagine that any other impressive yet deluded machine—like, for instance, the parachute seed—should by its apparent ingenuity succeed. Look at the parachute seed—this amazing seed actually flies off the insensate plant-mother! It sails on the wind! The seed itself hangs beneath such an intricate parasol, it is carried from the roots of its mother to land on fertile ground far away and set up there an emissary generation! And more—when it lands, this engine is o constructed that draughts inch-close to the soil drag, drag, drag at the little parachute, so that the seed beneath actually erodes the earth, digs for itself a little trench of shelter, buries itself! Amazing! And what if the clever little seed is borne on the wrong wind to a basin of basalt?

Claeys was thinking: "The rule of natural anarchy—a few succeed, many waste and die. No material waste: only a huge waste of effort. The only sure survival is the survival of the greater framework that includes the seed and all other things on the earth—the furious landcrab, the bright young eskimo, the Antiguan cornbroker—every thing and body . . . and these thrive and decay and compensate . . . just as we, on the threshold of some golden age of reason, just as we are the ones to harness some little nuclear genius, pack it into neat canisters, store it ready to blow up all those sunny new clinics when the time comes, the time for compensation. . . ."

Just then the car drove into a small town on the bank of a broad river. Instantly, in a matter of yards, the green withered and the party found themselves abruptly in what seemed to be some sort of a quarry, dry, dug-about, dust-pale, slagged up on either side with excavated stones.

It was indeed an excavation: it was of course the street of a town. This town was dead. It had been bombed by a thousand aircraft, shelled by an entire corps of artillery, and then fought through by land soldiers. No houses were left, no streets. The whole had been churned up, smashed and jig-sawed down again, with some of the jig-saw pieces left upended—those gaunt walls remaining—and the rest of the pieces desiccated into mounds and hollows and flats. No grass grew. The air hung sharp with vaporised dust. A few new alleys had been bulldozed through: these seemed pointless, for now there was no traffic, the armies had passed through, the town was deserted. Somewhere in the centre Claeys stopped the car. He held up his hand for silence. The four men listened. Throughout that wasted city there was no sound. No distant muttering, no murmur. No lost hammering, no drowned cry. No word, no footstep. No wheels. No wind shifting a branch—for there were no trees. No flapping of torn cloth, this avalanche had covered all the cloth. No birds—but one, a small bird that flew straight over, without singing; above such a desert it moved like a small vul-

ture, a shadow, a bird without destination. Brick, concrete
gravel-dust—with only two shaped objects as far all round
as they could see: one, an intestinal engine of fat iron pipes
black and big as an upended lorry, something thrown out
of a factory; and leaning on its side a pale copper-green
byzantine cupola like a gigantic sweet-kiosk blown over by
the wind, the tower fallen from what had been the town
church. This—in a town that had been the size of Reading.

Almost reverently, as on sacred ground, they started the
car and drove off again. Through the pinkish-white mounds
the sound of the motor seemed now to intrude garishly.
Claeys wanted only to be out of the place. Again, this de
struction seemed to have occurred years before; but now
because of the very absence of green, of any life at all, of
any reason to believe that people had ever lived there. Not
even a torn curtain. They wormed through and soon, as
abruptly as before, the country began and as from a season-
less pause the summer embraced them once more.

Claeys stood up off his seat to look over the passing hedges.
The camp was somewhere near now. The driver said, two
kilometres. Surely, Claeys thought, surely with that dead
town so near the men in this camp could realise the extent
of the upheaval, the need for a pause before their journey
could be organised? Surely they must see the disruption, this
town, the one-way bridges over every stream far around,
the roads pitted and impassable? Yet . . . what real meaning
had these evidences? Really, they were too negative to be
understood, too much again of something long finished. It
was not as if something positive, like an army passing, held
up one's own purpose; not even a stream of aircraft, showing that at least somewhere there was an effort and direction. No, over these fields there was nothing, not even the
sense of a pause, when something might be restarted; instead
a vacuity stretched abroad, a vacuum of human endeavour,
with the appalling contrast of this vegetable growth continuing evenly and unconcerned. That was really the compre-
hensible evidence, this sense of the land and of the essence
of life continuing, so that one must wish to be up and walking away, to be off to take part not in a regrowth but in a
simple continuation of what had always been. For every
immediate moment there was food to be sought, the pleasures
of taste to be enjoyed: what was more simple than to walk

out and put one's hands on a cap-full of eggs, a pig, a few fat hens? And if a grey uniform intervened, then it was above all a grey uniform, something instinctively obstructive, in no real sense connected with the dead town. The only real sympathy that ever came sometimes to soften the greyness of this grey was a discovery, felt occasionally with senses of wonder and unease, that this uniform went walking and working through its own mined cornfields and sometimes blew itself up—that therefore there must be a man inside it, a farmer more than a soldier. But the grey was mostly an obstruction to be ordinary daily desire for food, for fun, for something to be tasted. The day for these men was definitely a day. It was no twenty-four hours building up to a day in the future when something would happen. No future day had been promised. There was, therefore, no succession of days, no days for ticking off, for passing through and storing in preparation. There were in fact the days themselves, each one a matter of living, each a separate dawning and tasting and setting.

Suddenly Claeys heard singing, a chorus of men's voices. A second later the driver down behind the windshield heard it. He nodded, as though they had arrived. The singing grew louder, intimate—as though it came from round a corner that twisted the road immediately ahead. But it came from a lane just before, it flourished suddenly into a full-throated slavic anthem—and there was the lane crowded with men, some sitting, others marching four abreast out into the road. The car whirred down to a dead halt. The singing wavered and stopped. Claeys saw that the driver had only his left hand on the wheel—his other hand was down gripping the black butt of a revolver at his knee. (He had never done this driving through German crowds earlier.)

"It's not the camp," the driver said. "These are some of them, though. The camp's a kilometre up the road." He kept his eyes scanning slowly up and down the line of men crowding in the lane's entry, he never looked up at Claeys. Then the men came a few paces forward, though they looked scarcely interested. Probably they were pushed forward by the crowd behind, many of whom could not have seen the car, many of whom were still singing.

Claeys stood upright and said: "I'd like to talk to these

. . . you drive on, get round the corner and wait. I don't want that military feeling."

The men looked on with mild interest, as though they might have had many better things to do. They looked scarcely "displaced"; they had a self-contained air, an independence. There was no censure in their stare; equally no greeting; nor any love. Their clothes were simple, shirts and greyish trousers and boots; though these were weather-stained, they were not ragged.

Claeys jumped down. An interest seemed to quicken in some of the watching men as they saw how Claeys was dressed—béret, plus-fours, leather jacket. It was because of these clothes that the military in the car gave Claeys no salute as they drove off; also because they disapproved of this kind of nonsense, and this may have been why they neither smiled nor waved, but rather nodded impersonally and whirred off round the corner. They might, for instance, have been dropping Claeys after giving him some sort of a lift.

So that Claeys was left quite alone on the road, standing and smiling at the crowd of expatriates grouped at the entrance to the lane. The car had disappeared. It had driven off the road and round the corner. There, as often happens when a vehicle disappears from view, its noise had seemed to vanish too. Presumably it had stopped. But equally it might have been presumed far away on its journey to the next town.

The men took a pace or two forward, now beginning to form a crescent-shape round Claeys, while Claeys began to speak in English: "Good afternoon, mates. Excuse me, I'm Pieter Claeys—native of Belge." None of the men smiled. They only stared hard at him. They were too absorbed now even to mutter a word between themselves. They were searching for an explanation, a sign that would clarify this stranger. They were unsure, and certainly it seemed unimpressed. "Good afternoon, comrades," Claeys shouted. "Gentlemen, hello!"

Without waiting, for the silence was beginning to weigh, he turned into French. *"Suis Claeys de Belge. Je veux vous aider. Vous permettez—on peut causer un peu?"*

He repeated: *"Peut-être?"* And in the pause while no one answered he looked up and above the heads of these men, feeling that his smile might be losing its first flavour, that somehow an embarrassment might be dissolved if he looked away.

The country again stretched wide and green. Claeys was startled then to see sudden huge shapes of paint-box colour erecting themselves in the distance. But then immediately he saw what they were—the wings and fuselages of broken gliders, grounded and breathlessly still. Difficult at first to understand, for their shapes were strange and sudden, and of an artifice dangerously like something natural: brightly coloured, they might have been shapes torn from an abstract canvas and stuck wilfully on this green background: or the bright broken toys left by some giant child.

Claeys tried again: *"Gijmijneheeren zijt blijkbaar in moeilijkheden. Ik zou die gaarne vernemen. . . ."*

The Dutch words came ruggedly out with a revival of his first vigour, for Claeys was more used to Dutch and its familiarity brought some ease again to his smile. It brought also a first muttering from the men.

They began to mutter to each other in a Slav-sounding dialect—Polish, Ukrainian, Czech, Russian?—and as this muttering grew it seemed to become an argument. Claeys wanted instantly to make himself clearer, he seemed to have made some headway at last and so now again he repeated the Dutch. This time he nodded, raised his arm in a gesture, even took a pace forward in his enthusiasm. But now one of the men behind began to shout angrily, and would have pushed himself forward shaking his fist—had the others not held him.

It was not clear to Claeys—he felt that the Dutch had been understood, and yet what he had said was friendly . . . he began to repeat the words again. Then, half-way through, he thought of a clearer way. He broke into German. There was every chance that someone might understand German: they might have been working here for three years or more; or anyway it was the obvious second language. *". . . so bin ich hier um Ihnen zu hilfen gekommen. Bitte Kameraden, hören Sie mal. . . ."*

The muttering rose, they were plainly talking—and now not to each other but to him. The crescent had converged into a half-circle, these many men with livening faces were half round him. Claeys stood still. Overhead the summer sky

made its huge dome, under which this small group seemed
to make the pin-point centre. The green quiet stretched endlessly away to either side, the painted gliders stuck up brightly.
No traffic.

". . . *bitte ein moment . . . ich bin Freund, Freund,
FREUND . . .*" And as he repeated this word "friend" he
realised what his tongue had been quicker to understand—
that none of his listeners knew the meaning of these German
words. They knew only that he was speaking German, they
knew the intonation well.

He stopped. For a moment, as the men nudged each other
nearer, as the Slav words grew into accusation and impreca-
tion, Claeys' mind fogged up appalled by this muddle, help-
lessly overwhelmed by such absurdity, such disorder and mis-
understanding.

Then, making an effort to clear himself, he shook his head
and looked closely from one man to the other. But the com-
posure had gone: they were all mouths, eyes, anger and
desire—they were no longer independent. And this was
accumulating, breeding itself beyond the men as men. They
had become a crowd.

Knowing that words were of no further use, Claeys did
the natural thing—wearily, slowly he raised his arm in a last
despairing bid for silence.

An unfortunate gesture. The shouting compounded into
one confused roar. One of the men on the edge of the crowd
jumped out and swung something in the air—a scythe. It
cut Claeys down, and then all the pack of them were on him,
kicking, striking, grunting and shouting less.

Claeys must have screamed as the scythe hit him—two
shots thundered like two full stops into that muddle, there
was an abrupt silence and two men fell forward; and then
another shot and the men scattered crying into the lane.

Those three soldiers came running up to Claeys' body.
They shot again into the men crowding the lane; but then
the men, bottled up in the narrow lane, suddenly turned
and raised their arms above their heads. The soldiers held
their fire, their particular discipline actuated more strongly
than their emotions. Two of them kept their guns alert,
gestured the men forward. They came, hands raised, sham-
bling awkwardly. The other officer bent down to Claeys.

He was almost finished, messed with blood and blue-white where the flesh showed. He was breathing, trying to speak; and the officer knelt down on both his knees and raised Claeys' head up. But Claeys never opened his eyes—they were bruised shut, anyway. And no words came from his lips, though the officer lowered his head and listened very carefully.

Through the pain, through his battered head, one thought muddled out enormously. "Mistake . . . mistake. . . ." And this split into two other confused, unanswered questions, weakening dulling questions. Broadly, if they could have been straightened out, these questions would have been: "Order or Disorder? Those fellows were the victims of an attempt to rule men into an impeccable order, my killing was the result of the worst, that is, the most stupid disorder. . . ."

But he couldn't get the words out, or any like them. Only —weakly, slowly he raised his right hand. He groped for the officer's hand, and the officer knew what he wanted and met the hand with his own in a handshake. Claeys just managed to point at the place where the men had been, where they still were. Then his head sank deep on to his neck. Again the officer knew what he wanted. He rose, his hand still outstretched from Claeys' grasp, like a hand held out by a splint. Then he started over towards the men.

Instinctively, for this hand of his was wet with blood, he wiped it on his tunic as he walked forward. Without knowing this, he raised his hand again into its gesture of greeting. There was a distasteful expression on his face, for he hardly liked such a duty.

So that when he shook hands with the first of the men, proffering to them, in fact, Claeys' handshake, none of these expatriates knew whether the officer was giving them Claeys' hand or whether he had wiped Claeys' gesture away in distaste and was now offering them his congratulation for killing such a common enemy as Claeys.

May Sarton

THE TORTURED

Cried Innocence, "Mother, my thumbs, my thumbs!
The pain will make me wild."
And Wisdom answered, "Your brother-man
Is suffering, my child."

Screamed Innocence, "Mother, my eyes, my eyes!
Someone is blinding me."
And Wisdom answered, "Those are your brother's eyes,
The blinded one is he."

Cried Innocence, "Mother, my heart, my heart!
It bursts with agony."
And Wisdom answered, "That is your brother's heart
Breaking upon a tree."

Screamed Innocence, "Mother, I want to die.
I cannot bear the pain."
And Wisdom answered, "They will not let him die.
They bring him back again."

Cried Innocence, "Mother, I cannot bear
It now. My flesh is wild!"
And Wisdom answered, "His agony is endless
For your sake, my child."

Then whispered Innocence, "Mother, forgive,
Forgive my sin, forgive—"
And Wisdom wept. "Now do you understand, Love,
How you must live?"

Siegfried Sassoon

THE REAR-GUARD

(Hindenburg Line, April 1917)

Groping along the tunnel, step by step,
He winked his prying torch with patching glare
From side to side, and sniffed the unwholesome air.

Tins, boxes, bottles, shapes too vague to know;
A mirror smashed, the mattress from a bed;
And he, exploring fifty feet below
The rosy gloom of battle overhead.

Tripping, he grabbed the wall; saw some one lie
Humped at his feet, half-hidden by a rug,
And stooped to give the sleeper's arm a tug.
'I'm looking for headquarters.' No reply.
'God blast your neck!' (For days he'd had no sleep.)
'Get up and guide me through this stinking place.'

Savage, he kicked a soft, unanswering heap,
And flashed his beam across the livid face
Terribly glaring up, whose eyes yet wore
Agony dying hard ten days before;
And fists of fingers clutched a blackening wound.

Alone he staggered on until he found
Dawn's ghost that filtered down a shafted stair
To the dazed, muttering creatures underground
Who hear the boom of shells in muffled sound.
At last, with sweat of horror in his hair,
He climbed through darkness to the twilight air,
Unloading hell behind him step by step.

THE EFFECT

'The effect of our bombardment was terrific. One man told me he had never seen so many dead before.'
—War Correspondent.

'He'd never seen so many dead before.'
They sprawled in yellow daylight while he swore
And gasped and lugged his everlasting load
Of bombs along what once had been a road.
'How peaceful are the dead.'
Who put that silly gag in some one's head?

'He'd never seen so many dead before.'
The lilting words danced up and down his brain,
While corpses jumped and capered in the rain.
No, no; he wouldn't count them any more . . .
The dead have done with pain:
They've choked; they can't come back to life again.

When Dick was killed last week he looked like that,
Flapping along the fire-step like a fish,
After the blazing crump had knocked him flat . . .
'How many dead? As many as ever you wish.
Don't count 'em; they're too many.
Who'll buy my nice fresh corpses, two a penny?'

BASE DETAILS

If I were fierce, and bald, and short of breath,
    I'd live with scarlet Majors at the Base,
And speed glum heroes up the line to death.
    You'd see me with my puffy petulant face,
Guzzling and gulping in the best hotel,
    Reading the Roll of Honour. 'Poor young chap,'
I'd say—'I used to know his father well;
    Yes, we've lost heavily in this last scrap.'
And when the war is done and youth stone dead,
I'd toddle safely home and die—in bed.

THE GENERAL

'Good-morning; good-morning!' the General said
When we met him last week on our way to the line.
Now the soldiers he smiled at are most of 'em dead,
And we're cursing his staff for incompetent swine.
'He's a cheery old card,' grunted Harry to Jack
As they slogged up to Arras with rifle and pack.

. . . . .

But he did for them both by his plan of attack.

EVERYONE SANG

Everyone suddenly burst out singing;
And I was filled with such delight
As prisoned birds must find in freedom,
Winging wildly across the white
Orchards and dark-green fields; on—on—and out of sight.

Everyone's voice was suddenly lifted;
And beauty came like the setting sun;
My heart was shaken with tears; and horror
Drifted away . . . O, but Everyone
Was a bird; and the song was wordless; the singing will never
be done.

Louis Simpson

THE ASH AND THE OAK

When men discovered freedom first
The fighting was on foot,
They were encouraged by their thirst
And promises of loot,
And when it feathered and bows boomed
Their virtue was a root.

O the ash and the oak and the willow tree
And green grows the grass on the infantry!

At Malplaquet and Waterloo
They were polite and proud,
They primed their guns with billets-doux
And, as they fired, bowed.
At Appomattox too, it seems
Some things were understood.

O the ash and the oak and the willow tree
And green grows the grass on the infantry!

But at Verdun and at Bastogne
There was a great recoil,
The blood was bitter to the bone,
The trigger to the soul,
And death was nothing if not dull,
A hero was a fool.

O the ash and the oak and the willow tree
And that's an end of the infantry.

THE MAKING OF A SOLDIER USA

One January morning I left my steam-heated room at Columbia University and took the subway down to the Armory, a black building with castellated walls on Fourth Avenue. There I joined a line of draftees. We were loaded on trucks and transported to Fort Dix, New Jersey. We removed our clothing and stood in line. The line moved forward; supply sergeants thrust olive-drab clothing, eating utensils, and gas masks at us, and we emerged at the end of the line as soldiers.

For a few days we sluiced the barracks floors and "policed the area," picking up bits of fluff from the gravel between the buildings. Then we were divided in groups, marched to the railhead, and sent off in boxcars. All day the train clickety-clacked, hooting across a wilderness with shacks straggling away from the rails. At night, when the stopping train jerked me awake, I looked out on the stilly lights of strange cities.

My destination was a tank regiment in Texas. On the first evening in camp, for want of anything else to do, I sat in the room where men were writing letters home—how intently they bent their heads and wrote!—and looked at the tank-training manuals. There were diagrams of tank tactics, trajectories of fire, *et cetera*. It didn't look like much of a future. A bugle sounded us to bed.

Before dawn I woke, shivering with cold. I had never been so cold in my life. While it was still dark, the bugle sounded reveille. Though we had worn our long johns to bed—a garment of gray-white woolen underwear—getting out was like getting into a cold bath. The naked moment of putting your feet to the floor! Someone threw lumps of coal into the iron stove and lit it. We dressed as close to the heat as we could, then fell out under the frosty stars, and were shoved and commanded by the sergeants into the semblance of a company formation.

Before dawn the tanks loomed as shadows against the sky, with high turrets and cannons like elephants' trunks. When morning filtered through the bleak sky, the shadows parted, revealing machines of a remarkable ugliness, lop-sided metal boxes studded with rivets. These were the General

Grants, created on a design exactly opposite to that which was needed in tanks. In a tank you want a low silhouette and a long gun; the Grant had a short gun and a high silhouette.

But I was not concerned with field problems. What troubled me was the machinery—for example, the track, a belt of iron teeth which, our sergeant informed us, would sometimes break; we would then have to kink it together again, as though it were a watch strap. My fingers, crammed into my pockets where I was trying to warm them, were anticipating being flattened between the sledgehammer and teeth of broken track. We climbed into the turret. The gun breeches, with a cold rap now and then, promised to knock our brains out. Here, the sergeant explained, shells would be stacked all around us. I could see myself being blown to smithereens, or, more likely, fried to a crisp. I have met infantrymen who wanted to be in the Air Force; for my part, I yearned for a transfer to a mere rifle company.

We were given instruction in tank driving. The idea was simple. You pulled on a lever that braked one track; the other track would keep going and the tank would lurch in the braked direction. The farm boys, fresh from tractors, had no trouble with this, neither did truck drivers from Brooklyn; but I had never driven anything but a bicycle. At one point my instructor shouted, "Jesus Christ!" and swung at my head with a monkey wrench—though I don't believe he was really trying to kill me; it was just self-defense. They listed me not as a driver, but as loader and radioman.

Meanwhile we were learning to roll a pack and march; to take apart, put together, and shoot a tommy gun, rifle, pistol, and .30 caliber machine gun. Also we did KP, the bane of enlisted men, which calls you out of bed in the freezing dark to go and serve the cook—and all cooks are ill-tempered—clearing away swill, and scouring greasy pots, and peeling potatoes, until—when it seems you will never escape—you have scrubbed down the last table, and are released to grope your way back to bed by starlight. During this period, also, we were trotted, in our heavy overcoats, from the drill field to heated rooms, where we were shown movies. I remember one about the consequences of fornication. Who was the fine actor with half a face who made such an impression on the theatergoers of Camp Bowie? He was

more appalling than the Phantom of the Opera. When he
told in a mournful voice how he had got that way, even the
married men blanched.

THE COLONEL ASKED . . .

The aim of military training is not just to prepare men
for battle, but to make them long for it. Inspections are one
way to achieve this. When you've washed the barracks windows and floor till they are speckless, you arrange your clothing and equipment in symmetrical patterns on and around
a bed made tight as a drum. You stand at attention while a
colonel and your company officers pass by. Sometimes the
colonel stops in front of you. He may ask you to recite one
of the sacred orders of guard duty; he may look through
the barrel of your weapon, or harass you in a new way.

The colonel stopped in front of me.

"Soldier," he said, "do you believe in God?"

For weeks no one had asked my opinion about anything.
My vanity was roused and I seized the opportunity to star.
I hesitated, then said, "No, sir."

In a moment the air seemed to have become as fragile as
glass. I had already begun to be sorry. The colonel spoke
again. "Soldier, look out of that window."

I looked. There was a brown glimpse of Texas and a slice
of sky. There were the tanks drawn up in rows.

"Who made all that?"

Someone else might have replied, "General Motors," but
I didn't. Retreating from my expressed position as fast as
possible, I said, "I suppose it was God, sir."

The colonel told me that He had, and not to forget it, and
proceeded on his way.

When the officers had left the barracks, my platoon sergeant stared at me and exclaimed bitterly, "Why did he have
to ask *him!*"

The sergeant was a Regular Army man. The war, which
I thought of as a personal experience which was adding to
my education, was just another job to him, and the only important thing was to do it right. Of such is the Kingdom of
Heaven.

WHERE WE BEAT THE GERMANS

The regiment was sent to Hood. Today, in city apartments, housing developments, offices and gas stations and supermarkets, there are hundreds of thousands of men joined by one silent name—Hood! Conceive a plain of absolute brown, broken only by clumps of thorn and stunted trees, and in the middle of this desert, white barracks laid out in perfect rectangles; a city in the middle of Nowhere, housing eighty thousand souls. The sun rises and stirs this ant heap; men march here and there; they enter machines, and the machines proceed in files into the desert, where, in clouds of dust, they dart to and fro, or stand immobile. At noon the plain is burning with heat. Then the machines return to the center; the ant files wind back to their nests. Stars swim out, and the plain is gripped with cold.

Hood was for the training of tank destroyers and a handful of tanks. The tank destroyers were open armored cars with wheels in front and tracks in the rear, mounting a cannon. They were supposed to knock out tanks with one or two well-placed projectiles, and depart at speed before they could be hit. That, at least, was the theory. Our tanks were supposed to maneuver with or against them.

We turned out in the freezing dawn. I climbed into the tank turret, put on my helmet, and strapped myself to the seat. The tank lurched with whining engines and jingling, squeaking tracks over the plain. When the sun rose, through the periscope I glimpsed jigsaw pieces of sky and earth. We traveled in clouds of dust. Dust entered by every crack; it turned our green fatigues brown and filled our nostrils. Through the earphones which as radioman I wore, came sounds of command, drawling Tennessee and nervous New Jersey, exchanged by the lieutenants and sergeants. At noon we panted in universal heat. At the end of day, we joggled home, and came to a stop. But the task was not over. The tank guns then had to be cleaned and greased—the seventy-five by pushing a ramrod down its snout—and sometimes a track had to be repaired. While the infantryman returned to barracks, cleaned his rifle, showered, and went his way to chow and a movie, we struggled with our monster, cursing, shoving, sledgehammering.

Hood! It was there we beat the Germans. There, shivering at dawn and sweating at noon, we endured the climates of Africa and pestilent Kwajalein. The iron of which those tanks were made entered our souls. Hood was our university. There we got our real education, which set us off from the men who came before and the men who came after. Sometimes in speaking to older men I have sensed there is a veil between us; and to a man of twenty-five, there are things I cannot explain.

Under certain conditions human nature can be changed into something else. A man can be changed from a political animal into a machine—articulated to climb or leap from a height, to swing a sledgehammer, to dig with a shovel. His instincts can be trained so that with fingers from which all doubt has departed he can pick apart a machine gun under a blanket and assemble it again. Turn men out of their offices, separate them from the flesh of women, and books, and chairs; expose them to the naked sky and set them to drudging at physical tasks, and in a few months you can change the mind itself. Religion, philosophy, mathematics, art, and all the other abstractions, can be blotted out as though they never existed. This is how Ur and Karnak vanished and this is how the Ice Age will return.

For recreation in the evenings I'd take a bus—you couldn't walk the distances—to the main PX, and fill myself with beer and ice cream, and smoke a cigar. Or go to the movies. At that time Hollywood was producing patriotic musical comedies; in the finale, soldiers, sailors, marines, and chorus girls marked time with a hand salute, while Old Glory spread fluttering on the screen.

On our rare two-day passes, we went on desperate expeditions. The nearest settlement, Killeen, was not a town but a street trodden into muck by boot soles, like a cattle wallow. There were no women in Killeen. So we swarmed to towns hundreds of miles away—Fort Worth, or sparkling new, skyscrapered Dallas, or Houston—there, after prowling the streets and parks, once more to enter a theater and gaze at pictures. The aroma of popcorn . . . the slumped shoulders of the soldier snoring in the seat before you . . . then the propulsion once more into the streets, the glare of afternoon, with nothing to do but eat in a greasy restaurant and return to camp . . .

Most accounts of Army life describe a variety of characters, but I do not remember any who were remarkable. My tank crew included a soft-spoken, Southern sergeant; a driver with a rugged build and a face like a boot; and a half-witted fellow named Maniscalco. When I went to town, it was usually with a fat boy from New York named Marvin and a Jersey boy named Bob. Marvin sprinkled his conversation with French words got out of books. We made a rakish threesome in the streets, threatening the virtue of stenographers, but nothing came of it.

All at once, by a stroke of good fortune, Marvin, Bob, and I were taken out of the tanks. The Army had instituted a program of specialized training in order to turn enlisted men into technicians. I applied for language training. When the orders came we were all listed for engineering. I did not quibble; I packed my bags and left.

There is an epilogue to this history of the tanks. Years later in Manhattan, when I was on the subway, I saw the face of Maniscalco, the half-wit of my crew. I asked him what had happened to the company after I left.

"We went overseas," he said. "You was lucky to get out. The tank was hit by a shell. We was all wounded, and the driver was killed."

The specialized training program was a fraction of the sum of waste, the incalculable extravagance of war. Bob, Marvin, and I were sent to Louisiana State University and housed among lawns and flowering shrubs. In the morning we marched to classes, and for an hour in the afternoon we did calisthenics. It must have rapidly become clear that most of the trainees were not qualified to be engineers, yet the program continued while, around half the world, slender battalions, gasping for relief, bore the brunt of the fighting.

We knew how lucky we were and had no qualms about it. In our spare time we loafed around the swimming pool. This easy life, together with heavy army meals, began to make us puffy. Marvin discovered that some of the Louisiana girls spoke a kind of French; his line of French patter struck them as hilarious, and in no time at all we had dates. In the evenings on the banks of the Mississippi I found myself wrestling with a young woman who smelled like a cosmetics counter. These conflicts left me weak, and it was as much as I could do to get out of bed at reveille.

"FIND YOUR OUTFIT"

But, for all I know, Louisiana belles may still be as chaste as Diana, for the training program was scrapped as suddenly as it started, and I was sent off to an infantry division in Missouri. Bob and Marvin were shipped to an armored division; I congratulated myself on having the better luck.

It was the middle of winter. Somehow I got delayed in transit, and when I wandered into the headquarters of my new division, at Fort Leonard Wood, on a freezing December night, I was received with anything but joy.

"Your outfit is out there," said a first sergeant, pointing into the black Missouri woods and hills. "Find it."

Lugging my pack and rifle, I wandered through the night. It was snowing fitfully; here and there, campfires burned. Inquiring the way, at last I arrived at the right company, the right platoon, and the right squad, huddled round a fire in their blankets, with their boots practically in the embers. The squad corporal, a wiry young Italian, seemed possessed by devils. Uttering a stream of obscenity, he showed me a machine gun mounted on a tripod.

"You're the ammo bearer," he said. "Stand guard over that gun. What are you, one of those fuggin ASTP jerks? I don't want any of your fuggin crap!"

I stood over the gun in the cutting wind, with snow driving into my face. The bleak day rose. Men stirred, groaned, and got to their feet. They dragged dry branches to the fire and heated their rations in blackened mess kits. They were like a company of the dead. I had been assigned, it seemed, to the worst fuggin company, of the worst fuggin division, in the Army.

Experience confirmed this impression. The outfit was a kind of factory for turning out infantry replacements who would go overseas. The division itself never hoped to move. On the muddy, snow-covered hills of Missouri, it stumbled to and fro, cursing obscenely. The air had a smell of coal smoke and rusty iron. I stepped along in the files of the damned, carrying ammunition boxes that grew heavy as lead. And behind me, or in front, or to one side, howled the infernal corporal, Fugg.

One day I found my name on the bulletin board; I was to

gather my equipment and present myself at company headquarters. There the captain made a speech, disclaiming all responsibility for our incapacity, saluted with a final downward motion of the arm as though consigning us to hell, and released us from his jurisdiction. We were marched onto a train, and a few days later reached the Atlantic. Carrying our heavy barracks bags over one shoulder, we filed up a ramp, onto the deck of a ship, and groped our way down ladders into the hold. So, at last I went to war.

"Military servitude"—Vigny's phrase—how well it describes life in barracks! Details, drill, inspections, field problems, parades—the way of life of Regular Army men—all this was intolerable.

Action was better. In training you were always anticipating combat; you were oppressed by many anxieties. In action you confronted the worst and could hope for an end of things.

Who is the soldier with my face? He is strangely galvanized.

Holland . . . the churchyard at Veghel . . . We have turned off the road into a churchyard. It seems we are to dig in here, between the gravestones. Not at all conscious of the irony—irony and other defense mechanisms fade under pressure—we begin our excavations. I am about a foot down, when an airburst cracks over our heads and fragments of metal hum by, thwack against the tree trunks, slice into the ground.

In a wink, the company has vanished. We are lying on our faces in a hot passion of burrowing.

The airbursts follow one after the other. It's a trap, and we're caught in it. The Germans must have eighty-eights looking right down our throats.

Someone is shouting, "Medic!"

There's a tap on my left shoulder blade, and something trickles down my back. Blood. I've been hit.

I hear my name being called. It's the sergeant. I crawl out of my hole and approach him, on knees and elbows, cradling my rifle in my arms.

"Go back to Headquarters Section. Tell them that the mortars are out of ammunition."

I get to my feet and run crouching between the graves. I'm aware of explosions all around and a humming of jagged iron. But I have a strange feeling of joy. I've been tagged already—I'm safe. But, more than this, I'm exhilarated at the prospect of doing something.

I get to Headquarters, and find the first sergeant kneeling over cloverleaf containers of mortar shells.

"Take these up," he says.

A container under each arm, my rifle slung over my shoulder, I begin the return journey. More airbursts. Bullets are flying too, but I don't hear them.

I get to the mortars, and let the containers down into the hands of the crew. They look grateful. I start back for more.

And now I've lost count of the trips. As I run I feel like a broken-field runner on his lucky day.

Edith Sitwell

LULLABY

Though the world has slipped and gone.
Sounds my loud discordant cry
Like the steel birds' song on high:
"Still one thing is left—the Bone!"
Then out danced the Babioun.

She sat in the hollow of the sea—
A socket whence the eye's put out—
She sang to the child a lullaby
(The steel birds' nest was thereabout).

"Do, do, do, do—
Thy mother's hied to the vaster race:
The Pterodactyl made its nest
And laid a steel egg in her breast—
Under the Judas-coloured sun.
She'll work no more, no dance, nor moan,
And I am come to take her place
Do, do.

There's nothing left but earth's low bed—
(The Pterodactyl fouls its nest):
But steel wings fan thee to thy rest,
And wingless truth and larvae lie
And eyeless hope and handless fear—
All these for thee as toys are spread,
Do—do—

Red is the bed of Poland, Spain,
And thy mother's breast, who has grown wise
In that fouled nest. If she could rise,
Give birth again,

In wolfish pelt she'd hide thy bones
To shield thee from the world's long cold,
And down on all fours shouldst thou crawl
For thus from no height canst thou fall—
Do, do.

She'd give no hands: there's naught to hold,
And naught to make: there's dust to sift,
But no food for the hands to lift.
Do, do.

Heed my ragged lullaby,
Fear not living, fear not chance;
All is equal—blindness, sight,
There is no depth, there is no height:
Do, do,

The Judas-coloured sun is gone,
And with the Ape thou art alone—
Do,
    Do."

Robert Southey

AFTER BLENHEIM

It was a summer evening,
  Old Kaspar's work was done,
And he before his cottage door
  Was sitting in the sun;
And by him sported on the green
His little grandchild Wilhelmine.

She saw her brother Peterkin
  Roll something large and round
Which he beside the rivulet
  In playing there had found;
He came to ask what he had found
That was so large and smooth and round.

Old Kaspar took it from the boy
  Who stood expectant by;
And then the old man shook his head,
  And with a natural sigh
' 'Tis some poor fellow's skull,' said he;
'Who fell in the great victory.

'I find them in the garden,
  For there's many here about;
And often when I go to plough
  The ploughshare turns them out.
For many thousand men,' said he,
'Were slain in that great victory.'

'Now tell us what 'twas all about,'
  Young Peterkin he cries;
And little Wilhelmine looks up
  With wonder-waiting eyes;
'Now tell us all about the war,
And what they fought each other for.'

'It was the English,' Kaspar cried,
  'Who put the French to rout;
But what they fought each other for
  I could not well make out.
But everybody said,' quoth he,
'That 'twas a famous victory.

'My father lived at Blenheim then,
  Yon little stream hard by;
They burnt his dwelling to the ground,
  And he was forced to fly:
So with his wife and child he fled,
Nor had he where to rest his head.

'With fire and sword the country round
  Was wasted far and wide,
And many a childing mother then
  And new-born baby died:
But things like that, you know, must be
At every famous victory.

'They say it was a shocking sight
  After the field was won;
For many thousand bodies here
  Lay rotting in the sun:
But things like that, you know, must be
After a famous victory.

'Great praise the Duke of Marlbro' won
  And our good Prince Eugene;'
'Why, 'twas a very wicked thing!'
  Said little Wilhelmine;
'Nay . . . nay . . . my little girl,' quoth he,
'It was a famous victory.

'And everybody praised the Duke
  Who this great fight did win.'
'But what good came of it at last?'
  Quoth little Peterkin:—
'Why, that I cannot tell,' said he,
'But 'twas a famous victory!'

Theodore Spencer

THE INFLATABLE GLOBE

When the allegorical man came calling,
He told us all he would show us a trick,
And he showed us a flat but inflatable ball.
'Look at this ball,' he told us all;
'Look at the lines marked out on this ball.'
We looked at the ball and the lines on the ball:
England was red, and France was blue;
Germany orange and Russia brown:
'Look at this ball,' he told us all,
'With a blow of my breath I inflate this ball.'
He blew, and it bounced, and bouncing, falling,
He bounced it against the wall with a kick.
'But without my breath it will flatten and fall,'
Said the allegorical man; and down
Flat came his hand and squashed the ball,
And it fell on the floor with no life at all
Once his breath had gone out of the ball . . .
It seemed to us all a stupid trick.

THE WAR GOD

Why cannot the one good
Benevolent feasible
Final dove descend?

And the wheat be divided?
And the soldiers sent home?
And the barriers torn down?
And the enemies forgiven?
And there be no retribution?

Because the conqueror
Is an instrument of power,
With merciless heart hammered
Out of former fear,
When to-day's vanquished
Destroyed his noble father,
Filling his cradle with anguish.

His irremediable victory
Chokes back sobbing anxiety
Lest children of the slain
(When the ripe ears grow high
To the sickles of his own
And the sun goes down)
Rise in iron morning
To stain with blood the sky
And avenge their fathers again.

His heart broke before
His raging splendour.
The virgins of prayer

Fumble vainly for that day
Buried under ruins,
Of his pride's greatest murder
When his heart which was a child
Asking and tender,
He hunted and killed.

The lost filled with lead
On the helpless field
May dream the pious reason
Of mercy, but also
Their eyes know what they did
In their own proud season,
Their dead teeth bite the earth
With semen of new hatred.

For the world is the world
And not the slain
Nor the slayer, forgive,
Nor do wild shores
Of passionate histories
Close on endless love;
Though hidden under seas
Of chafing despair,
Love's need does not cease.

Gertrude Stein

I WAS TALKING

I was talking to a woman the other day we were both walking carrying our baskets and intending to bring home something, and she told me of her two brothers and her husband who had all three escaped before the prisoners were taken to Germany, she said some families suffered so much and some not at all, she said it was fate. She herself had five children four of them girls. That too does happen very frequently in this country we both agreed. And then we got talking about the strange thing, that so many of the comparatively few Frenchmen killed in this war were only sons of widows whose husbands had fallen in the last war. Why I said. Well she said, it is probably because they went into the war more worried than those whose fathers had not been killed in the last war. It could be that. And she said might it not be that being raised by a widow they would naturally be more spoilt and not so active as those raised by father and mother. Naturally she said, a mother can never really dominate a son, a mother is bound to spoil children because she is with them all the time and she cannot always be saying no so she ends up by not saying no at all. And besides she said, if a mother had lost her husband in the war her little boy had been impressed by her crying so much and that would make him nervous, when he too had gone to war. It certainly is true that a very considerable percentage of the relatively few Frenchmen killed in this war were the only sons of widowed mothers who had had their husbands killed in the last war.

To-night Francis Malherbe who had been sent to Germany to work came to see us just back and very interesting, January nineteenth forty-four. One of the things he said was that in Paris he had come home that way they all said that there would be a landing on the twentieth of January. Of course everybody supposed it was going to be in France, and at the same time we had word that the man who always knows what the Germans expect to happen said that there was to be a landing between the sixteenth and the twentieth of January forty-four and he always knows what they know and so we were quite excited and there was a landing only it was in Italy instead of in France. Pretty good deception that, because and that must never be forgotten people do know what is going to happen and so far the Americans have been pretty good at it, twice we have known it was going to happen and the right date and everything but not the right place. We are very pleased with our countrymen, it is a good poker game. Very good indeed and we like them to play poker well. It pleases us.

However that was not all that Francis Malherbe told us. He described Germany the way it is now and the way the French who are compulsorily working there are. He gave such a good description, he said of course there was no food no fat, and the cooking of vegetables always in water, the German workmen were given fats but not the Frenchmen, but I said is there no black market no way of getting any, oh yes he said plenty of that among all the foreign workmen but never with the Germans, but I said where do the foreign workmen get it, how do they get it, they steal it, he said, each one who can steals a certain quantity of something and sells it or trades it with others for something else, and that is all the black market there is but and he laughed it is considerable, and we said how do they the Germans feel, still convinced of victory especially the young, he said but why should they not the world is made for the young, the fifteen year old boys have older men get up in the street cars to give them seats, naturally they are convinced that they will win, if you have such a position in the world as that at fifteen of course you are bound to win. And really we said really he said they certainly can hold out six months longer, certainly. My brother he said he is a military prisoner a lieutenant, and as I was what they call the man of trust, that is to say I had to judge and patch up the incessant quarrels between French and German workers they gave me leave to go and see my brother. He had been a prisoner for four years and of course I had not seen him and now I saw him. He came in with two soldiers with guns and fixed bayonets at his back and it upset me so I began to cry but he said to me sternly control yourself do not show emotion, and we sat down at a table together and we talked and we compared photographs those he had of the family and those I had with me, and the adjutant who was there to listen to us said suddenly he is giving you photographs, how dare you said my brother accuse me of such a thing, apologise I insist that you apologise, first examine these photographs and then apologise, and the man said but it is all right, no said my brother look, look at them count them and examine them and then apologise, which the adjutant had to do. I was proud of my brother. When he told us this we were of course much moved, it was so real so normal, like a piece out of Dumas and yet happening, happening to a boy we knew very well and are very fond of, and then he went on describing, and telling about the different nationalities with which he was working and making it all real and the Russians he said, they are the most interesting, we Frenchmen get along better with them than with any others except Frenchmen, and they do impress us with their courage and their tenacity and the simple way they say naturally we expect to occupy this country and when we do and we think we will, we will make them very unhappy. And so he talked on and then he had to leave and he has to go back and he has to go back because he has two officer brothers as prisoners and something might happen to them if he did not and so he will go back. We hope to have him back again we are very very fond of him. He is a nice neighbor.

These days everybody hears from their sons or their nephews who are working there, one who really was too small and too weak to go but go he did, his father had been in the navy and then had been in a garage as electrician and we had liked him and when the French were defeated the shock killed him he could not believe it and this only son writes to his mother dear mother I am hungry, I was never hungry before but I am hungry now always hungry so hungry. And then there is a nephew of some one here we know he is an intelligent fellow a designer of machines, and he writes that he is in the capital and that the sky is sad, it is a cold sad sky, and he he plays the violin and draws a little and hopes not very much but a little as most of his compatriots have been killed in a bombardment, and so every day is another day which passes in that way.

Yesterday I went my usual twelve kilometers to get some bread and cake and I met three or four who were on a farm wagon being drawn by a mule and they said come and sit, and I said can the mule stand one more, why not they said and I sat it was very comfortable. Basket the white poodle was completely upset but finally he decided to follow along and we jogged along and it was a pleasant day although it was January and I said you know you French people you can make a pleasant thing out of anything, but we are not rich like the Americans no I said but you can go on working the kind of working you do until you are ninety or a hundred and you complain but any day is a pleasant enough day which it is not in every other country, and they said perhaps but they would like to be rich like the Americans and then we were on the top of the hill and I went to get my bread and cake and they went on to get their flour and it was a pleasant day.

The young ones who come back from Germany on leave are puzzled by one thing, any Frenchman would be why are the Germans so sentimental, when they are what they are why are they so sentimental. No Frenchman can understand that.

Yesterday I was out walking and I met a man I used to know, a casual country acquaintance, that is to say he and his family were cousins of some very old friends of ours, and they own a place around here, they used to be here for only a few weeks in the summer but now, things being as they are, they live here altogether. The father is a big gay man about town, who has lots of property is a good business man and used to spend all his life between here and other places and the Cote d'Azur. His wife was born in Washington U.S.A. her father having been in the French embassy and he is an amusing man, of course he says we live here now, the country is lovely in winter, I never saw it before but it is, it is like English pastels such a delicate color, and besides we all get all we want to eat, dont you, and I agreed that we did, as much of everything that we want, butter eggs meat cake and cheese, and I had to agree that we all did because we all do. Just why we do now when the years before we did not nobody seems to be able to ex-

plain but we do, is it because the army of occupation is
getting smaller and smaller or is it, that everybody knows
how now better and better, anyway it is undoubtedly true
everywhere in France now, everywhere and nobody seems
to know quite why. Well anyway, the other day I met him
M. Labadie, he saw Basket and he waited for us he was
on his bicycle and I was on foot, and we stopped to talk
together. I thought he had very funny clothes on and when
I came nearer I said to him these are funny clothes that
you are wearing what are they. Ah he said you would never
guess look at the buttons and I did, they were large American army buttons with the eagle and the shield, nice brass
buttons on a khaki coat and I said when in the name of
wonder did you get that. Ah he said I bought it after the
other war from the American stocks and I kept it here in
the country and now it is very handy, and it was, some
German soldiers on patrol had just passed but M. Labadie
did not mind that, you know he said everybody wants to
buy one off me, look he said counting them there are
twelve of them, quite a little fortune, just to-day again they
offered me forty francs for one, but not I, I keep them and
wear them. Well we went on talking and I said your boy
who is twenty-one, has he gone, oh dear no, he said, you
see I keep him traveling, that is the way you do you either
go off to some little bit of a place and stay there quietly
and nobody bothers you or you keep moving, now I keep
my boy moving, I have lots of business to attend to, and
I send him around to attend to it, and if you keep on traveling for business your papers all always have to be in order
which of course they are so no one bothers, that is the
way he said, and of course he is right that is the way. And
then we went on talking. We talked about the war, why
not since there is this war. He said of course the Germans
cannot win, which is natural enough because their country
is so poor they know nothing about cooking and eating,
people who know nothing about cooking and eating naturally cannot win. He went on reflectively, France always seems
to be beaten but really a country that can see and shut
one eye and then shut the other eye opening the first eye,
is bound to come out of any mess not too badly, you see
he went on meditatively, one must take care of oneself and
be brave and be excited and at the same time must take

care of one's business must not be poor. War said he is inevitably connected with money and naturally when two people want the same money or more money they must fight, and he said reflectively nowadays when one wants to spend so much money when everybody wants automobiles and electrical installations and everything else well naturally the more money everybody wants to spend the more men have to be killed when it comes to a war. People who spend little money when they make war kill few people, but the more money you want to spend, the more men you have to kill when you begin to go to war. And there is another thing if you can really spend the most money then you have less of your own men killed than the other side who wants to spend more money but has not got it to spend. And so America has less men killed and Germany more and that he said is natural enough. And just then another man whom we both knew was coming along, now said M. Labadie he is a poor thing an unfortunate man, he has a wife but one never sees her she is always away and a forsaken man and he shrugged his shoulders and we each of us went on our way.

To-day was another day, as usual in France feeling gets more and more complicated, and now when those who have taken to the hills come down and take food off the railways, well will it get them in the habit of stealing and should it, and they all worry, and there was one woman who was visiting and she quarreled with every one in Culoz, and when she left she said they needed the Germans to come to whip them into subjugation, and some one said and she an idler who has money what does she think will happen to her. Well anyway one thing is certain every day brings the war nearer and nearer to an ending but does any one around here believe that, certainly not, so little do they believe it that although we know it we do not really believe it ourselves. As one woman said well now as we have all made all our arrangements to live in a state of war I suppose the war will go on. We all suppose it will and it does this the first day of February in nineteen forty-four.

I have just been listening to a description of how the mountain boys captured two Germans and took them to the mountains as hostages and now the Germans even when they want to buy a piece of bread in a store they are all

armed and always at least six of them and one standing outside as a guard for them. It makes everybody laugh. Every
tenth birthday makes a man afraid and a woman too and
even children every tenth birthday does that. Be careful
everybody.

Everybody is feeling a little more cheerful about everything to-day even though it is a dark and gloomy day.

Breathes there a man with soul so dead who never to
himself has said, this is my own my native land.

Well yes, yesterday when the Swiss radio announced that
the Americans had landed on the Marshall Islands and that
these islands had belonged to Japan before the war I was
so pleased. It was midnight and I was so pleased. As an
American and as a Californian I was so pleased. I went up
stairs and woke up Alice Toklas who was asleep, and I
said we have landed the Americans have landed on the
Marshall Islands, which before the war belonged to Japan
and Alice Toklas opened one eye slightly and said, well
then they are invaded, and slept gently again. Of course
that is what every one wants them to be that they are
invaded, when that does come to pass it will be a comfort to every one, yes every one but them and they do not
want at least their feelings are of no account no account.
So that made this day a nice day. Otherwise not such a
nice day because they are trying to take younger and younger
men away to work but mostly they do not go this is undoubtedly so.

Wallace Stevens

THE DEATH OF A SOLDIER

Life contracts and death is expected,
As in a season of autumn.
The soldier falls.

He does not become a three-days personage,
Imposing his separation,
Calling for pomp.

Death is absolute and without memorial,
As in a season of autumn,
When the wind stops,

When the wind stops and, over the heavens,
The clouds go, nevertheless,
In their direction.

Jonathan Swift

A SATIRICAL ELEGY
ON THE DEATH OF A LATE FAMOUS GENERAL

His Grace! impossible! what, dead!
Of old age too, and in his bed!
And could that Mighty Warrior fall?
And so inglorious, after all!
Well, since he's gone, no matter how,
The last loud trump must wake him now:
And, trust me, as the noise grows stronger,
He'd wish to sleep a little longer.
And could he be indeed so old
As by the news-papers we're told?
Threescore, I think, is pretty high;
'Twas time in conscience he should die.
This world he cumber'd long enough;
He burnt his candle to the snuff;
And that's the reason, some folks think,
He left behind *so great a s - - - k.*
Behold his funeral appears,
Nor widow's sighs, nor orphan's tears,
Wont at such times each heart to pierce,
Attend the progress of his herse.
But what of that, his friends may say,
He had those honours in his day.
True to his profit and his pride,
He made them weep before he dy'd.

Come hither, all ye empty things,
Ye bubbles rais'd by breath of Kings;
Who float upon the tide of state,
Come hither, and behold your fate.
Let pride be taught by this rebuke,
How very mean a thing's a Duke;
From all his ill-got honours flung,
Turn'd to that dirt from whence he sprung.

Alfred, Lord Tennyson

LINES FROM "LOCKSLEY HALL"

For I dipt into the future, far as human eye could see,
Saw the Vision of the world, and all the wonder that would be;
Saw the heavens fill with commerce, argosies of magic sails,
Pilots of the purple twilight, dropping down with costly bales;
Heard the heavens fill with shouting, and there rain'd a ghastly dew
From the nations' airy navies grappling in the central blue;
Far along the world-wide whisper of the south-wind rushing warm,
With the standards of the peoples plunging thro' the thunder storm;
Till the war-drum throbb'd no longer, and the battle flags were furl'd
In the Parliament of man, the Federation of the world.
There the common sense of most shall hold a fretful realm in awe,
And the kindly earth shall slumber, lapt in universal law.

Dylan Thomas

A REFUSAL TO MOURN THE DEATH, BY FIRE, OF A CHILD IN LONDON

Never until the mankind making
Bird beast and flower
Fathering and all humbling darkness
Tells with silence the last light breaking
And the still hour
Is come of the sea tumbling in harness

And I must enter again the round
Zion of the water bead
And the synagogue of the ear of corn
Shall I let pray the shadow of a sound
Or sow my salt seed
In the least valley of sackcloth to mourn

The majesty and burning of the child's death.
I shall not murder
The mankind of her going with a grave truth
Nor blaspheme down the stations of the breath
With any further
Elegy of innocence and youth

Deep with the first dead lies London's daughter,
Robed in the long friends,
The grains beyond age, the dark veins of her mother
Secret by the unmourning water
Of the riding Thames.
After the first death, there is no other.

Henry David Thoreau

BATTLE OF ANTS

From "Brute Neighbors"

I was witness to events of a less peaceful character. One day when I went out to my wood-pile, or rather my pile of stumps, I observed two large ants, the one red, the other much larger, nearly half an inch long, and black, fiercely contending with one another. Having once got hold they never let go, but struggled and wrestled and rolled on the chips incessantly. Looking farther, I was surprised to find that the chips were covered with such combatants, that it was not a *duellum,* but a *bellum,* a war between two races of ants, the red always pitted against the black, and frequently two red ones to one black. The legions of these Myrmidons covered all the hills and vales in my wood-yard, and the ground was already strewn with the dead and dying, both red and black. It was the only battle which I have ever witnessed, the only battle-field I ever trod while the battle was raging; internecine war; the red republicans on the one hand, and the black imperialists on the other. On every side they were engaged in the deadly combat, yet without any noise that I could hear, and human soldiers never fought so resolutely. I watched a couple that were fast locked in each other's embraces, in a little sunny valley amid the chips, now at noon-day prepared to fight till the sun went down, or life went out. The smaller red champion had fastened himself like a vice to his adversary's front, and through all the tumblings on that field never for an instant ceased to gnaw at one of his feelers near the root, having already caused the other to go by the board; while the stronger black one dashed him from side to side, and, as I saw on looking nearer, had already divested him of several of his members. They fought with more pertinacity than bull-dogs.

Neither manifested the least disposition to retreat. It was evident that their battle-cry was Conquer or die. In the mean while there came along a single red ant on the hill-side of this valley, evidently full of excitement, who either had despatched his foe, or had not yet taken part in the battle; probably the latter, for he had lost none of his limbs; whose mother had charged him to return with his shield or upon it. Or perchance he was some Achilles, who had nourished his wrath apart, and had now come to avenge or rescue his Patroclus. He saw this unequal combat from afar,—for the blacks were nearly twice the size of the red,—he drew near with rapid pace till he stood on his guard within half an inch of the combatants; then watching his opportunity, he sprang upon the black warrior, and commenced his operations near the root of his right fore-leg, leaving the foe to select among his own members; and so there were three united for life, as if a new kind of attraction had been invented which put all other locks and cements to shame. I should not have wondered by this time to find that they had their respective musical bands stationed on some eminent chip, and playing their national airs the while, to excite the slow and cheer the dying combatants. I was myself excited somewhat even as if they had been men. The more you think of it, the less the difference. And certainly there is not the fight recorded in Concord history, at least, if in the history of America, that will bear a moment's comparison with this, whether for the numbers engaged in it, or for the patriotism and heroism displayed. For numbers and for carnage it was an Austerlitz or Dresden. Concord Fight! Two killed on the patriots' side, and Luther Blanchard wounded! Why here every ant was a Buttrick,—"Fire! for God's sake fire!"—and thousands shared the fate of Davis and Hosmer. There was not one hireling there. I have no doubt that it was a principle they fought for, as much as our ancestors, and not to avoid a three-penny tax on their tea; and the results of this battle will be as important and memorable to those whom it concerns as those of the battle of Bunker Hill, at least.

I took up the chip on which the three I have particularly described were struggling, carried it into my house, and placed it under a tumbler on my window-sill, in order to see the issue. Holding a microscope to the first-mentioned red ant, I saw that, though he was assiduously gnawing at the near fore-leg of his enemy, having severed his remaining feeler, his own breast was all torn away, exposing what vitals he had there to the jaws of the black warrior, whose breast-plate was apparently too thick for him to pierce; and the dark carbuncles of the sufferer's eyes shone with ferocity such as war only could excite. They struggled half an hour longer under the tumbler, and when I looked again the black soldier had severed the heads of his foes from their bodies, and the still living heads were hanging on either side of him like ghastly trophies at his saddle-bow, still apparently as firmly fastened as ever, and he was endeavoring with feeble struggles, being without feelers and with only the remnant of a leg, and I know not how many other wounds, to divest himself of them; which at length, after half an hour more, he accomplished. I raised the glass, and he went off over the window-sill in that crippled state. Whether he finally survived that combat, and spent the remainder of his days in some Hotel des Invalides, I do not know; but I thought that his industry would not be worth much thereafter. I never learned which party was victorious, nor the cause of the war; but I felt for the rest of that day as if I had had my feelings excited and harrowed by witnessing the struggle, the ferocity and carnage, of a human battle before my door.

James Thurber

THE LAST FLOWER

A PARABLE IN PICTURES

FOR ROSEMARY

*IN THE WISTFUL HOPE THAT HER WORLD
WILL BE BETTER THAN MINE*

WORLD WAR XII, AS EVERYBODY KNOWS,

BROUGHT ABOUT THE COLLAPSE OF CIVILIZATION

TOWNS, CITIES, AND VILLAGES DISAPPEARED FROM THE EARTH

ALL THE GROVES AND FORESTS WERE DESTROYED

AND ALL THE GARDENS

AND ALL THE WORKS OF ART

MEN, WOMEN, AND CHILDREN BECAME LOWER THAN THE LOWER ANIMALS

DISCOURAGED AND DISILLUSIONED, DOGS DESERTED THEIR FALLEN MASTERS

EMBOLDENED BY THE PITIFUL CONDITION
OF THE FORMER LORDS OF THE EARTH,
RABBITS DESCENDED UPON THEM

BOOKS, PAINTINGS, AND MUSIC DISAPPEARED
FROM THE EARTH, AND HUMAN BEINGS
JUST SAT AROUND, DOING NOTHING

YEARS AND YEARS WENT BY

EVEN THE FEW GENERALS WHO WERE LEFT
FORGOT WHAT THE LAST WAR HAD DECIDED

BOYS AND GIRLS GREW UP TO STARE AT EACH OTHER
BLANKLY, FOR LOVE HAD PASSED FROM THE EARTH

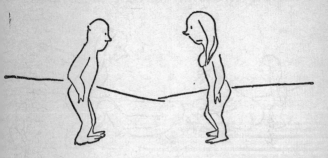

ONE DAY A YOUNG GIRL WHO HAD NEVER
SEEN A FLOWER CHANCED TO COME
UPON THE LAST ONE IN THE WORLD

SHE TOLD THE OTHER HUMAN BEINGS
THAT THE LAST FLOWER WAS DYING

THE ONLY ONE WHO PAID ANY ATTENTION
TO HER WAS A YOUNG MAN SHE
FOUND WANDERING ABOUT

TOGETHER THE YOUNG MAN AND THE GIRL
NURTURED THE FLOWER AND IT BEGAN
TO LIVE AGAIN

ONE DAY A BEE VISITED THE FLOWER,
AND A HUMMINGBIRD

BEFORE LONG THERE WERE TWO FLOWERS, AND
THEN FOUR, AND THEN A GREAT MANY

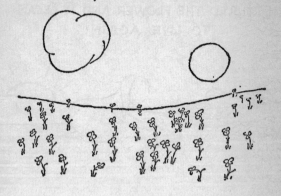

GROVES AND FORESTS FLOURISHED AGAIN

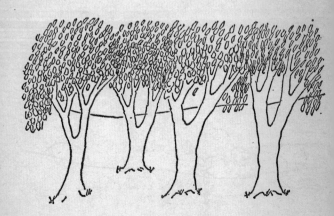

THE YOUNG GIRL BEGAN TO TAKE AN INTEREST IN HOW SHE LOOKED

THE YOUNG MAN DISCOVERED THAT TOUCHING THE GIRL WAS PLEASURABLE

LOVE WAS REBORN INTO THE WORLD

THEIR CHILDREN GREW UP STRONG AND HEALTHY
AND LEARNED TO RUN AND LAUGH

DOGS CAME OUT OF THEIR EXILE

THE YOUNG MAN DISCOVERED, BY PUTTING ONE STONE UPON ANOTHER, HOW TO BUILD A SHELTER

PRETTY SOON EVERYBODY WAS BUILDING SHELTERS

TOWNS, CITIES, AND VILLAGES SPRANG UP

SONG CAME BACK INTO THE WORLD

AND TROUBADOURS AND JUGGLERS

AND TAILORS AND COBBLERS

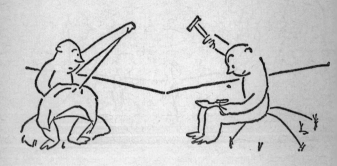

AND PAINTERS AND POETS

AND SCULPTORS AND WHEELWRIGHTS

AND SOLDIERS

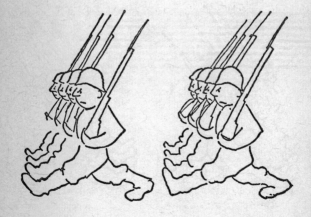

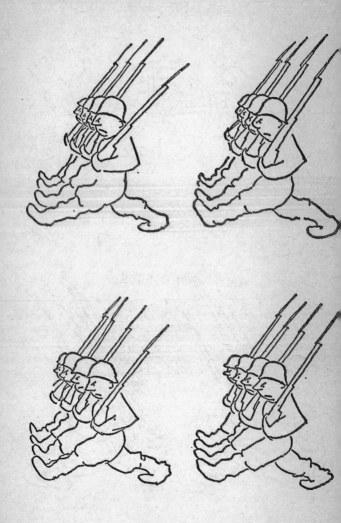

266

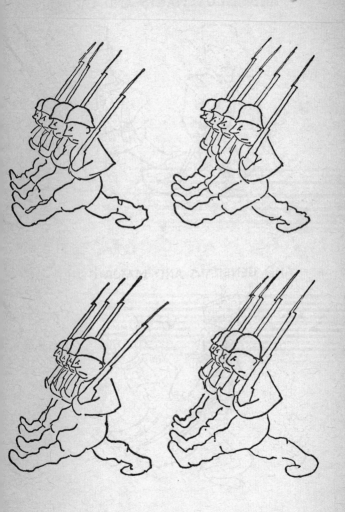

267

AND LIEUTENANTS AND CAPTAINS

AND GENERALS AND MAJOR-GENERALS

AND LIBERATORS

SOME PEOPLE WENT ONE PLACE TO LIVE, AND SOME ANOTHER

BEFORE LONG, THOSE WHO WENT TO LIVE IN THE VALLEYS
WISHED THEY HAD GONE TO LIVE IN THE HILLS

AND THOSE WHO HAD GONE TO LIVE IN THE HILLS
WISHED THEY HAD GONE TO LIVE IN THE VALLEYS

THE LIBERATORS, UNDER THE GUIDANCE OF GOD, SET FIRE TO THE DISCONTENT

SO PRESENTLY THE WORLD WAS AT WAR AGAIN

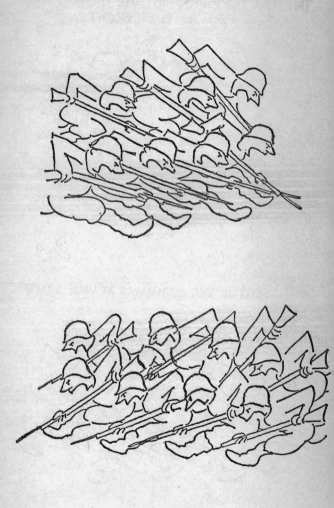

THAT NOTHING AT ALL WAS LEFT IN THE WORLD

EXCEPT ONE MAN

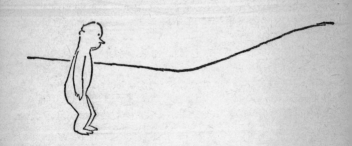

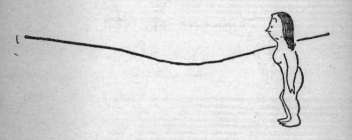

AND ONE FLOWER

Leo Tolstoy

ADVICE TO A DRAFTEE

The letter by Leo Tolstoy dramatizes the frequent fact that what is past is prologue. Written in 1899 to a desperate young candidate for conscription, Tolstoy's words will seem to some to bear a relevance to America today. In conjunction we publish on page 294 a carefully reasoned examination of civil disobedience from a federal judge directly confronted with the issue today.

Count Tolstoy's letter was addressed to a young Hessian named Ernst Schramm, whose earlier correspondence with the great writer has been lost; Schramm evidently wrote a second time in an effort to evade Tolstoy's argument that he refuse conscription. The letter printed here is Tolstoy's response to Schramm's second letter, and it seems to have terminated the exchange. In reading Tolstoy's words against killing, one should bear in mind that both parties understood that the Hessian army in 1899 was a peacetime army, but that the penalty for evading conscription was death. Tolstoy addressed the letter to Schramm in Darmstadt, and the Hessian post office forwarded it to Aschaffenburg in Bavaria, leaving us to infer that Schramm decided not to join up but to change countries instead.

In my last letter I answered your question as well as I could. It is not only Christians but all just people who must refuse to become soldiers—that is, to be ready on another's command (for this is what a soldier's duty actually consists of) to kill all those one is ordered to kill. The question as you state it—which is more useful, to become a good teacher or to suffer for rejecting conscription?—is falsely stated. The question is falsely stated because it is wrong for us to determine our actions according to their results, to view actions merely as useful or destructive. In the choice of our actions we can be led by their advantages or disadvantages only when the actions themselves are not opposed to the demands of morality.

We can stay home, go abroad, or concern ourselves with farming or science according to what we find useful for ourselves or others; for neither in domestic life, foreign travel, farming, nor science is there anything immoral. But under no circumstance can we inflict violence on people, torture or kill them because we think such acts could be of use to us or to others. We cannot and may not do such things, especially because we can never be sure of the results of our actions. Often actions which seem the most advantageous of all turn out in fact to be destructive; and the reverse is also true.

The question should not be stated: which is more useful, to be a good teacher or to go to jail for refusing conscription? but rather: what should a man do who has been called upon for military service—that is, called upon to kill or to prepare himself to kill?

And to this question, for a person who understands the true meaning of military service and who wants to be moral, there is only one clear and incontrovertible answer: such a person must refuse to take part in military service no matter what consequences this refusal may have. It may seem to us that this refusal could be futile or even harmful, and that it would be a far more useful thing, after serving one's time, to become a good village teacher. But in the same way, Christ could have judged it more useful for himself to be a good carpenter and submit to all the principles of the Pharisees than to die in obscurity as he did, repudiated and forgotten by everyone.

Moral acts are distinguished from all other acts by the fact that they operate independently of any predictable advantage to ourselves or to others. No matter how dangerous the situation may be of a man who finds himself in the power of robbers who demand that he take part in plundering, murder, and rape, a moral person cannot take part. Is not military service the same thing? Is one not required to agree to the deaths of all those one is commanded to kill?

But how can one refuse to do what everyone does, what everyone finds unavoidable and necessary? Or, must one do what no one does and what everyone considers unnecessary or even stupid and bad? No matter how strange it sounds, this strange argument is the main one offered against those moral acts which in our times face you and every other person called up for military service. But this argument is even more incorrect than the one which would make a moral action dependent upon considerations of advantage.

If I, finding myself in a crowd of running people, run with the crowd without knowing where, it is obvious that I have given myself up to mass hysteria; but if by chance I should push my way to the front, or be gifted with sharper sight than the others, or receive information that this crowd was racing to attack human beings and toward its own corruption, would I really not stop and tell the people what might rescue them? Would I go on running and do these things which I knew to be bad and corrupt? This is the situation of every individual called up for military service, if he knows what military service means.

I can well understand that you, a young man full of life, loving and loved by your mother, friends, perhaps a young woman, think with a natural terror about what awaits you if you refuse conscription; and perhaps you will not feel strong enough to bear the consequences of refusal, and knowing your weakness, will submit and become a soldier. I understand completely, and I do not for a moment allow myself to blame you, knowing very well that in your place I might perhaps do the same thing. Only do not say that you did it because it was useful or because everyone does it. If you did it, know that you did wrong.

In every person's life there are moments in which he can know himself, tell himself who he is, whether he is a man who values his human dignity above his life or a weak creature who does not know his dignity and is concerned merely with being useful (chiefly to himself). This is the situation of a man who goes out to defend his honor in a duel or a soldier who goes into battle (although here the concepts of life are wrong). It is the situation of a doctor or a priest called to someone sick with plague, of a man in a burning house or a sinking ship who must decide whether to let the weaker go first or shove them aside and save himself. It is the situation of a man in poverty who accepts or rejects a bribe. And in our times, it is the situation of a man called to military service. For a man who knows its significance, the call to the army is perhaps the only opportunity for him to behave as a morally free creature and fulfill the highest requirement of his life—or else merely to keep his advantage in sight like an animal and thus remain slavishly submissive and servile until humanity becomes degraded and stupid.

For these reasons I answered your question whether one has to refuse to do military service with a categorical "yes" —if you understand the meaning of military service (and if you did not understand it then, you do now) and if you want to behave as a moral person living in our times must.

Please excuse me if these words are harsh. The subject is so important that one cannot be careful enough in expressing oneself so as to avoid false interpretation.

April 7, 1899   LEO TOLSTOY

Translated by Rodney Dennis

Walt Whitman

BEAT! BEAT! DRUMS!

Beat! beat! drums!—blow! bugles! blow!
Through the windows—through doors—burst like a ruth-
    less force,
Into the solemn church, and scatter the congregation,
Into the school where the scholar is studying;
Leave not the bridegroom quiet—no happiness must he have
    now with his bride,
Nor the peaceful farmer any peace, ploughing his field or
    gathering his grain,
So fierce you whirr and pound you drums—so shrill you
    bugles blow.

Beat! beat! drums!—blow! bugles! blow!
Over the traffic of cities—over the rumble of wheels in the
    streets;
Are beds procured for sleepers at night in the houses? no
    sleepers must sleep in those beds,
No bargainers' bargains by day—no brokers or speculators
    —would they continue?
Would the talkers be talking? would the singer attempt to
    sing?
Would the lawyer rise in the court to state his case before
    the judge?
Then rattle quicker, heavier drums—you bugles wilder blow.

Beat! beat! drums!—blow! bugles! blow!
Make no parley—stop for no expostulation,
Mind not the timid—mind not the weeper or prayer,
Mind not the old man beseeching the young man,
Let not the child's voice be heard, nor the mother's en-
    treaties,

Make even the trestles to shake the dead where they lie
    awaiting the hearses,
So strong you thump O terrible drums—so loud you bugles
    blow.

VIGIL STRANGE I KEPT ON THE FIELD ONE NIGHT

Vigil strange I kept on the field one night;
When you my son and my comrade dropt at my side that day,
One look I but gave which your dear eyes return'd with a
    look I shall never forget,
One touch of your hand to mine O boy, reach'd up as you
    lay on the ground,
Then onward I sped in the battle, the even-contested battle,
Till late in the night reliev'd to the place at last again I made
    my way,
Found you in death so cold dear comrade, found your body
    son of responding kisses, (never again on earth respond-
    ing,)
Bared your face in the starlight, curious the scene, cool
    blew the moderate night-wind,
Long there and then in vigil I stood, dimly around me the
    battlefield spreading,
Vigil wondrous and vigil sweet there in the fragrant silent
    night,
But not a tear fell, not even a long-drawn sigh, long, long
    I gazed,
Then on the earth partially reclining sat by your side lean-
    ing my chin in my hands,
Passing sweet hours, immortal and mystic hours with you
    dearest comrade—not a tear, not a word,
Vigil of silence, love and death, vigil for you my son and
    my soldier,
As onward silently stars aloft, eastward new ones upward
    stole,
Vigil final for you brave boy, (I could not save you, swift
    was your death,
I faithfully loved you and cared for you living, I think we
    shall surely meet again,)

Till at latest lingering of the night, indeed just as the dawn
    appear'd,
My comrade I wrapt in his blanket, envelop'd well his form,
Folded the blanket well, tucking it carefully over head and
    carefully under feet,
And there and then and bathed by the rising sun, my son in
    his grave, in his rude-dug grave I deposited,
Ending my vigil strange with that, vigil of night and battle-
    field dim,
Vigil for boy of responding kisses, (never again on earth
    responding,)
Vigil for comrade swiftly slain, vigil I never forget, how as
    day brighten'd,
I rose from the chill ground and folded my soldier well in
    his blanket,
And buried him where he fell.

AS TOILSOME I WANDER'D VIRGINIA'S WOODS

As toilsome I wander'd Virginia's woods,
To the music of rustling leaves kick'd by my feet, (for 'twas
    autumn,)
I mark'd at the foot of a tree the grave of a soldier;
Mortally wounded he and buried on the retreat, (easily all
    could I understand,)
The halt of a mid-day hour, when up! no time to lose—yet
    this sign left,
On a tablet scrawl'd and nail'd on the tree by the grave,
Bold, cautious, true, and my loving comrade.

Long, long I muse, then on my way go wandering,
Many a changeful season to follow, and many a scene of
    life,
Yet at times through changeful season and scene, abrupt,
    alone, or in the crowded street,
Comes before me the unknown soldier's grave, comes the
    inscription rude in Virginia's woods,
Bold, cautious, true, and my loving comrade.

THE WOUND-DRESSER

1

An old man bending I come among new faces,
Years looking backward resuming in answer to children,
Come tell us old man, as from young men and maidens that
    love me,
(Arous'd and angry, I'd thought to beat the alarum, and
    urge relentless war,
But soon my fingers fail'd me, my face droop'd and I re-
    sign'd myself,
To sit by the wounded and soothe them, or silently watch the
    dead;)
Years hence of these scenes, of these furious passions, these
    chances,
Of unsurpass'd heroes, (was one side so brave? the other
    was equally brave;)
Now be witness again, paint the mightiest armies of earth,
Of those armies so rapid so wondrous what saw you to tell
    us?
What stays with you latest and deepest? of curious panics,
Of hard-fought engagements or sieges tremendous what deep-
    est remains?

2

O maidens and young men I love and that love me,
What you ask of my days those the strangest and sudden
    your talking recalls,
Soldier alert I arrive after a long march cover'd with sweat
    and dust,
In the nick of time I come, plunge in the fight, loudly shout
    in the rush of successful charge,
Enter the captur'd works—yet lo, like a swift-running river
    they fade,
Pass and are gone they fade—I dwell not on soldiers' perils
    or soldiers' joys,
(Both I remember well—many the hardships, few the joys,
    yet I was content.)

But in silence, in dreams' projections,
While the world of gain and appearance and mirth goes on,
So soon what is over forgotten, and waves wash the imprints
    off the sand,
With hinged knees returning I enter the doors, (while for
    you up there,
Whoever you are, follow without noise and be of strong
    heart.)

Bearing the bandages, water and sponge,
Straight and swift to my wounded I go,
Where they lie on the ground after the battle brought in,
Where their priceless blood reddens the grass the ground,
Or to the rows of the hospital tent, or under the roof'd hos-
    pital,
To the long rows of cots up and down each side I return,
To each and all one after another I draw near, not one do
    I miss,
An attendant follows holding a tray, he carries a refuse
    pail,
Soon to be fill'd with clotted rags and blood, emptied, and
    fill'd again.

I onward go, I stop,
With hinged knees and steady hand to dress wounds,
I am firm with each, the pangs are sharp yet unavoidable,
One turns to me his appealing eyes—poor boy! I never knew
    you,
Yet I think I could not refuse this moment to die for you,
    if that would save you.

3

On, on I go, (open doors of time! open hospital doors!)
The crush'd head I dress, (poor crazed hand tear not the
    bandage away,)
The neck of the cavalry-man with the bullet through and
    through I examine,
Hard the breathing rattles, quite glazed already the eye, yet
    life struggles hard,
(Come sweet death! be persuaded O beautiful death!
In mercy come quickly.)

rom the stump of the arm, the amputated hand,
  undo the clotted lint, remove the slough, wash off the
    matter and blood,
ack on his pillow the soldier bends with curv'd neck and
    side falling head,
Iis eyes are closed, his face is pale, he dares not look on
    the bloody stump,
And has not yet look'd on it.

dress a wound in the side, deep, deep,
But a day or two more, for see the frame all wasted and
    sinking,
And the yellow-blue countenance see.

dress the perforated shoulder, the foot with the bullet-
    wound,
Cleanse the one with a gnawing and putrid gangrene, so
    sickening, so offensive,
While the attendant stands behind aside me holding the tray
    and pail.

am faithful, I do not give out,
The fractur'd thigh, the knee, the wound in the abdomen,
These and more I dress with impassive hand, (yet deep in
    my breast a fire, a burning flame.)

4

Thus in silence in dreams' projections,
Returning, resuming, I thread my way through the hospitals,
The hurt and wounded I pacify with soothing hand,
sit by the restless all the dark night, some are so young,
Some suffer so much, I recall the experience sweet and sad,
Many a soldier's loving arms about this neck have cross'd
    and rested,
Many a soldier's kiss dwells on these bearded lips.)

RECONCILIATION

Word over all, beautiful as the sky,
Beautiful that war and all its deeds of carnage must in time
    be utterly lost,
That the hands of the sisters Death and Night incessantly
    softly wash again, and ever again, this soil'd world;
For my enemy is dead, a man divine as myself is dead,
I look where he lies white-faced and still in the coffin—I
    draw near,
Bend down and touch lightly with my lips the white face
    in the coffin.

A GLIMPSE OF WAR'S HELL-SCENES

In one of the late movements of our troops in the valley
(near Upperville, I think), a strong force of Moseby's
mounted guerrillas attacked a train of wounded and the guard
of cavalry convoying them. The ambulances contained about
60 wounded, quite a number of them officers of rank. The
rebels were in strength, and the capture of the train and its
partial guard after a short snap was effectually accomplished.
No sooner had our men surrendered, the rebels instantly
commenced robbing the train and murdering their prisoners,
even the wounded. Here is the scene or a sample of it, ten
minutes after. Among the wounded officers in the ambulances were one, a lieutenant of regulars, and another of
higher rank. These two were dragged out on the ground on
their backs, and were now surrounded by the guerrillas, a
demoniac crowd, each member of which was stabbing them
in different parts of their bodies. One of the officers had his
feet pinned firmly to the ground by bayonets stuck through
them and thrust into the ground. These two officers, as afterward found on examination, had received about twenty such
thrusts, some of them through the mouth, face, etc. The
wounded had all been dragged (to give a better chance also
for plunder) out of their wagons; some had been effectually

dispatched, and their bodies were lying there lifeless and bloody. Others, not yet dead, but horribly mutilated, were moaning or groaning. Of our men who surrendered, most had been thus maimed or slaughtered.

At this instant a force of our cavalry, who had been following the train at some interval, charged suddenly upon the secesh captors, who proceeded at once to make the best escape they could. Most of them got away, but we gobbled two officers and seventeen men, in the very acts just described. The sight was one which admitted of little discussion, as may be imagined. The seventeen captured men and two officers were put under guard for the night, but it was decided there and then that they should die. The next morning the two officers were taken in the town, separate places, put in the center of the street, and shot. The seventeen men were taken to an open ground, a little one side. They were placed in a hollow square, half-encompassed by two of our cavalry regiments, one of which regiments had three days before found the bloody corpses of three of their men hamstrung and hung up by the heels to limbs of trees by Moseby's guerrillas, and the other had not long before had twelve men, after surrendering, shot and then hung by the neck to limbs of trees, and jeering inscriptions pinned to the breast of one of the corpses, who had been a sergeant. Those three, and those twelve, had been found, I say, by these environing regiments. Now, with revolvers, they formed the grim cordon of the seventeen prisoners. The latter were placed in the midst of the hollow square, unfastened, and the ironical remark made to them that they were now to be given "a chance for themselves." A few ran for it. But what use? From every side the deadly pills came. In a few minutes the seventeen corpses strewed the hollow square. I was curious to know whether some of the Union soldiers, some few (some one or two at least of the youngsters), did not abstain from shooting on the helpless men. Not one. There was no exultation, very little said, almost nothing, yet every man there contributed his shot.

Multiply the above by scores, aye hundreds—verify it in all the forms that different circumstances, individuals, places, could afford—light it with every lurid passion, the wolf's, the lion's lapping thirst for blood—the passionate, boiling

volcanoes of human revenge for comrades, brothers slain—
with the light of burning farms, and heaps of smutting
smoldering black embers—and in the human heart everywhere
black, worse embers—and you have an inkling of this war.

THE REAL WAR WILL NEVER GET IN THE BOOKS

And so good-by to the war. I know not how it may have
been, or may be, to others—to me the main interest I found
(and still, on recollection, find) in the rank and file of the
armies, both sides, and in those specimens amid the hospitals,
and even the dead on the field. To me the points illustrating
the latent personal character and eligibilities of these states.
in the two or three millions of American young and middle-
aged men, North and South, embodied in those armies—and
especially the one-third or one-fourth of their number
stricken by wounds or disease at some time in the course of
the contest—were of more significance even than the political
interests involved. (As so much of a race depends on how it
faces death, and how it stands personal anguish and sickness. As, in the glints of emotions under emergencies, and
the indirect traits and asides in Plutarch, we get far pro-
founder clues to the antique world than all its more formal
history.)

Future years will never know the seething hell and the
black infernal background of countless minor scenes and
interiors (not the official surface courteousness of the generals, not the few great battles) of the Secession War; and
it is best they should not—the real war will never get in the
books. In the mushy influences of current times, too, the
fervid atmosphere and typical events of those years are in
danger of being totally forgotten. I have at night watched by
the side of a sick man in the hospital, one who could not
live many hours. I have seen his eyes flash and burn as he
raised himself and recurred to the cruelties on his surrendered
brother, and mutilations of the corpse afterwards. (See, in
the preceding pages, the incident at Upperville—the seventeen killed as in the description were left there on the ground.
After they dropped dead, no one touched them—all were

made sure of, however. The carcasses were left for the citizens to bury or not, as they chose.)

Such was the war. It was not a quadrille in a ballroom. Its interior history will not only never be written—its practicality, minutiæ of deeds and passions, will never be even suggested. The actual soldier of 1862-'65, North and South, with all his ways, his incredible dauntlessness, habits, practices, tastes, language, his fierce friendship, his appetite, rankness, his superb strength and animality, lawless gait, and a hundred unnamed lights and shades of camp, I say, will never be written—perhaps must not and should not be.

The preceding notes may furnish a few stray glimpses into that life, and into those lurid interiors, never to be fully conveyed to the future. The hospital part of the drama from '61 to '65 deserves to be recorded. Of that many-threaded drama, with its sudden and strange surprises, its confounding of prophecies, its moments of despair, the dread of foreign interference, the interminable campaigns, the bloody battles, the mighty and cumbrous and green armies, the drafts and bounties—the immense money expenditure, like a heavy-pouring constant rain—with, over the whole land, the last three years of the struggle, an unending, universal mourning wail of women, parents, orphans—the marrow of the tragedy concentrated in those Army Hospitals (it seemed sometimes as if the whole interest of the land, North and South, was one vast central hospital, and all the rest of the affair but flanges)—those forming the untold and unwritten history of the war—infinitely greater (like life's) than the few scraps and distortions that are ever told or written. Think how much, and of importance, will be—how much, civic and military, has already been—buried in the grave, in eternal darkness.

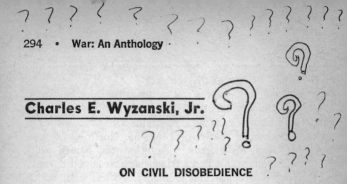

Charles E. Wyzanski, Jr.

ON CIVIL DISOBEDIENCE

Disobedience is a long step beyond dissent. In this country, at least in theory, no one denies the right of any person to differ with the government, or his right to express that difference in speech, in the press, by petition, or in an assembly.

But civil disobedience, by definition, involves a deliberate and punishable breach of a legal duty. However much they differ in other respects, both passive and violent resisters intentionally violate the law. So, in general, it is unnecessary in considering the moral qualities of disobedience to spend much time in determining what is the correct construction of the law. By hypothesis the law has been broken, and broken knowingly.

The virtual exclusion of legal topics makes it possible to discuss the morality of resistance to the Vietnam War without answering the question whether the President as Commander in Chief under the Constitution, or as the Chief Executive authorized by the Congress, or otherwise has power to send to Vietnam armed forces regularly enlisted or conscripted, or whether the Constitution gives power to draft men to serve in a conflict not covered by a formal declaration of war, or whether there is any rule of international or domestic law which inhibits the President or the Congress or the armed forces either from conducting in Vietnam any operations whatsoever or any particular operations, or from using any specific methods of fighting or injuring other persons, military or civilian.

There cannot be an issue of civil disobedience unless there is a conscious choice to violate not merely a governmental policy but a technically valid law or order. Only such laws and orders as are ultimately held valid under our Constitution are subject to genuine civil disobedience.

Of course, until the Supreme Court has spoken, a person may not know whether a particular law or order is valid. If because he believes the law is invalid under the Constitution he refuses to obey it until the order has been upheld, he is not in the strictest sense engaged in civil disobedience. Thus many of the recent refusals of Negroes to obey segregation orders of local authorities, though they are popularly referred to as examples of civil disobedience, have been, in fact, nothing more than challenges to laws believed to be and often found to be unconstitutional.

If it turns out that the Supreme Court should hold that the government lacks power to order the induction of men into military training and service for the Vietnam War, then one who had refused to obey the induction order would not have been guilty of civil disobedience. He would merely have been vindicating his constitutional rights.

But if, as I suppose the majority of informed lawyers expect, the Supreme Court, at least during the continuation of hostilities, does not hold an induction order void on the ground of lack of legislative or executive power, then one who continues willfully to disobey is engaged in civil disobedience. The same would be true of one who, on the ground that the funds were used for war, refused to pay taxes, or who in protesting war deliberately injured another's person or property, or who went beyond argument and persuasion to advocate resistance to lawful orders.

There are many people who have asserted that a man always has an undeniable moral claim to disobey any law to which he is consciously opposed. Antigone, Thoreau, and Gandhi are cited. It is contended that resistance to the law is the proper response to the still small voice of conscience.

That extreme position seems untenable. Every time that a law is disobeyed by even a man whose motive is solely ethical, in the sense that it is responsive to a deep moral conviction, there are unfortunate consequences. He himself becomes more prone to disobey laws for which he has no profound repugnance. He sets an example for others who may not have his pure motives. He weakens the fabric of society.

Those disadvantages are so serious that in *Principia Ethica* G. E. Moore, the English philosopher who set the tone for twentieth-century thought on ethics, concluded that in most instances civil disobedience is immoral. A dramatic precursor of Moore was Socrates. He swallowed hemlock pursuant to an arbitrary Athenian decree rather than refuse obedience to the laws of the city-state which had formed and protected him.

However, it is not here suggested that disobedience is always morally wrong, or that it is never ethically proper for a man to organize opposition to an immoral law even before the state brings its command directly to his door.

There are situations when it seems plainly moral for a man to disobey an evil law promulgated by a government which is entirely lacking in ethical character. If a man has lost confidence in the integrity of his society, or if he fears that unless he acts forthwith there will not come a later day when he can effectively protest, or if (in terms reminiscent of Burke's metaphor) he seeks to terminate the partnership of the American dead, the American living, and the as yet unborn Americans, then there is much justification for his disobedience.

The gangster state operated by the Nazis presented such a picture to many conscientious men. But no unprejudiced observer is likely to see the American government in its involvement in Vietnam as in a posture comparable with that of the Nazi regime. Nor is there reason to suppose that men must act now or forever be silenced. We are not moving either torrentially or glacially toward despotism.

It is, of course, conceivable that if men resist forthwith, they may forestall grave consequences. It is certain that many, many Americans and Asians will lose their lives if the war continues. It is possible that if fighting is not promptly stopped, the scale will increase dramatically, and at worst, might produce a holocaust of worldwide dimensions.

But what is by no means assured is that resistance would avert those consequences. Historical prediction is clouded by ambiguities. Political developments move to a heterogeneity of ends. No one can tell whether, as the resisters would hope, they, by rallying widespread support, would prove that in a democracy substantial segments of public opinion have the residual power to terminate or veto a war, or, as less impli- cated observers fear, the resisters, by provoking the responsive passions of the belligerent, would set the stage for a revival of a virulent McCarthyism, an administrative system of

pressment into the armed forces, and the establishment of
despotic tyranny bent on impairing traditional civil liberties
d civil rights.

Most thoughtful men have always been aware how danger-
s it is to go beyond persuasion and to defy the law by
her peaceful or violent resistance. If the effort is success-
l, as with the Revolution of the American colonists, then
story accepts the claims of the victors that they acted
orally. But if the effort not merely fails but produces a
rrible reaction, then history is likely to ask whether there
ere not other courses that could have been more wisely
llowed.

To illustrate how perplexing is the problem, nothing is
ore illuminating than the struggle in America in the 1850s
d 1860s over the slavery question. Abraham Lincoln
ought laws enforcing slavery were immoral. Yet he declared
e would endure, and thus aid the enforcement of, slavery
the Southern states if that would preserve the Union. His
sition was shared by two great jurists of my state who
ere his contemporaries: Lemuel Shaw, Chief Justice of
assachusetts, and Benjamin Robbins Curtis, Associate Jus-
e of the Supreme Court of the United States, both of
hom enforced the Fugitive Slave Law.

But Lincoln's position was challenged by, among others,
o men whom the city of Boston has honored by statues
ected after their death—Wendell Phillips and William
loyd Garrison, each of whom disobeyed the Fugitive Slave
aw and wrote approvingly of the murderous violence of
hn Brown. What should give us even greater pause is that
liver Wendell Holmes, Jr., the future Justice, in effect
hered to the Abolitionist cause when he joined the small
oup of Abolitionists who, during the winter of 1860–1861,
ade themselves responsible for securing the physical safety
f Wendell Phillips against the threats of the Boston mobs,
protection which the Boston police seemed unlikely to pro-
de. The details are set forth in Professor Mark Howe's
scriminating biography of Holmes.

If it was morally right to break the laws supporting slavery
ven when it cost the nation its unity and helped precipitate
hat, despite W. H. Seward, may not have been an "irrepress-

ible conflict," one cannot be so certain that it is morall[y] wrong to resist the war in Vietnam if one deeply believe[s] its purposes or methods are wicked.

At any rate the Lincolnian analogy has not the final au[-] thority that it may seem to have on cursory inspection. I[n] 1860 and 1861 our country was in immediate grave peril[.] Lincoln adhered to the ancient Roman maxim that the safet[y] of the people is the highest law. But that maxim has n[o] obvious application today. Even the most ardent supporter[s] of our role in Vietnam would hardly aver that the threa[t] they see in Communism or Asian nationalism is one of suc[h] immediacy as existed when the Civil War erupted. Perhap[s] there are long-term dangers from the Asian and other Com[-] munist powers, but one may wonder if Mr. Justice Holme[s] would have regarded them as either "clear" or "present.["] Would not President Lincoln have invoked our recollectio[n] not of 1860 or 1861 but rather of 1863 when, the battle o[f] Antietam having made a change of policy practical, he issue[d] the Emancipation Proclamation?

In support of the moral right of resistance, another, [a] cognate, point must be made, however uncongenial it is t[o] me both temperamentally and officially. A man may con[-] scientiously believe that his deepest obligation is to do hi[s] utmost to eradicate an evil, to stand athwart a wicked action[,] forcefully to promote reform, or to establish a new social o[r] legal or religious order. Luther and Lenin serve as archetypes[.] They share to some degree the view Vanzetti on the eve o[f] his electrocution expressed to his lawyer Thompson: "that, a[s] he read history, every great cause for the benefit of humanit[y] had to fight for its existence against entrenched power an[d] wrong."

Perceptive observers may support Vanzetti's social theorem[.] Anguished souls may yield to its persuasiveness. Effective me[n] may make that vision once again prove its reality.

Yet the fierce passion which moves men to rebel is often[,] not always, dangerously mixed with vanity, self-righteousness[,] and blindness to possible, nay probable, consequences fa[r] different from those sought. The voice of reason urges, i[n] Cromwellian terms, "I beseech you, in the bowels of Chris[t] think it possible you may be mistaken."

Violent disorder once set in motion may spawn tyranny[,] not freedom. Rebellion may fail to gain its contemplate[d]

pport, and as surely as in other human relations, result
"the expense of spirit in a waste of shame."

Or, what is far harder to bear, the rebellion may in form
cceed but in substance impose a new oppressive yoke, a
hilistic world regime, or chaos instead of a community of
ations. The wager on a finer, purer, more fraternal world
rder may be disastrously lost. Before one places all one's
rength behind the rebel's cause, he should have not only
aïve faith but that invincible insight which warrants martyr-
om.

For men of conscience there remains a less risky but not
ss worthy moral choice. Each of us may bide his time until
e personally is faced with an order requiring him as an
dividual to do a wrongful act. Such patience, fortitude,
nd resolution find illustration in the career of Sir Thomas
lore. He did not rush in to protest the Act of Henry VIII's
arliament requiring Englishmen to take an oath of suprem-
cy attesting to the King's, instead of the Pope's, headship
f the English Church. Only when attempt was made to force
im to subscribe to the oath did he resist. In present circum-
ances the parallel to not resisting the Act of Supremacy
efore it has been personally applied is to await at the very
ast an induction order before resisting. Indeed, since, when
aducted, one does not know if he will be sent to Vietnam,
r if sent, will be called upon directly to do what he regards
s an immoral act, it may well be that resistance at the
noment of induction is premature.

This waiting until an issue is squarely presented to an
dividual and cannot further be avoided will not be a course
ppealing to those who have a burning desire to intervene
ffirmatively to save this nation's honor and the lives of its
itizens and citizens of other lands. It seems at first blush a
ot very heroic attitude. But heroism sometimes lies in with-
olding action until it is compelled, and using the interval to
liscern competing interests, to ascertain their values, and to
eek to strike a balance that marshals the claims not only
f the accountant and of others in his society, but of men of
listant lands and times.

Such restraint will in no way run counter to the rules
pplied in the judgment of the Nuremberg Tribunal. That
udgment recognized that no one may properly be charged
vith a crime unless he personally participated in it by doing

the wrong or by purposefully aiding, abetting, and furthering the wrong. As the Nuremberg verdicts show, merely to fight in an aggressive war is no crime. What is a crime is personally to fight by foul means.

Those who look upon Sir Thomas More as one of the noblest exemplars of the human spirit reflecting the impact of the love of God may find a delayed civil disobedience the response most likely to give peace of mind and to evidence moral courage.

William Butler Yeats

AN IRISH AIRMAN FORESEES HIS DEATH

I know that I shall meet my fate
Somewhere among the clouds above;
Those that I fight I do not hate,
Those that I guard I do not love;
My country is Kiltartan Cross,
My countrymen Kiltartan's poor,
No likely end could bring them loss
Or leave them happier than before.
Nor law, nor duty bade me fight,
Nor public men, nor cheering crowds,
A lonely impulse of delight
Drove to this tumult in the clouds;
I balanced all, brought all to mind,
The years to come seemed waste of breath
A waste of breath the years behind
In balance with this life, this death.

ON BEING ASKED FOR A WAR POEM

I think it better that in times like these
A poet's mouth be silent, for in truth
We have no gift to set a statesman right;
He has had enough of meddling who can please
A young girl in the indolence of her youth,
Or an old man upon a winter's night.

THE STARE'S NEST BY MY WINDOW

The bees build in the crevices
Of loosening masonry, and there
The mother birds bring grubs and flies.
My wall is loosening; honey-bees,
Come build in the empty house of the stare.

We are closed in, and the key is turned
On our uncertainty; somewhere
A man is killed, or a house burned,
Yet no clear fact to be discerned:
Come build in the empty house of the stare.

A barricade of stone or of wood;
Some fourteen days of civil war;
Last night they trundled down the road
That dead young soldier in his blood:
Come build in the empty house of the stare.

We had fed the heart on fantasies,
The heart's grown brutal from the fare;
More substance in our enmities
Than in our love; O honey-bees,
Come build in the empty house of the stare.

ndex of Titles by Genre

Love - what is love?

Love is a bowl of cherries or a garden of flowers up to the moment it has not been touched & given you disappointment.